GRAPHIC CAPTAIN
Captain America & Iron Man

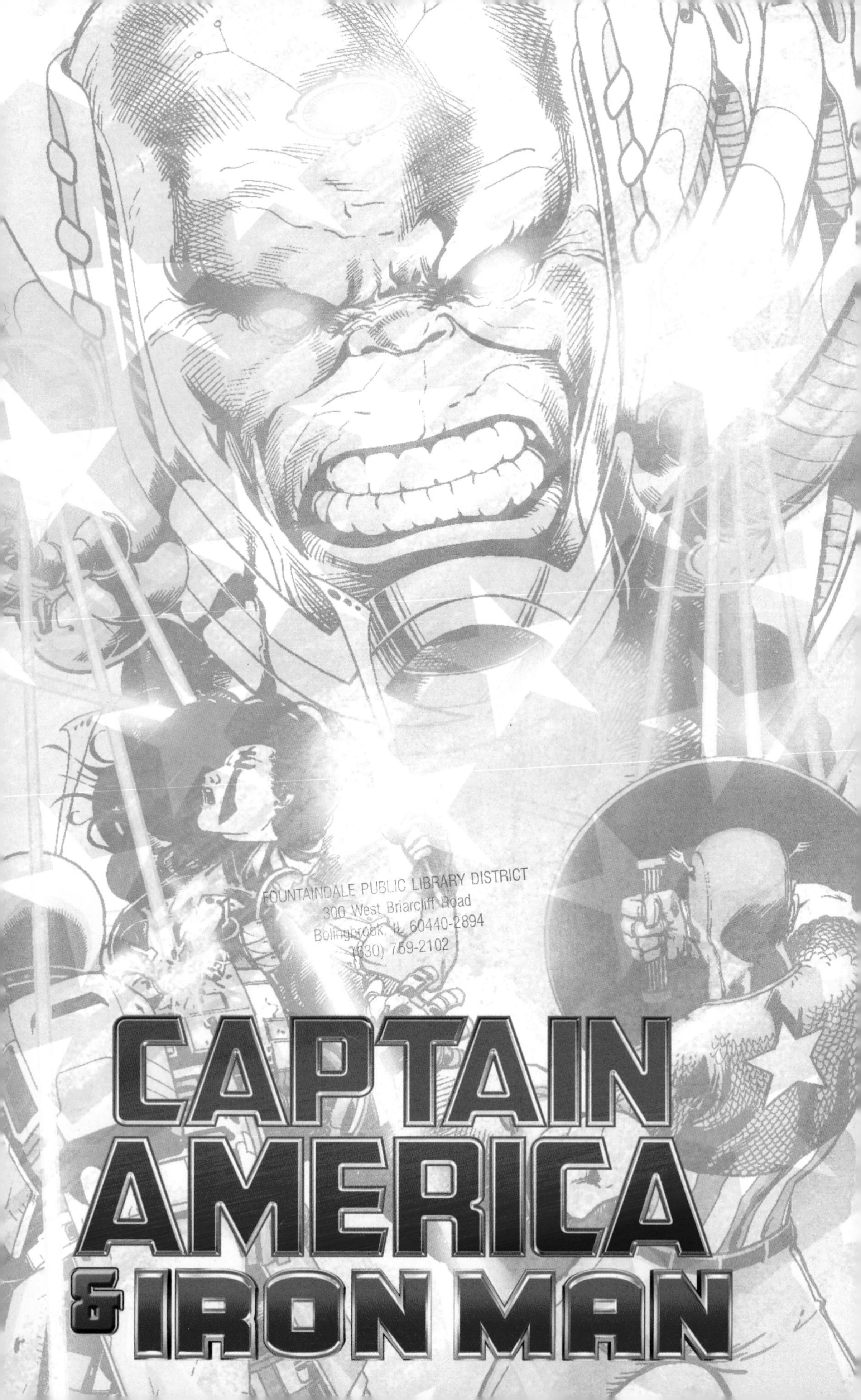
CAPTAIN AMERICA
& IRON MAN

CAPTAIN AMERICA & IRON MAN

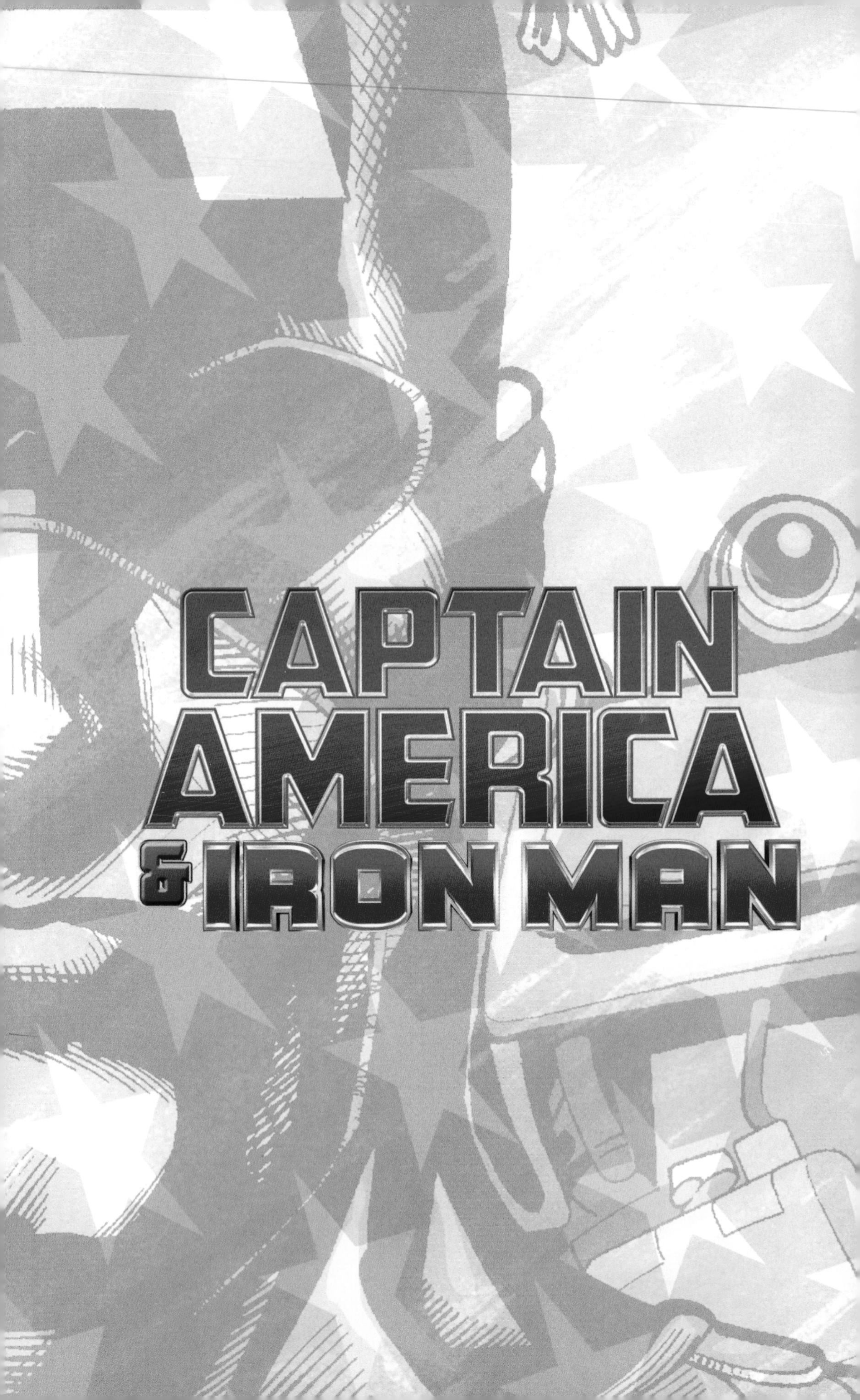

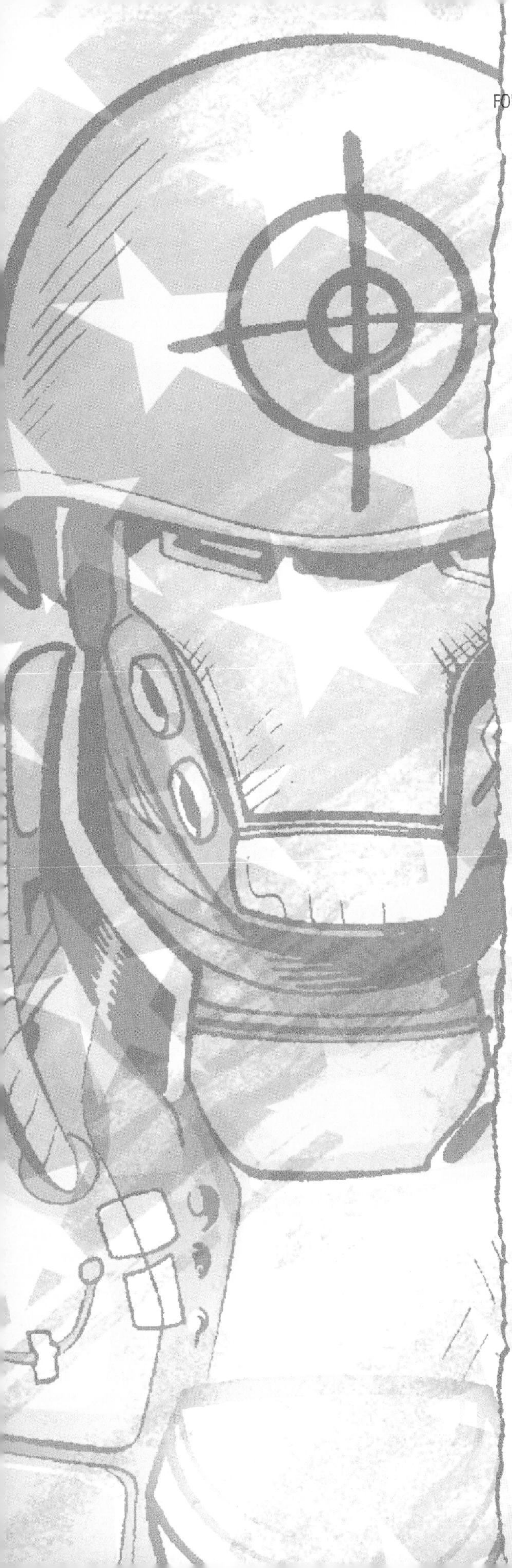

WRITER
CULLEN BUNN

ISSUES #633-635
ARTIST
BARRY KITSON
WITH **JAY LEISTEN**
(FINISHES, ISSUE #634)

COLOR ARTIST
JAVIER TARTAGLIA

ISSUE #635.1
ARTIST
WILL CONRAD

COLOR ARTIST
CRIS PETER

LETTERERS
VC'S JOE CARAMAGNA & JOE SABINO

COVER ARTISTS
KALMAN ANDRASOFSZKY
(ISSUES #633-635)
AND **STUART IMMONEN, WADE VON GRAWBADGER & MATTHEW WILSON**
(ISSUE #635.1)

ASSISTANT EDITORS
JOHN DENNING & JAKE THOMAS

EDITOR
LAUREN SANKOVITCH

CAPTAIN AMERICA CREATED BY
JOE SIMON & JACK KIRBY

COLLECTION EDITOR
CORY LEVINE
ASSISTANT EDITORS
ALEX STARBUCK & NELSON RIBEIRO
EDITORS, SPECIAL PROJECTS
JENNIFER GRÜNWALD & MARK D. BEAZLEY
SENIOR EDITOR, SPECIAL PROJECTS
JEFF YOUNGQUIST
SENIOR VICE PRESIDENT OF SALES
DAVID GABRIEL
SVP OF BRAND PLANNING
& COMMUNICATIONS
MICHAEL PASCIULLO
BOOK DESIGN
JEFF POWELL

EDITOR IN CHIEF
AXEL ALONSO
CHIEF CREATIVE OFFICER
JOE QUESADA
PUBLISHER
DAN BUCKLEY
EXECUTIVE PRODUCER
ALAN FINE

CAPTAIN AMERICA AND IRON MAN. Contains material originally published in magazine form as CAPTAIN AMERICA AND IRON MAN #633-635 and CAPTAIN AMERICA AND NAMOR #635.1. First printing 2012. ISBN# 978-0-7851-6578-1. Published by MARVEL WORLDWIDE, INC., a subsidiary of MARVEL ENTERTAINMENT, LLC. OFFICE OF PUBLICATION: 135 West 50th Street, New York, NY 10020. Copyright © 2012 Marvel Characters, Inc. All rights reserved. $14.99 per copy in the U.S. and $16.99 in Canada (GST #R127032852); Canadian Agreement #40668537. All characters featured in this issue and the distinctive names and likenesses thereof, and all related indicia are trademarks of Marvel Characters, Inc. No similarity between any of the names, characters, persons, and/or institutions in this magazine with those of any living or dead person or institution is intended, and any such similarity which may exist is purely coincidental. **Printed in the U.S.A.** ALAN FINE, EVP - Office of the President, Marvel Worldwide, Inc. and EVP & CMO Marvel Characters B.V.; DAN BUCKLEY, Publisher & President - Print, Animation & Digital Divisions; JOE QUESADA, Chief Creative Officer; TOM BREVOORT, SVP of Publishing; DAVID BOGART, SVP of Operations & Procurement, Publishing; RUWAN JAYATILLEKE, SVP & Associate Publisher, Publishing; C.B. CEBULSKI, SVP of Creator & Content Development; DAVID GABRIEL, SVP of Publishing Sales & Circulation; MICHAEL PASCIULLO, SVP of Brand Planning & Communications; JIM O'KEEFE, VP of Operations & Logistics; DAN CARR, Executive Director of Publishing Technology; SUSAN CRESPI, Editorial Operations Manager; ALEX MORALES, Publishing Operations Manager; STAN LEE, Chairman Emeritus. For information regarding advertising in Marvel Comics or on Marvel.com, please contact Niza Disla, Director of Marvel Partnerships, at ndisla@marvel.com. For Marvel subscription inquiries, please call 800-217-9158. **Manufactured between 10/11/2012 and 11/13/2012 by QUAD/GRAPHICS, DUBUQUE, IA, USA.**

10 9 8 7 6 5 4 3 2 1

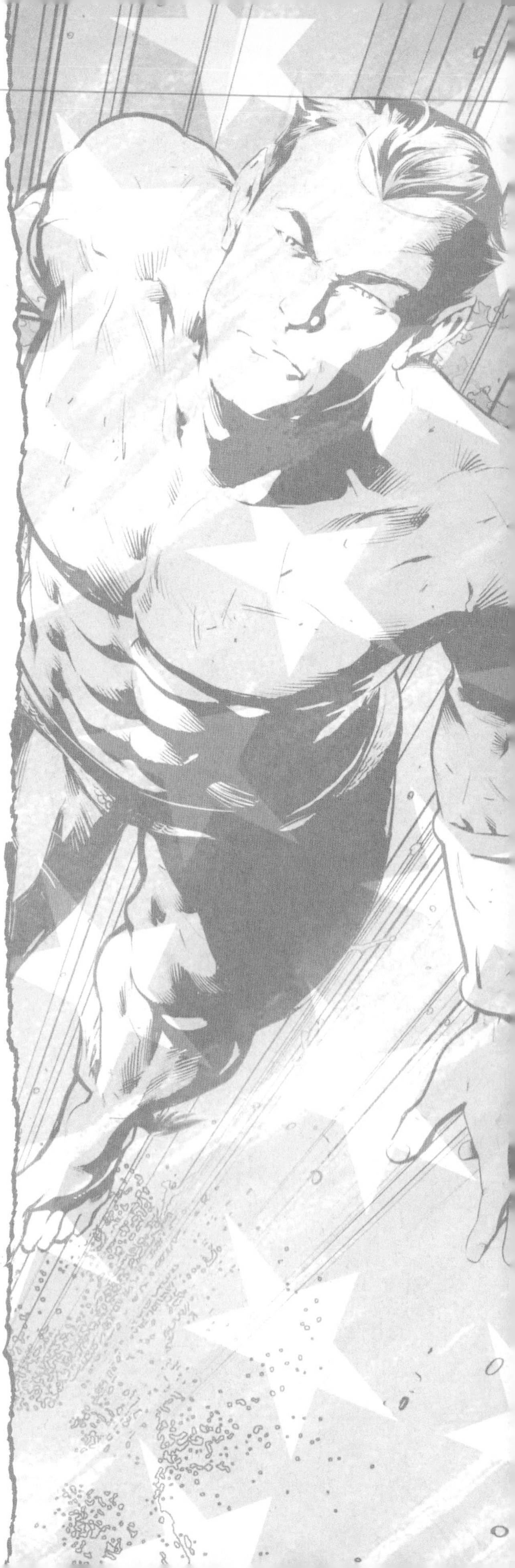

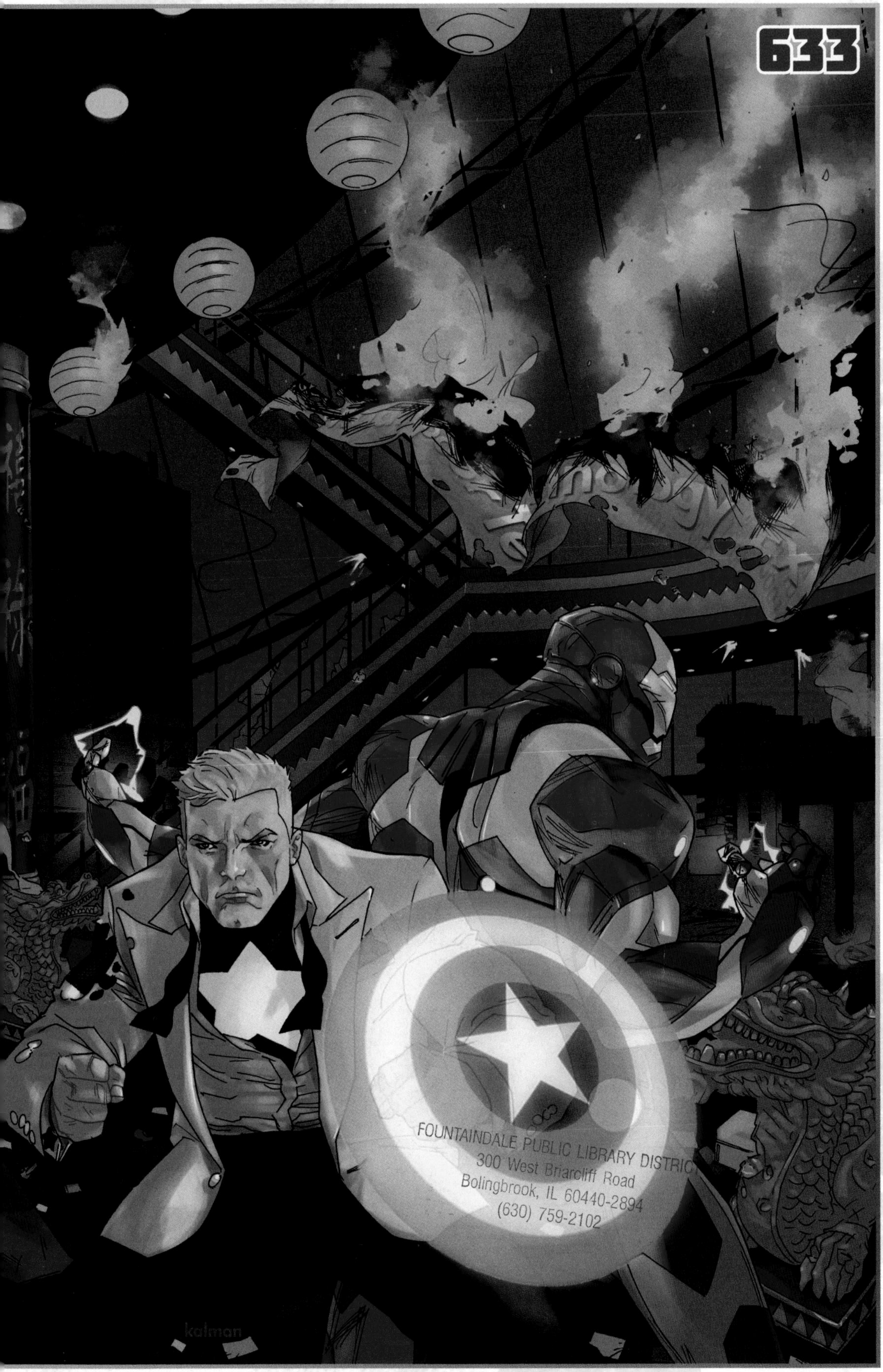
633
kalman

CAPTAIN AMERICA

STEVE ROGERS

PEAK STRENGTH, REFLEXES AND ENDURANCE. TACTICAL GENIUS.
THE SUPER-SOLDIER OF WORLD WAR II. LEADER OF THE AVENGERS.

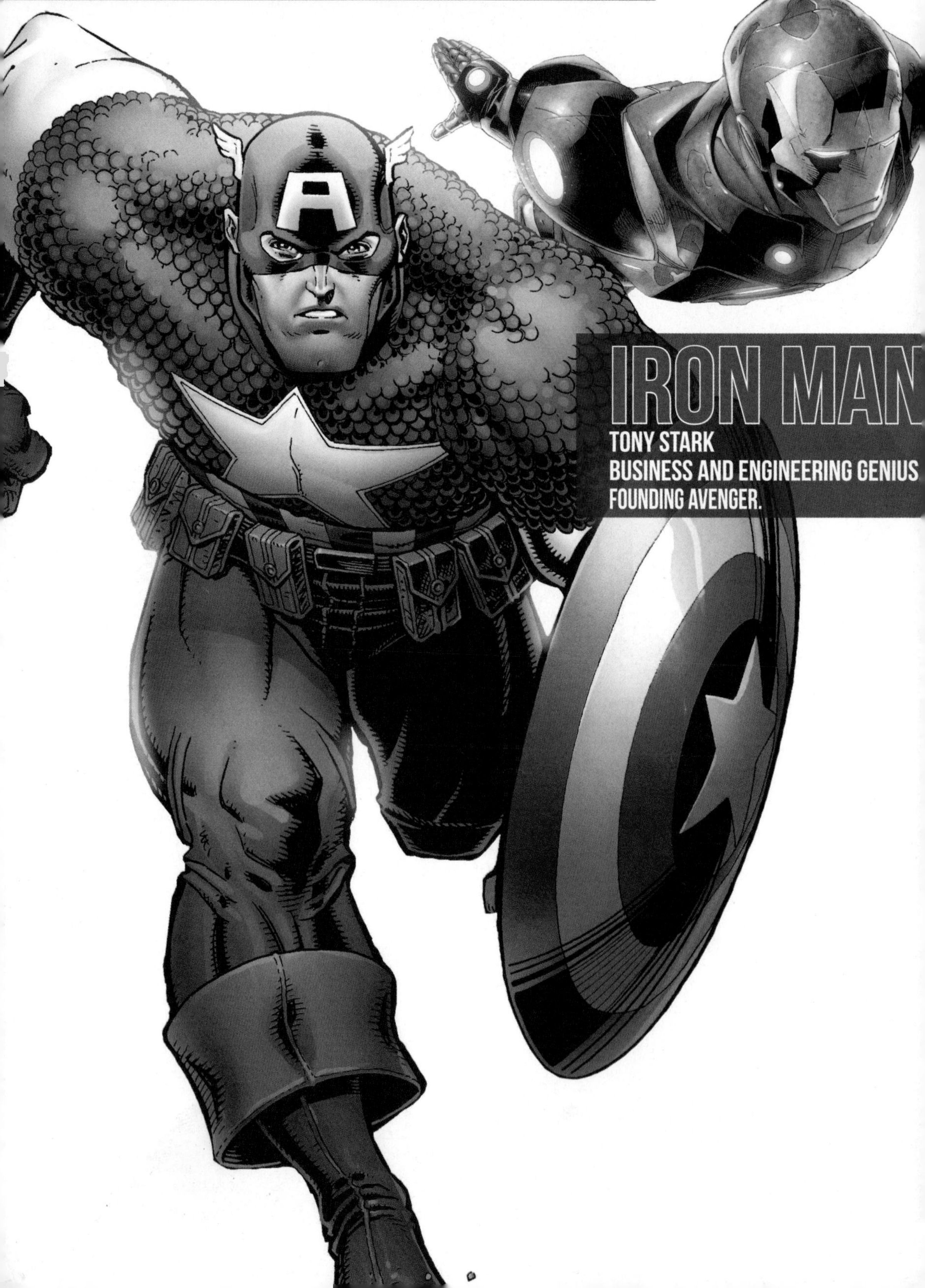

IRON MAN

TONY STARK

BUSINESS AND ENGINEERING GENIUS

FOUNDING AVENGER.

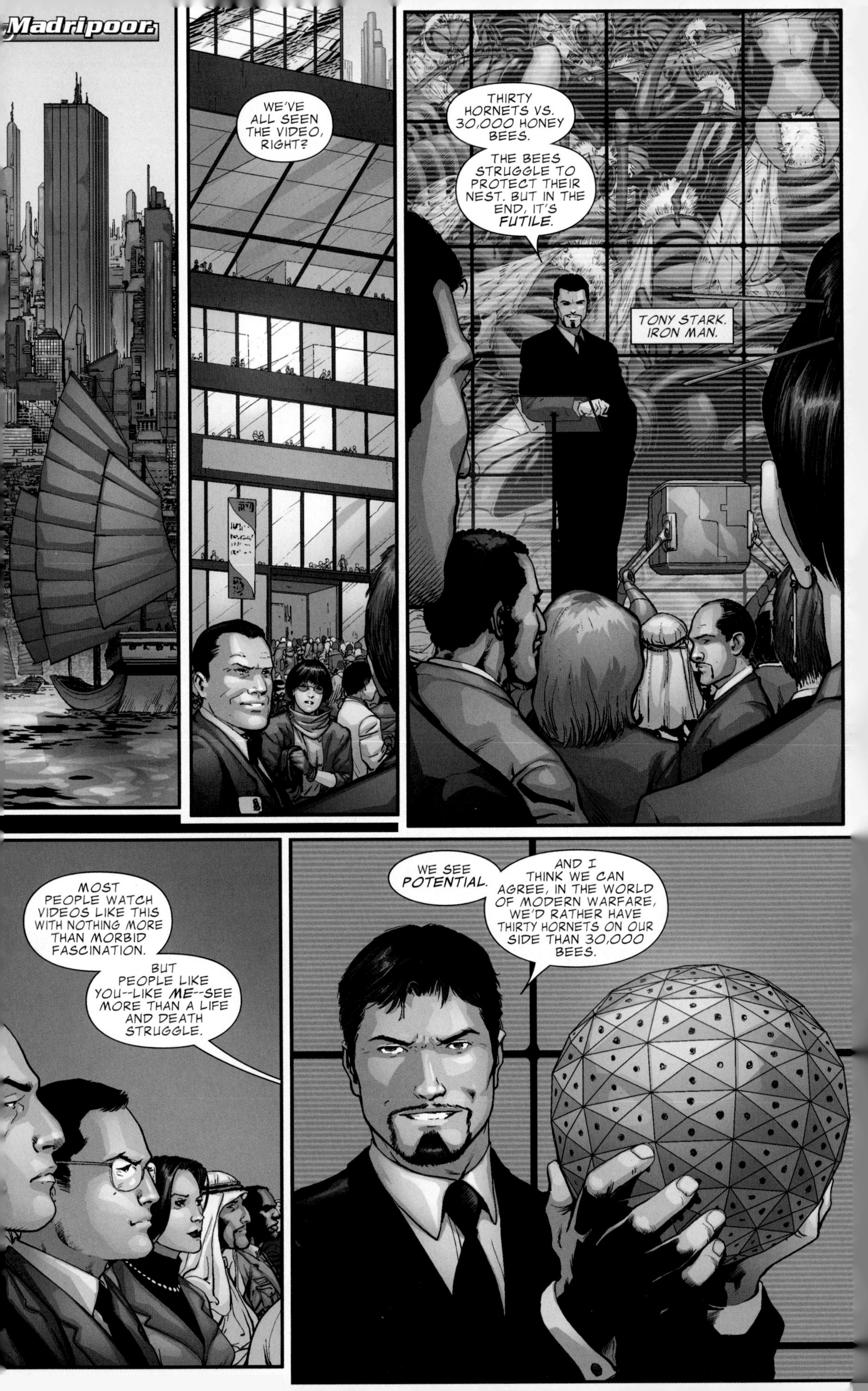
Madripoor.
WE'VE ALL SEEN THE VIDEO, RIGHT?
THIRTY HORNETS VS. 30,000 HONEY BEES.
THE BEES STRUGGLE TO PROTECT THEIR NEST. BUT IN THE END, IT'S FUTILE.
TONY STARK. IRON MAN.
MOST PEOPLE WATCH VIDEOS LIKE THIS WITH NOTHING MORE THAN MORBID FASCINATION.
BUT PEOPLE LIKE YOU--LIKE ME--SEE MORE THAN A LIFE AND DEATH STRUGGLE.
WE SEE POTENTIAL.
AND I THINK WE CAN AGREE, IN THE WORLD OF MODERN WARFARE, WE'D RATHER HAVE THIRTY HORNETS ON OUR SIDE THAN 30,000 BEES.

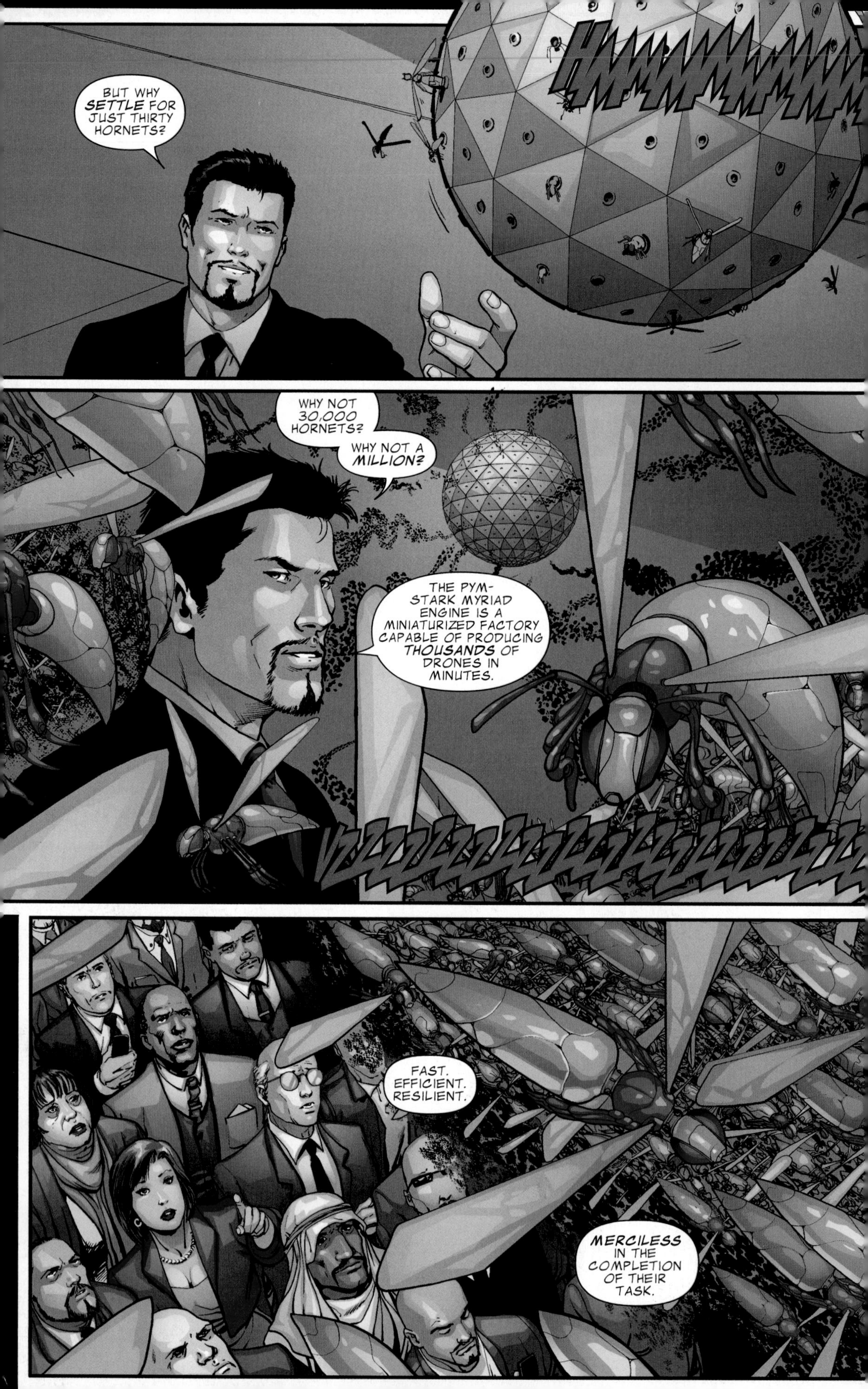
BUT WHY SETTLE FOR JUST THIRTY HORNETS?
HMMMMMMMM
WHY NOT 30,000 HORNETS?
WHY NOT A MILLION?
THE PYM-STARK MYRIAD ENGINE IS A MINIATURIZED FACTORY CAPABLE OF PRODUCING THOUSANDS OF DRONES IN MINUTES.
VZZZZZZZZZZZZZZZZZZZZZZZZZZ
FAST. EFFICIENT. RESILIENT.
MERCILESS IN THE COMPLETION OF THEIR TASK.

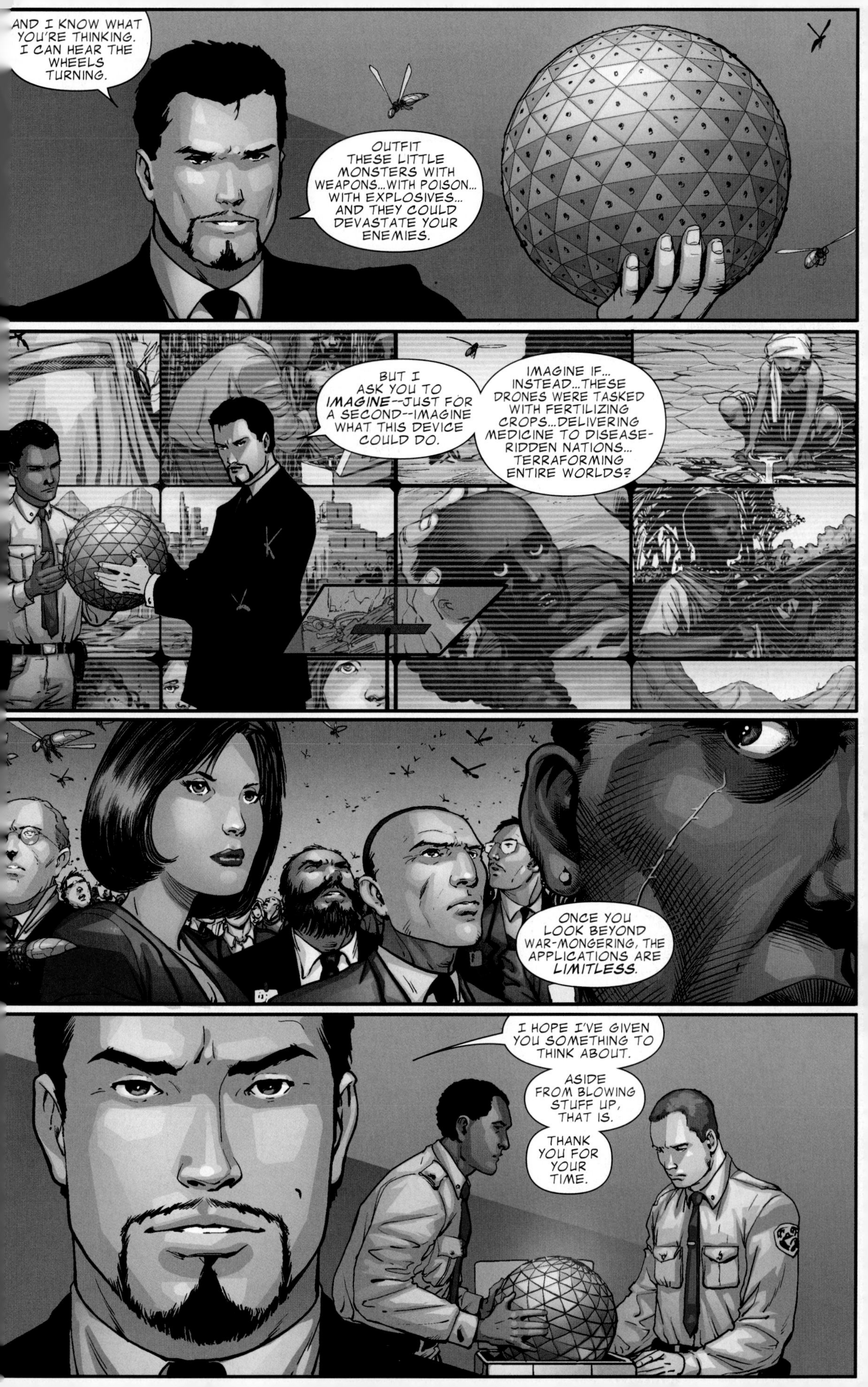
AND I KNOW WHAT YOU'RE THINKING. I CAN HEAR THE WHEELS TURNING.
OUTFIT THESE LITTLE MONSTERS WITH WEAPONS...WITH POISON... WITH EXPLOSIVES... AND THEY COULD DEVASTATE YOUR ENEMIES.
BUT I ASK YOU TO IMAGINE--JUST FOR A SECOND--IMAGINE WHAT THIS DEVICE COULD DO.
IMAGINE IF... INSTEAD...THESE DRONES WERE TASKED WITH FERTILIZING CROPS...DELIVERING MEDICINE TO DISEASE-RIDDEN NATIONS... TERRAFORMING ENTIRE WORLDS?
ONCE YOU LOOK BEYOND WAR-MONGERING, THE APPLICATIONS ARE LIMITLESS.
I HOPE I'VE GIVEN YOU SOMETHING TO THINK ABOUT.
ASIDE FROM BLOWING STUFF UP, THAT IS.
THANK YOU FOR YOUR TIME.

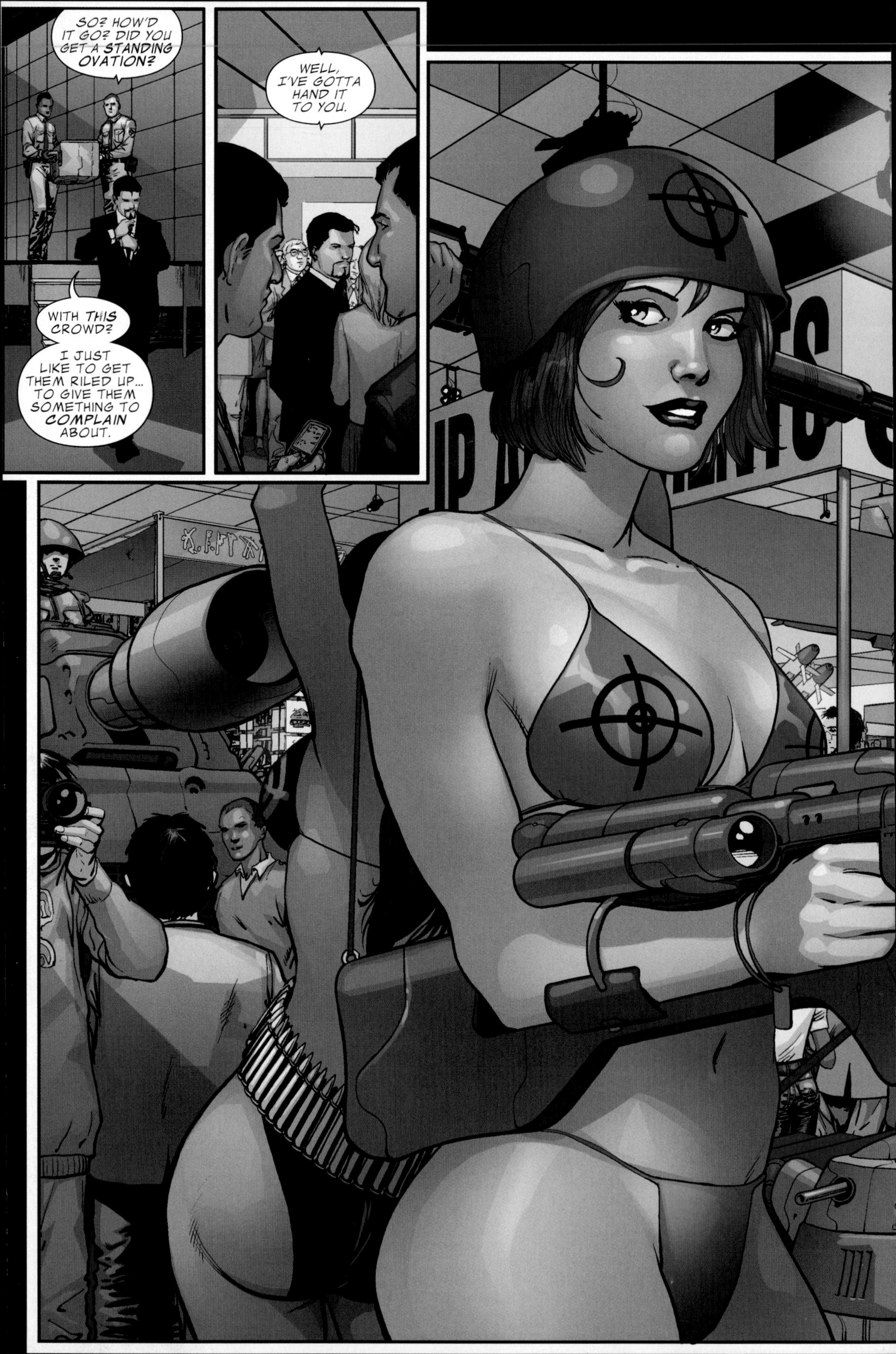
SO? HOW'D IT GO? DID YOU GET A STANDING OVATION?
WITH THIS CROWD?
I JUST LIKE TO GET THEM RILED UP... TO GIVE THEM SOMETHING TO COMPLAIN ABOUT.
WELL, I'VE GOTTA HAND IT TO YOU.

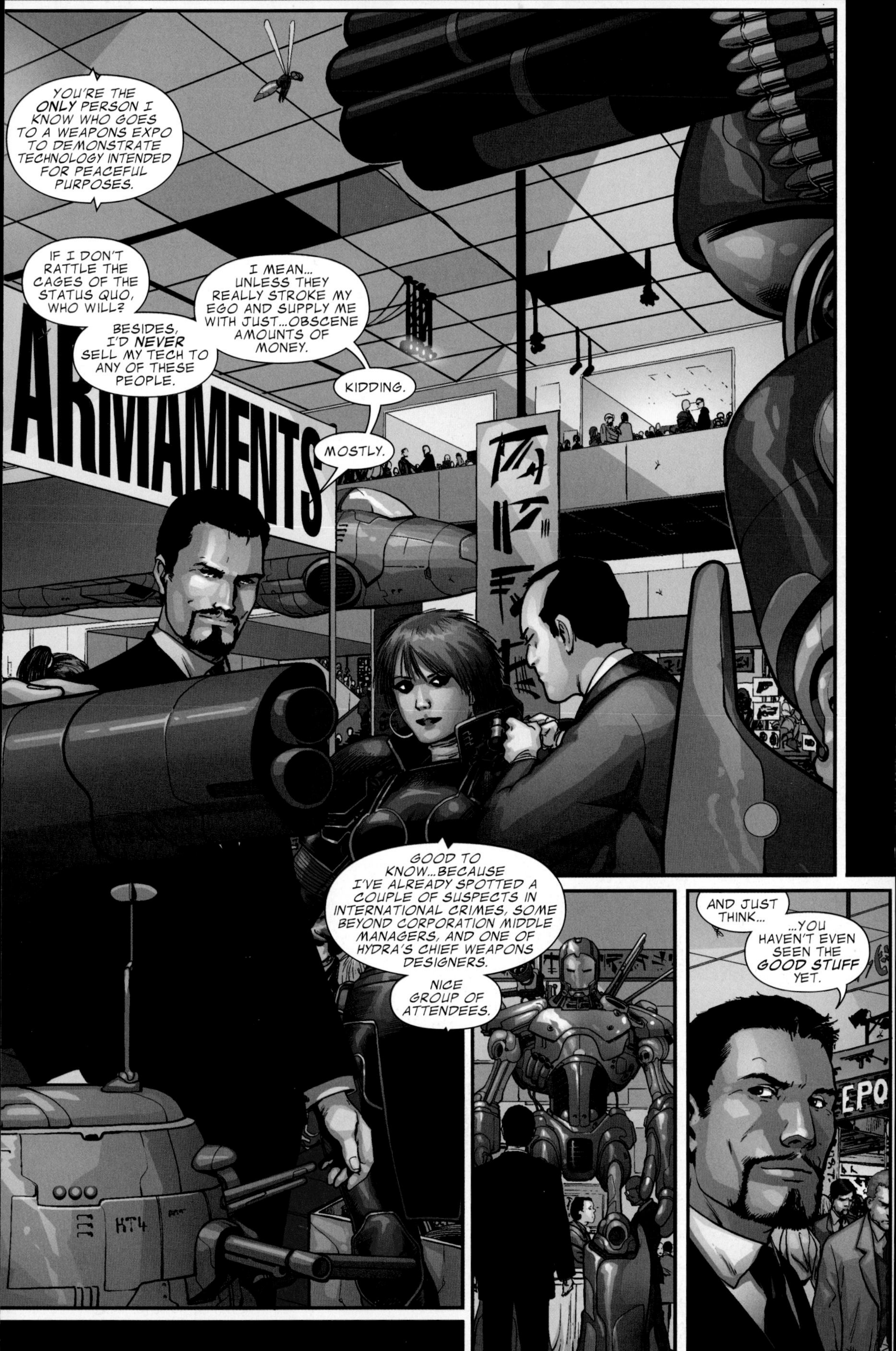
YOU'RE THE ONLY PERSON I KNOW WHO GOES TO A WEAPONS EXPO TO DEMONSTRATE TECHNOLOGY INTENDED FOR PEACEFUL PURPOSES.
IF I DON'T RATTLE THE CAGES OF THE STATUS QUO, WHO WILL?
BESIDES, I'D NEVER SELL MY TECH TO ANY OF THESE PEOPLE.
I MEAN... UNLESS THEY REALLY STROKE MY EGO AND SUPPLY ME WITH JUST...OBSCENE AMOUNTS OF MONEY.
KIDDING.
MOSTLY.
ARMAMENTS
GOOD TO KNOW...BECAUSE I'VE ALREADY SPOTTED A COUPLE OF SUSPECTS IN INTERNATIONAL CRIMES, SOME BEYOND CORPORATION MIDDLE MANAGERS, AND ONE OF HYDRA'S CHIEF WEAPONS DESIGNERS.
NICE GROUP OF ATTENDEES.
AND JUST THINK...
...YOU HAVEN'T EVEN SEEN THE GOOD STUFF YET.

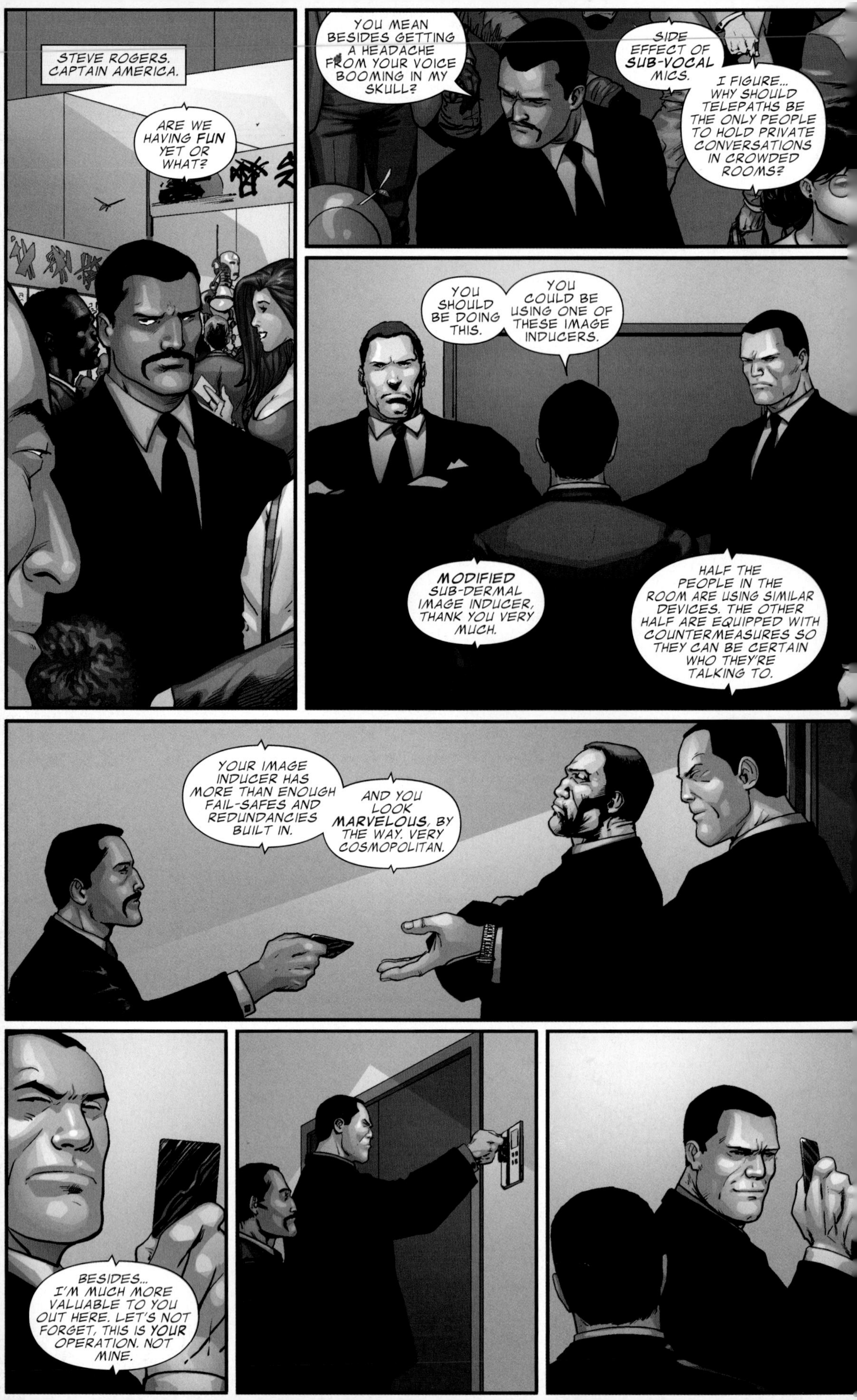
STEVE ROGERS. CAPTAIN AMERICA.
ARE WE HAVING FUN YET OR WHAT?
YOU MEAN BESIDES GETTING A HEADACHE FROM YOUR VOICE BOOMING IN MY SKULL?
SIDE EFFECT OF SUB-VOCAL MICS.
I FIGURE... WHY SHOULD TELEPATHS BE THE ONLY PEOPLE TO HOLD PRIVATE CONVERSATIONS IN CROWDED ROOMS?
YOU SHOULD BE DOING THIS.
YOU COULD BE USING ONE OF THESE IMAGE INDUCERS.
MODIFIED SUB-DERMAL IMAGE INDUCER, THANK YOU VERY MUCH.
HALF THE PEOPLE IN THE ROOM ARE USING SIMILAR DEVICES. THE OTHER HALF ARE EQUIPPED WITH COUNTERMEASURES SO THEY CAN BE CERTAIN WHO THEY'RE TALKING TO.
YOUR IMAGE INDUCER HAS MORE THAN ENOUGH FAIL-SAFES AND REDUNDANCIES BUILT IN.
AND YOU LOOK MARVELOUS, BY THE WAY. VERY COSMOPOLITAN.
BESIDES... I'M MUCH MORE VALUABLE TO YOU OUT HERE. LET'S NOT FORGET, THIS IS YOUR OPERATION. NOT MINE.

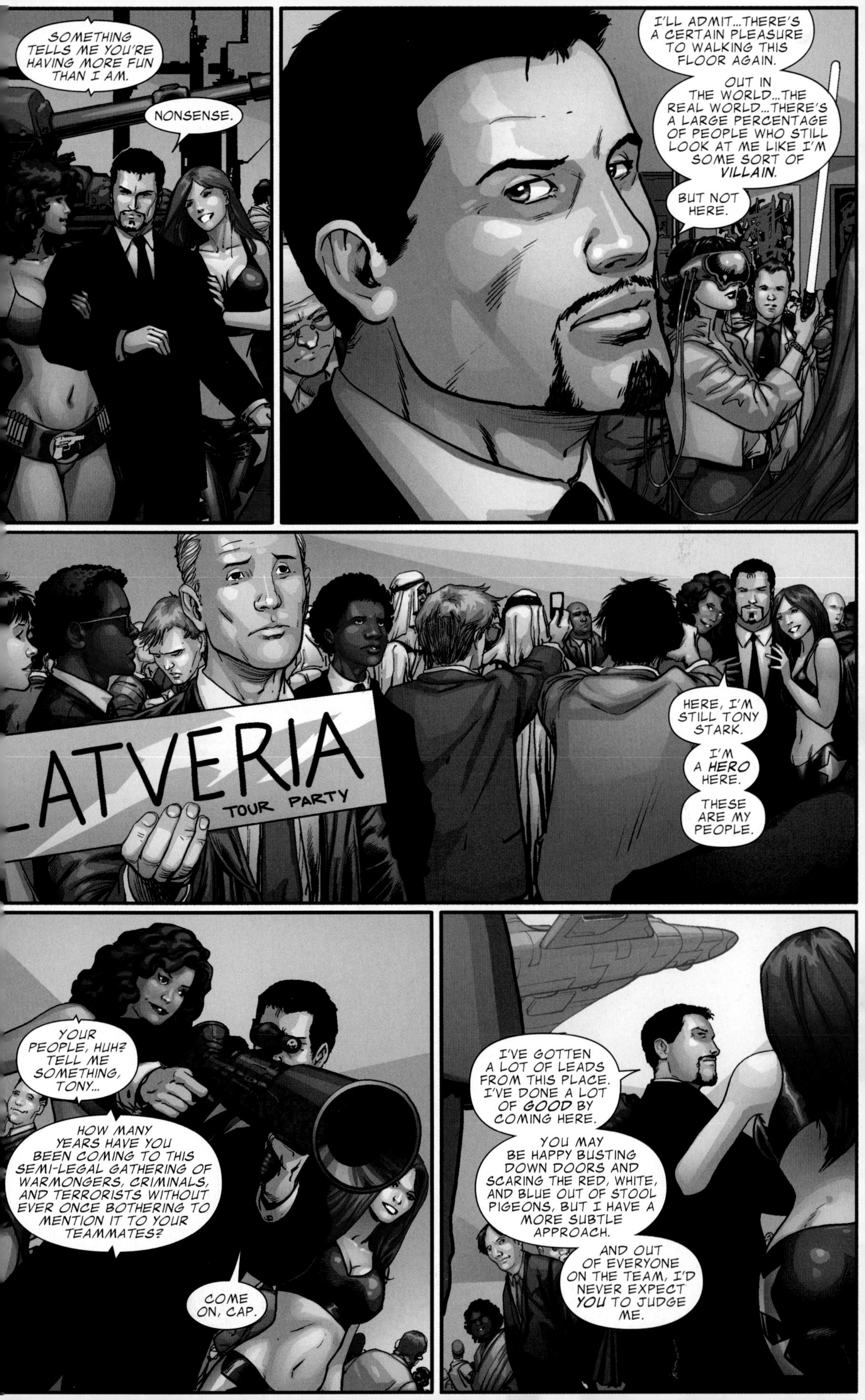
SOMETHING TELLS ME YOU'RE HAVING MORE FUN THAN I AM.
NONSENSE.
I'LL ADMIT...THERE'S A CERTAIN PLEASURE TO WALKING THIS FLOOR AGAIN.
OUT IN THE WORLD...THE REAL WORLD...THERE'S A LARGE PERCENTAGE OF PEOPLE WHO STILL LOOK AT ME LIKE I'M SOME SORT OF VILLAIN.
BUT NOT HERE.
LATVERIA
TOUR PARTY
HERE, I'M STILL TONY STARK.
I'M A HERO HERE.
THESE ARE MY PEOPLE.
YOUR PEOPLE, HUH? TELL ME SOMETHING, TONY...
HOW MANY YEARS HAVE YOU BEEN COMING TO THIS SEMI-LEGAL GATHERING OF WARMONGERS, CRIMINALS, AND TERRORISTS WITHOUT EVER ONCE BOTHERING TO MENTION IT TO YOUR TEAMMATES?
COME ON, CAP.
I'VE GOTTEN A LOT OF LEADS FROM THIS PLACE. I'VE DONE A LOT OF GOOD BY COMING HERE.
YOU MAY BE HAPPY BUSTING DOWN DOORS AND SCARING THE RED, WHITE, AND BLUE OUT OF STOOL PIGEONS, BUT I HAVE A MORE SUBTLE APPROACH.
AND OUT OF EVERYONE ON THE TEAM, I'D NEVER EXPECT YOU TO JUDGE ME.

WE'RE ALL FLAWED, TONY. I'M IN.

YOU'D BETTER BE. I HAD TO CALL IN MORE THAN ONE FAVOR FOR THAT INVITE.

OF COURSE, ONCE UPON A TIME I WAS ON THE GUEST LIST.

DON'T WORRY, THOUGH. I'M WITH YOU.

THE DRONES ARE EQUIPPED WITH SURVEILLANCE EQUIPMENT. I'VE GOT EYES EVERYWHERE.

YOU SURE SHE'LL BE HERE?

SURE? NO.

BUT I PICKED UP THE NAME YOU GAVE ME--KASHMIR VENNEMA--AMONG SOME CHATTER RELATED TO THIS EVENT.

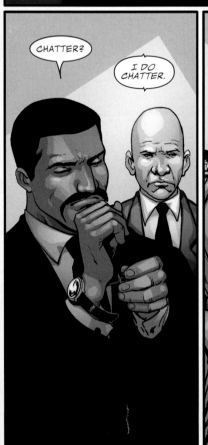

CHATTER?

I DO CHATTER.

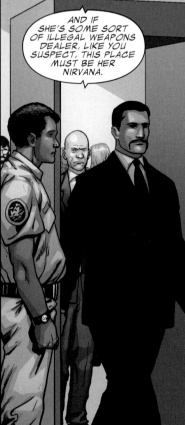

AND IF SHE'S SOME SORT OF ILLEGAL WEAPONS DEALER, LIKE YOU SUSPECT, THIS PLACE MUST BE HER NIRVANA.

YOUR WATCH, SIR.

THANK YOU.

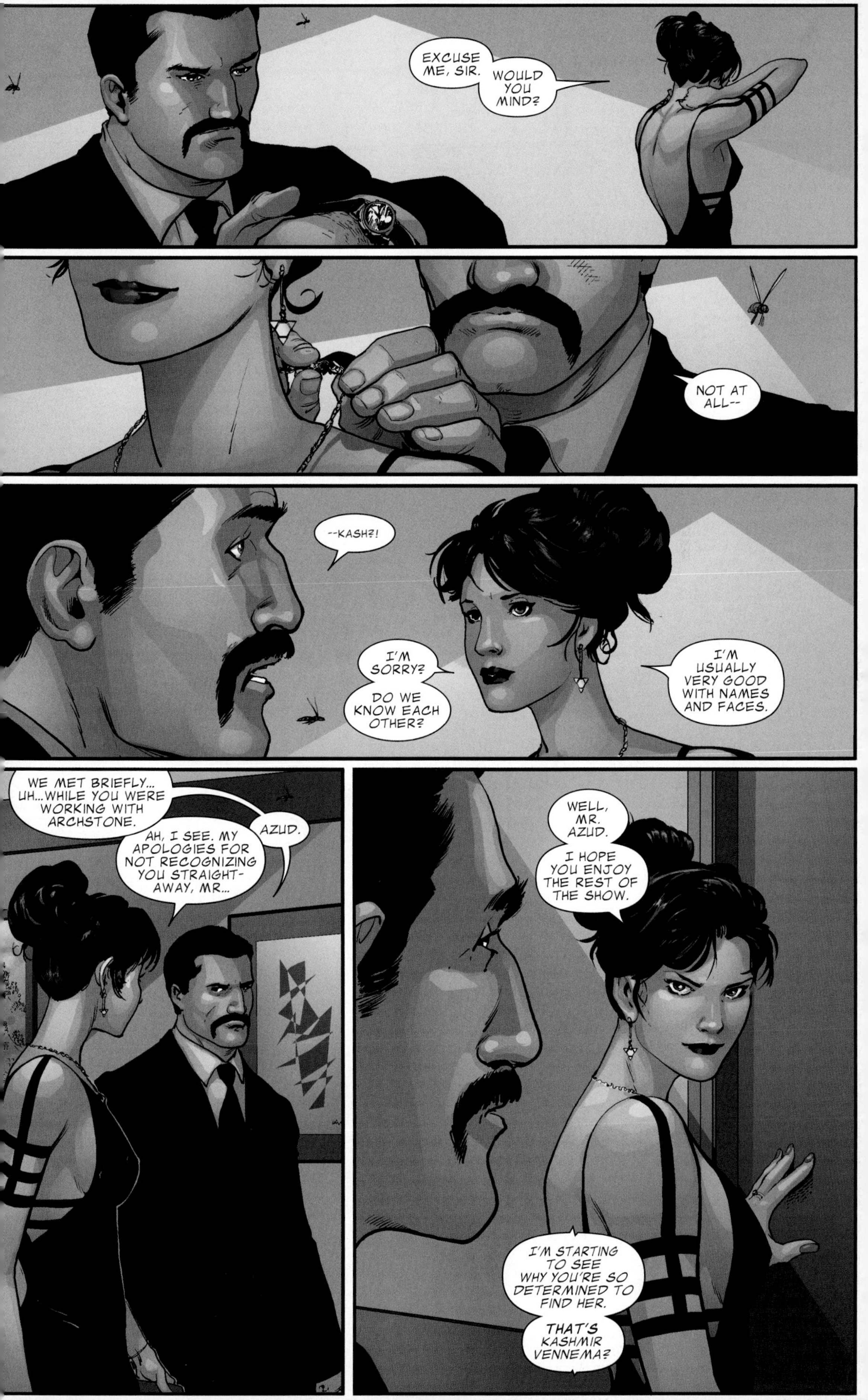
EXCUSE ME, SIR.
WOULD YOU MIND?
NOT AT ALL--
--KASH?!
I'M SORRY?
DO WE KNOW EACH OTHER?
I'M USUALLY VERY GOOD WITH NAMES AND FACES.
WE MET BRIEFLY... UH...WHILE YOU WERE WORKING WITH ARCHSTONE.
AH, I SEE. MY APOLOGIES FOR NOT RECOGNIZING YOU STRAIGHT-AWAY, MR...
AZUD.
WELL, MR. AZUD.
I HOPE YOU ENJOY THE REST OF THE SHOW.
I'M STARTING TO SEE WHY YOU'RE SO DETERMINED TO FIND HER.
THAT'S KASHMIR VENNEMA?

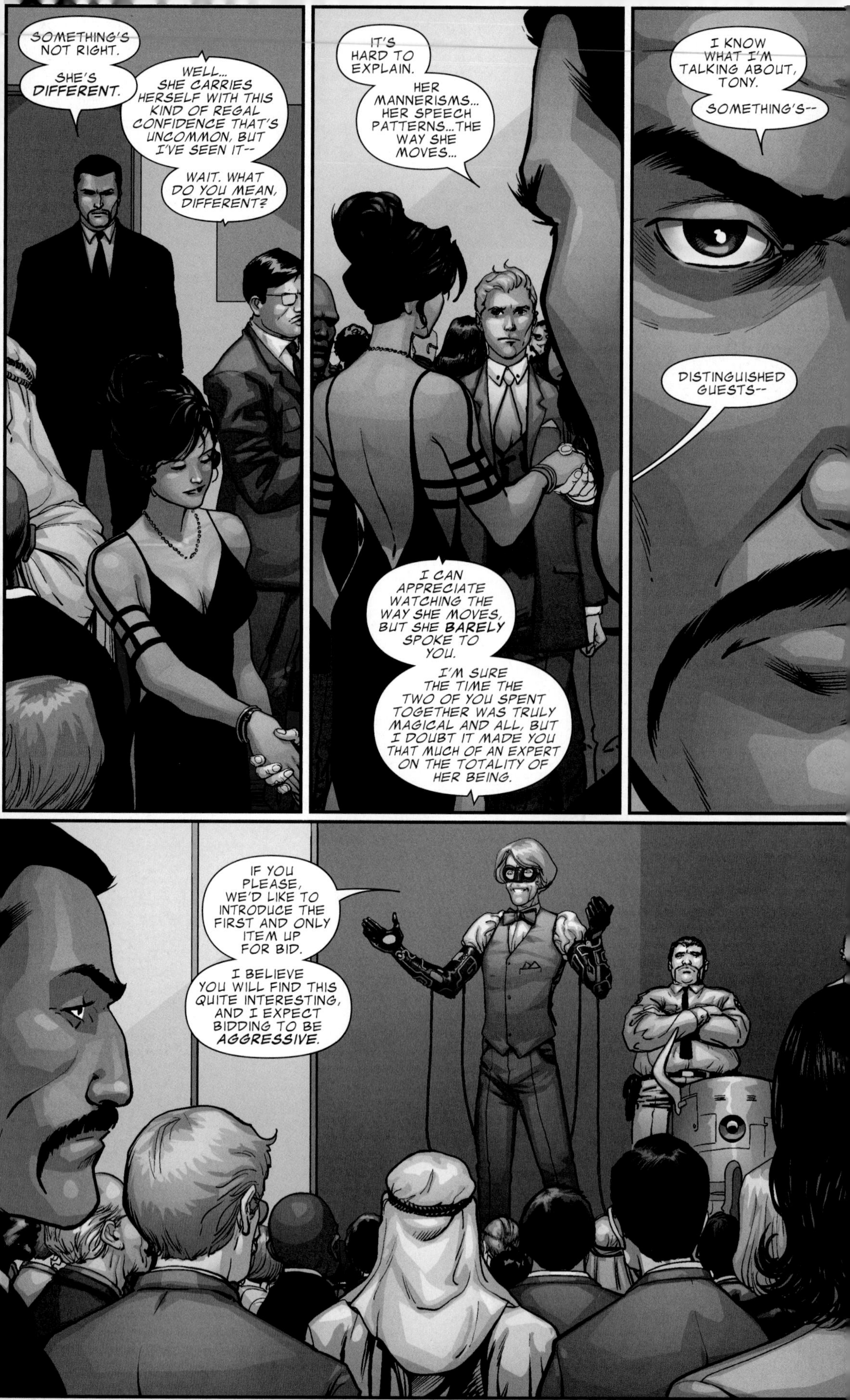
SOMETHING'S NOT RIGHT.
SHE'S DIFFERENT.
WELL... SHE CARRIES HERSELF WITH THIS KIND OF REGAL CONFIDENCE THAT'S UNCOMMON, BUT I'VE SEEN IT--
WAIT. WHAT DO YOU MEAN, DIFFERENT?
IT'S HARD TO EXPLAIN.
HER MANNERISMS... HER SPEECH PATTERNS...THE WAY SHE MOVES...
I CAN APPRECIATE WATCHING THE WAY SHE MOVES, BUT SHE BARELY SPOKE TO YOU.
I'M SURE THE TIME THE TWO OF YOU SPENT TOGETHER WAS TRULY MAGICAL AND ALL, BUT I DOUBT IT MADE YOU THAT MUCH OF AN EXPERT ON THE TOTALITY OF HER BEING.
I KNOW WHAT I'M TALKING ABOUT, TONY.
SOMETHING'S--
DISTINGUISHED GUESTS--
IF YOU PLEASE, WE'D LIKE TO INTRODUCE THE FIRST AND ONLY ITEM UP FOR BID.
I BELIEVE YOU WILL FIND THIS QUITE INTERESTING, AND I EXPECT BIDDING TO BE AGGRESSIVE.

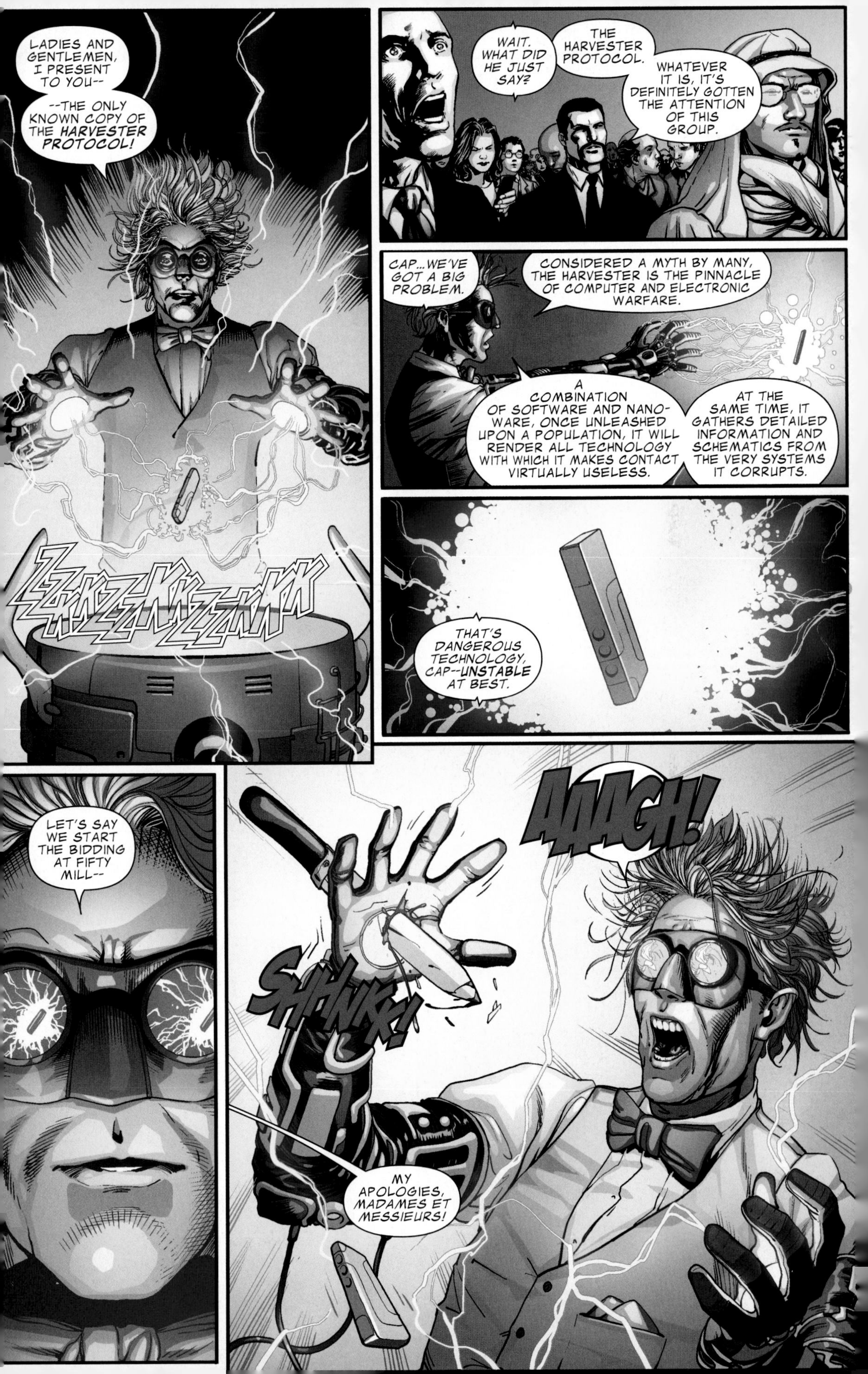
LADIES AND GENTLEMEN, I PRESENT TO YOU--
--THE ONLY KNOWN COPY OF THE HARVESTER PROTOCOL!
ZZKKZZKKZZKKK
WAIT. WHAT DID HE JUST SAY?
THE HARVESTER PROTOCOL.
WHATEVER IT IS, IT'S DEFINITELY GOTTEN THE ATTENTION OF THIS GROUP.
CAP...WE'VE GOT A BIG PROBLEM.
CONSIDERED A MYTH BY MANY, THE HARVESTER IS THE PINNACLE OF COMPUTER AND ELECTRONIC WARFARE.
A COMBINATION OF SOFTWARE AND NANO-WARE, ONCE UNLEASHED UPON A POPULATION, IT WILL RENDER ALL TECHNOLOGY WITH WHICH IT MAKES CONTACT VIRTUALLY USELESS.
AT THE SAME TIME, IT GATHERS DETAILED INFORMATION AND SCHEMATICS FROM THE VERY SYSTEMS IT CORRUPTS.
THAT'S DANGEROUS TECHNOLOGY, CAP--UNSTABLE AT BEST.
LET'S SAY WE START THE BIDDING AT FIFTY MILL--
AAAGH!
SHNKK!
MY APOLOGIES, MADAMES ET MESSIEURS!

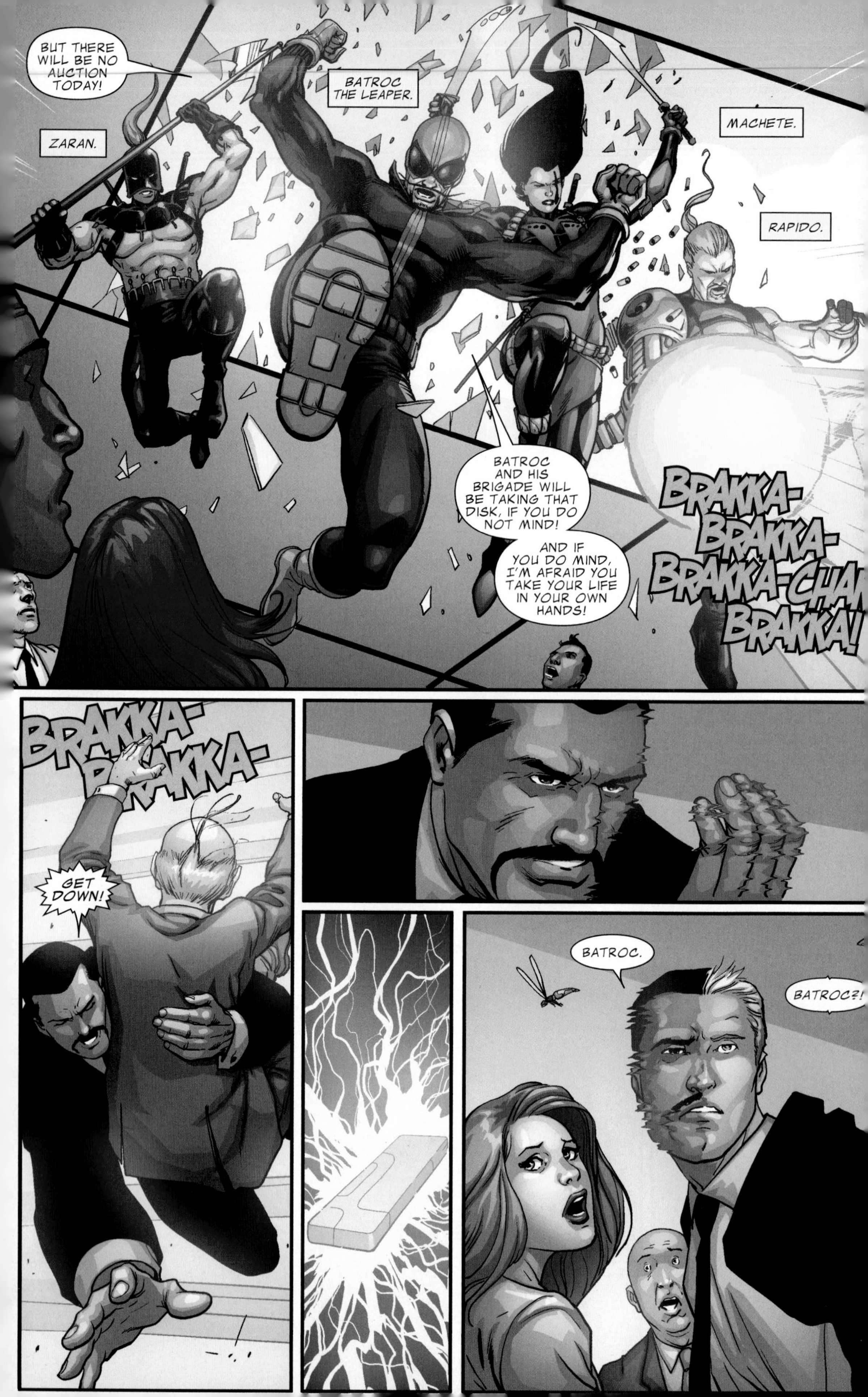
BUT THERE WILL BE NO AUCTION TODAY!
ZARAN.
BATROC THE LEAPER.
MACHETE.
RAPIDO.
BATROC AND HIS BRIGADE WILL BE TAKING THAT DISK, IF YOU DO NOT MIND!
AND IF YOU DO MIND, I'M AFRAID YOU TAKE YOUR LIFE IN YOUR OWN HANDS!
BRAKKA-BRAKKA-BRAKKA-CHA BRAKKA!
BRAKKA-BRAKKA-
GET DOWN!
BATROC.
BATROC?!

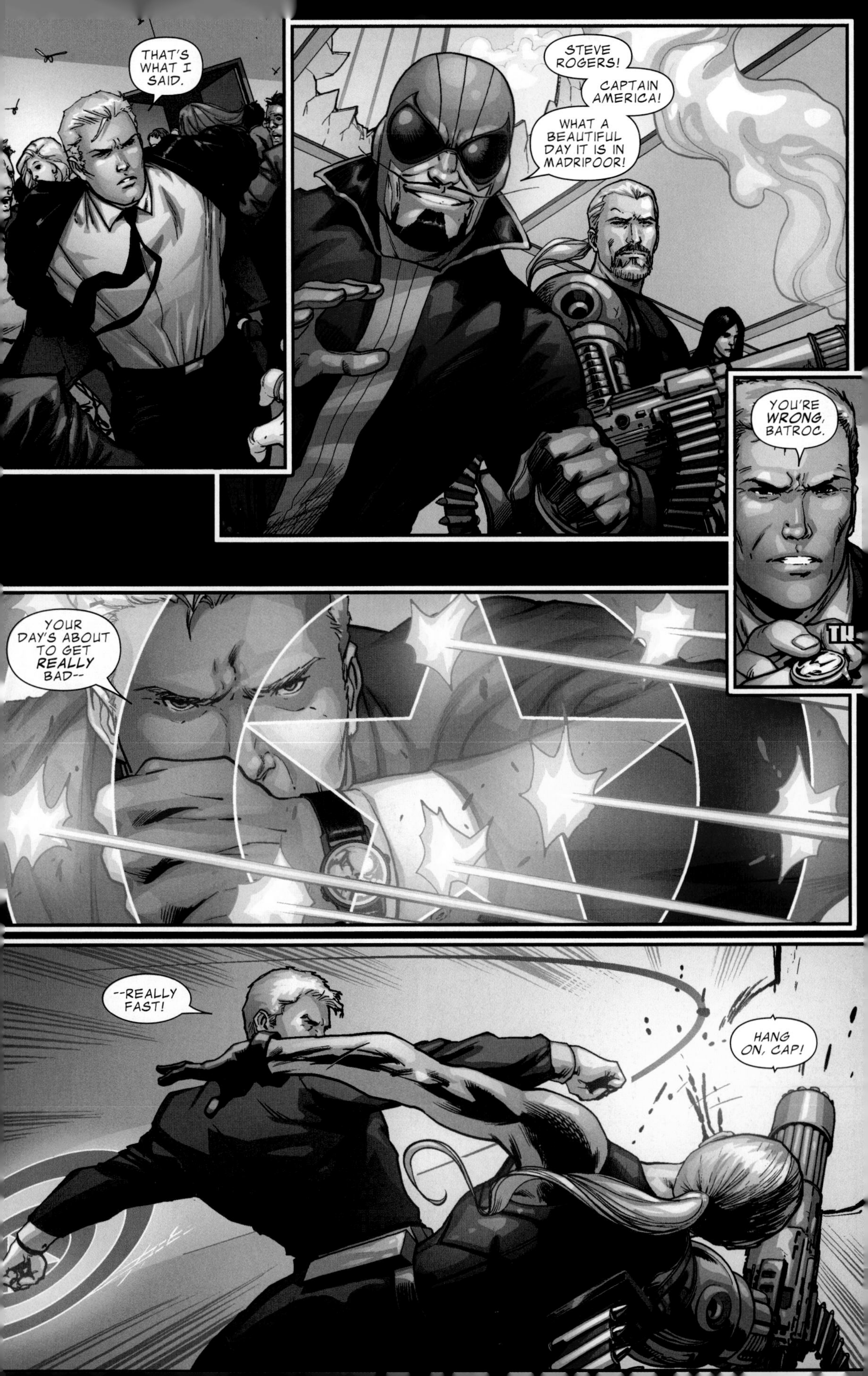

THAT'S WHAT I SAID.
STEVE ROGERS!
CAPTAIN AMERICA!
WHAT A BEAUTIFUL DAY IT IS IN MADRIPOOR!
YOU'RE WRONG, BATROC.
YOUR DAY'S ABOUT TO GET REALLY BAD--
--REALLY FAST!
HANG ON, CAP!

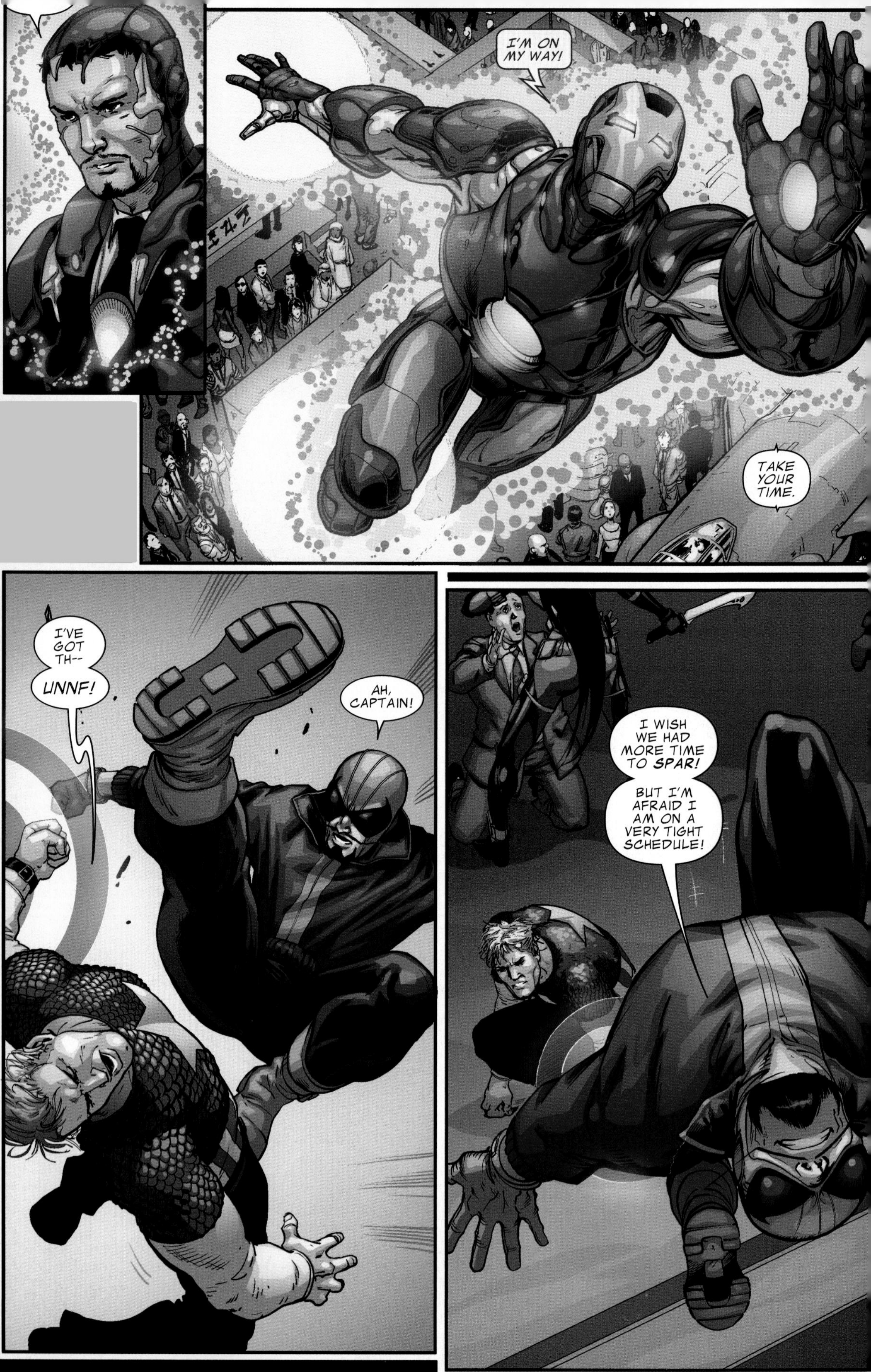
I'M ON MY WAY!
TAKE YOUR TIME.
I'VE GOT TH--
UNNF!
AH, CAPTAIN!
I WISH WE HAD MORE TIME TO SPAR!
BUT I'M AFRAID I AM ON A VERY TIGHT SCHEDULE!

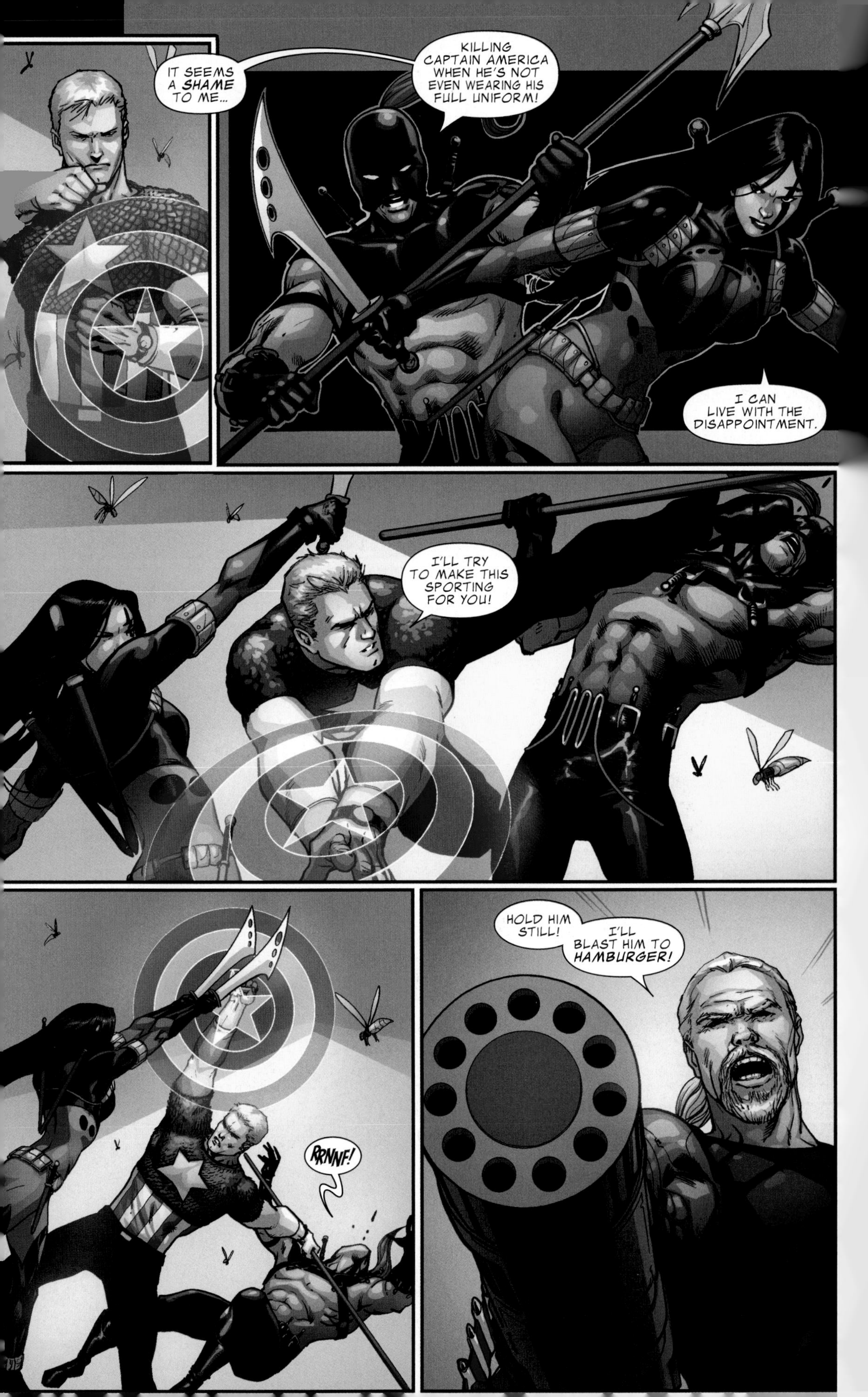
IT SEEMS A SHAME TO ME...
KILLING CAPTAIN AMERICA WHEN HE'S NOT EVEN WEARING HIS FULL UNIFORM!
I CAN LIVE WITH THE DISAPPOINTMENT.
I'LL TRY TO MAKE THIS SPORTING FOR YOU!
RRNNF!
HOLD HIM STILL!
I'LL BLAST HIM TO HAMBURGER!

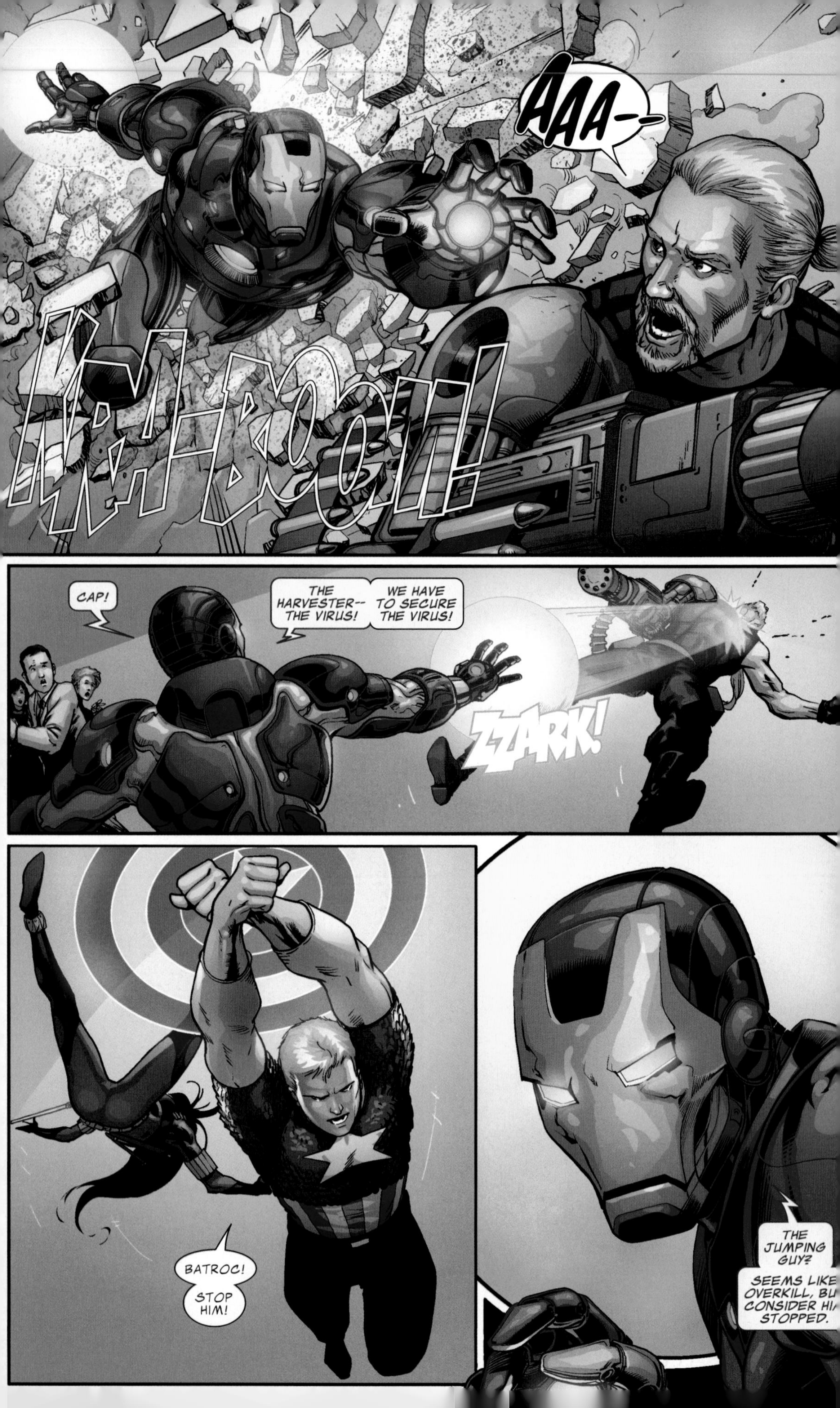
AAA--
K-THOOM!
CAP!
THE HARVESTER-- THE VIRUS!
WE HAVE TO SECURE THE VIRUS!
ZZARK!
BATROC!
STOP HIM!
THE JUMPING GUY?
SEEMS LIKE OVERKILL, BU
CONSIDER HI
STOPPED.

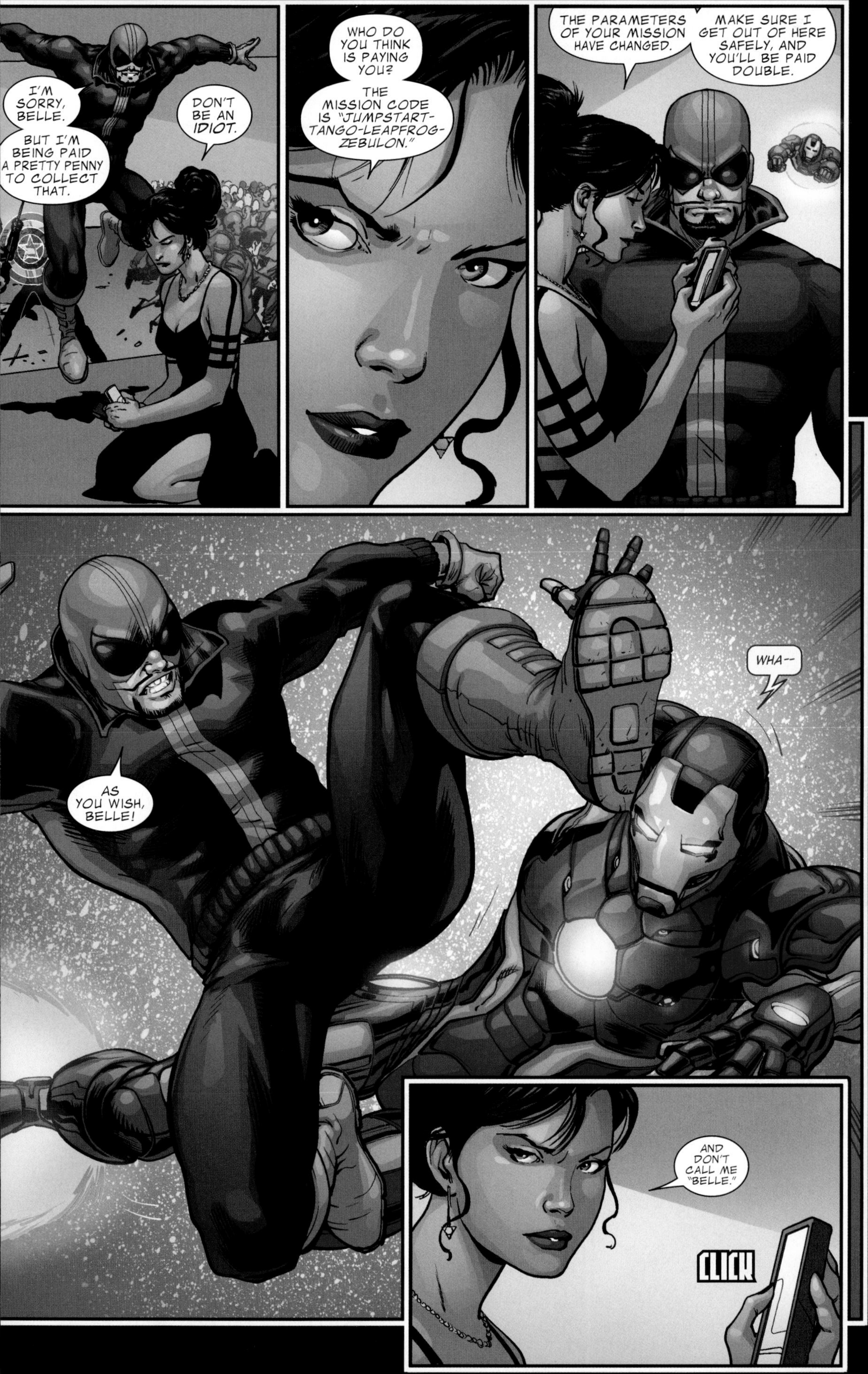
I'M SORRY, BELLE.
BUT I'M BEING PAID A PRETTY PENNY TO COLLECT THAT.
DON'T BE AN IDIOT.
WHO DO YOU THINK IS PAYING YOU?
THE MISSION CODE IS "JUMPSTART-TANGO-LEAPFROG-ZEBULON."
THE PARAMETERS OF YOUR MISSION HAVE CHANGED.
MAKE SURE I GET OUT OF HERE SAFELY, AND YOU'LL BE PAID DOUBLE.
AS YOU WISH, BELLE!
WHA--
AND DON'T CALL ME "BELLE."
CLICK

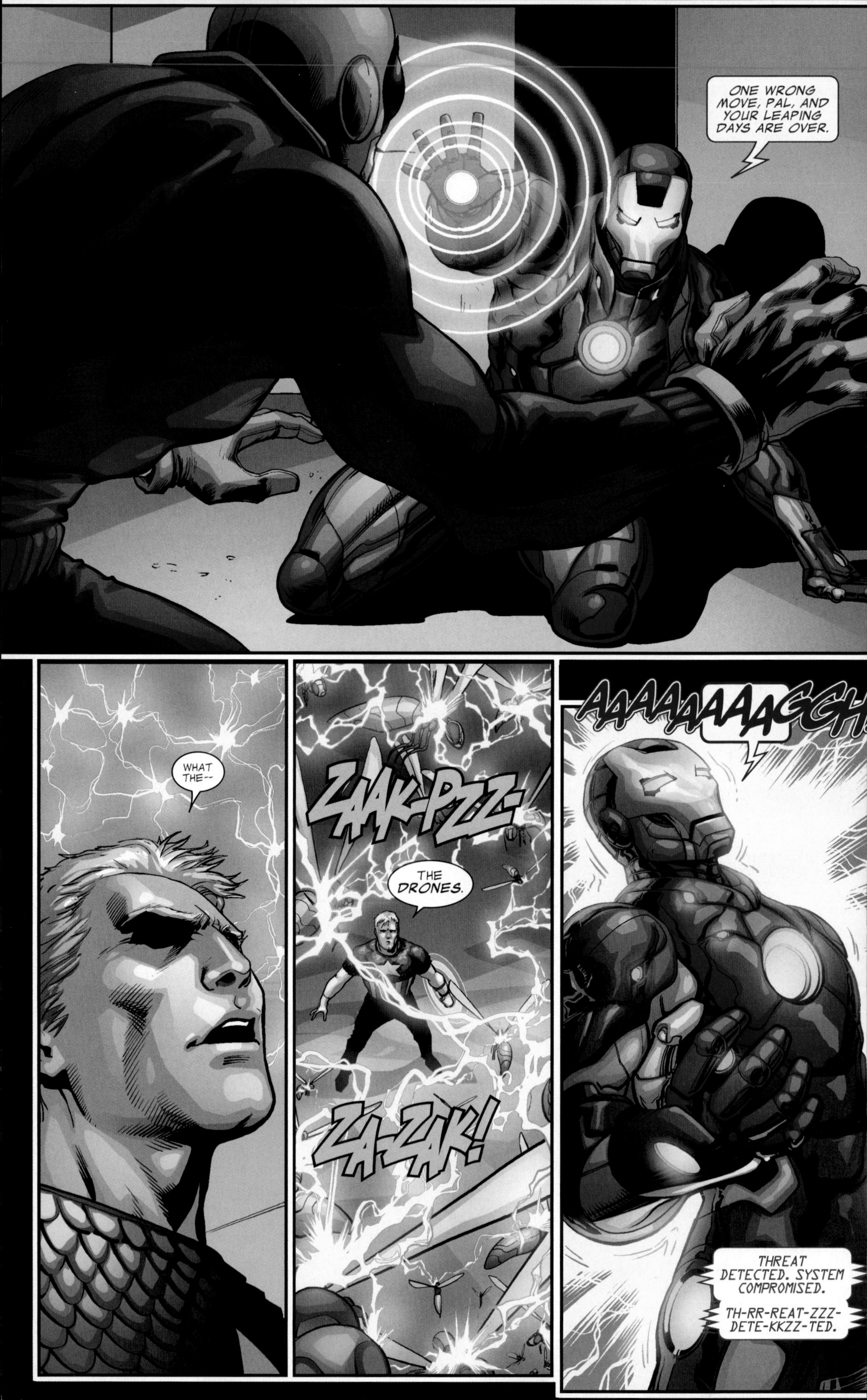
ONE WRONG MOVE, PAL, AND YOUR LEAPING DAYS ARE OVER.
WHAT THE--
ZAAK-PZZ-
THE DRONES.
ZA-ZAK!
AAAAAAAAGGH!
THREAT DETECTED. SYSTEM COMPROMISED.
TH-RR-REAT-ZZZ-DETE-KKZZ-TED.

VZZZZZZZZZZZZZZZZZZZZZZZZZZZZ

UNNNF!

...

ZZZK-ZZ-
KKK-
ZZZZ

HARD LIGHT SHIELD... INFECTED!

IT'S USELESS!

ARMOR... CORRUPTED--

--HAVE TO--

--SHUT DOWN!

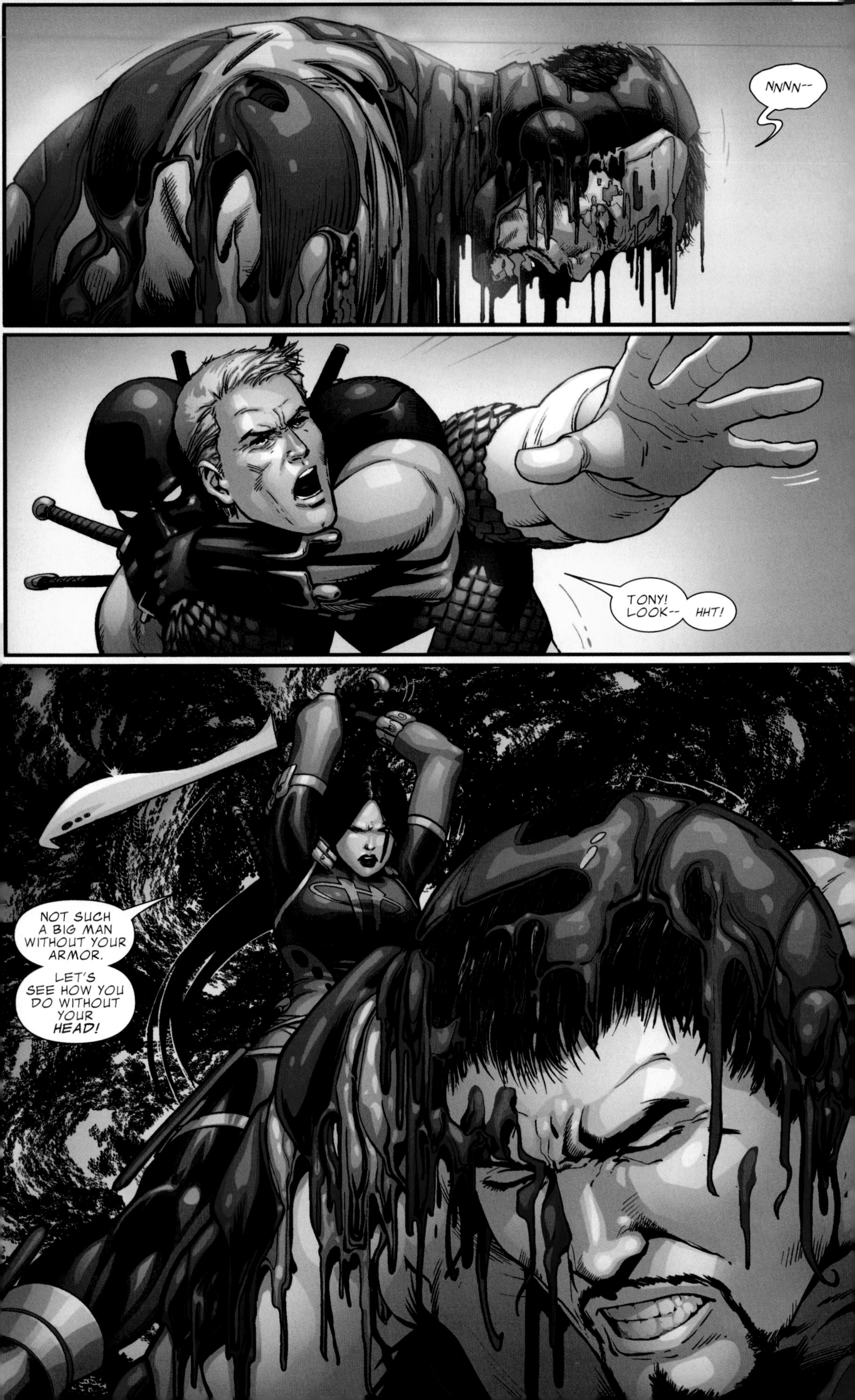
NNNN--
TONY! LOOK--
HHT!
NOT SUCH A BIG MAN WITHOUT YOUR ARMOR.
LET'S SEE HOW YOU DO WITHOUT YOUR HEAD!

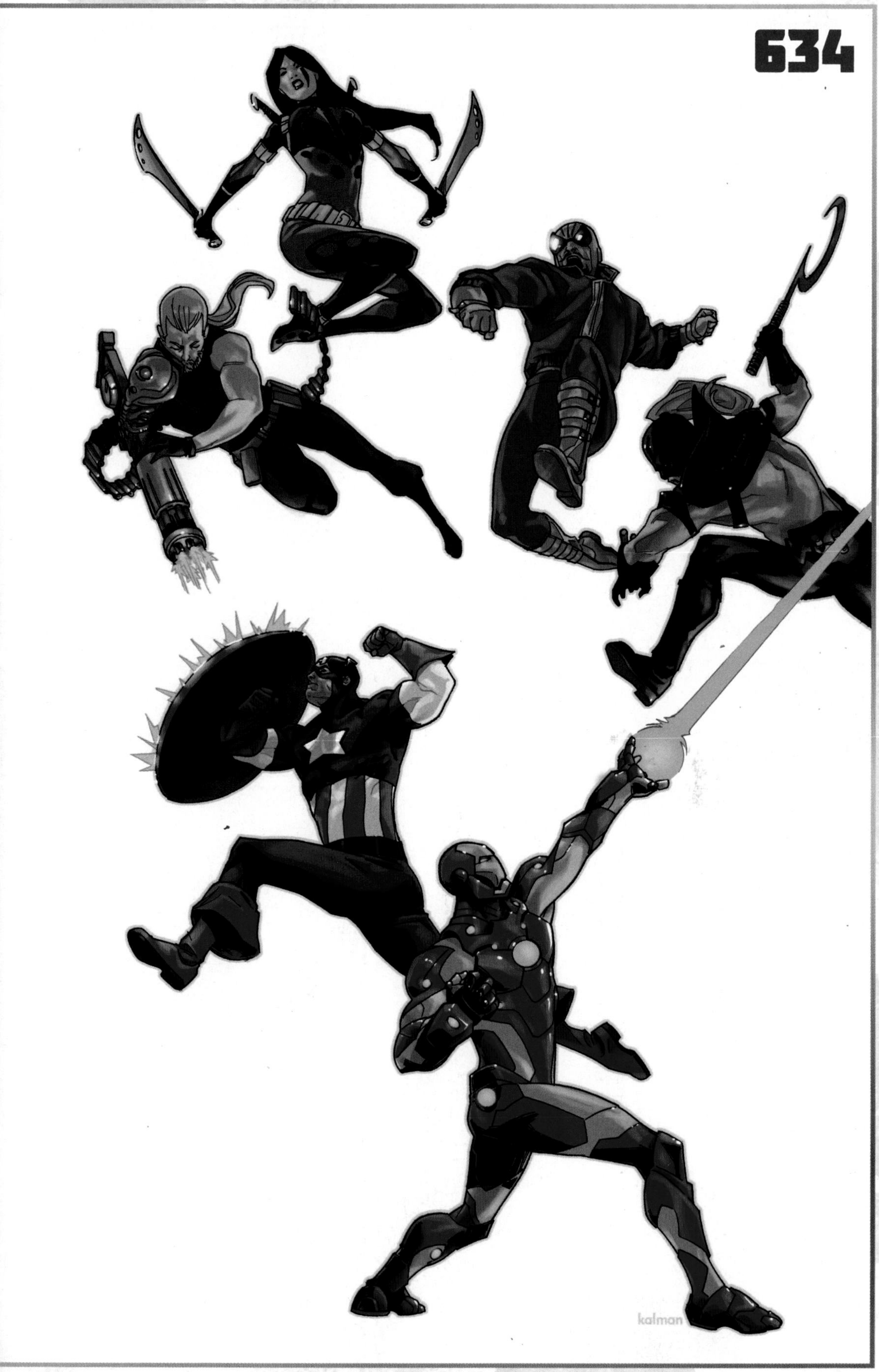
634
kalman

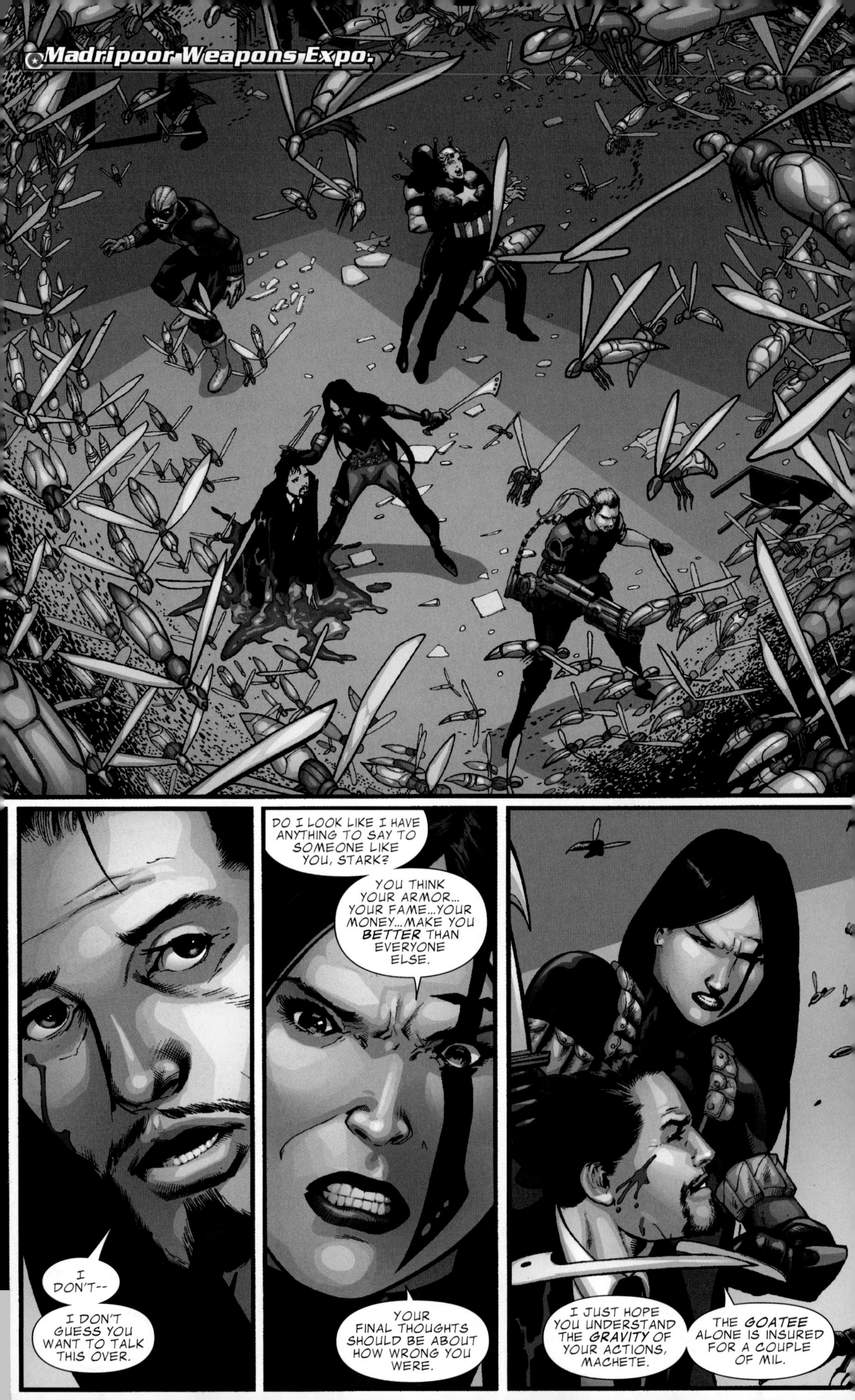
Madripoor Weapons Expo.
I DON'T--
I DON'T GUESS YOU WANT TO TALK THIS OVER.
DO I LOOK LIKE I HAVE ANYTHING TO SAY TO SOMEONE LIKE YOU, STARK?
YOU THINK YOUR ARMOR... YOUR FAME...YOUR MONEY...MAKE YOU BETTER THAN EVERYONE ELSE.
YOUR FINAL THOUGHTS SHOULD BE ABOUT HOW WRONG YOU WERE.
I JUST HOPE YOU UNDERSTAND THE GRAVITY OF YOUR ACTIONS, MACHETE.
THE GOATEE ALONE IS INSURED FOR A COUPLE OF MIL.

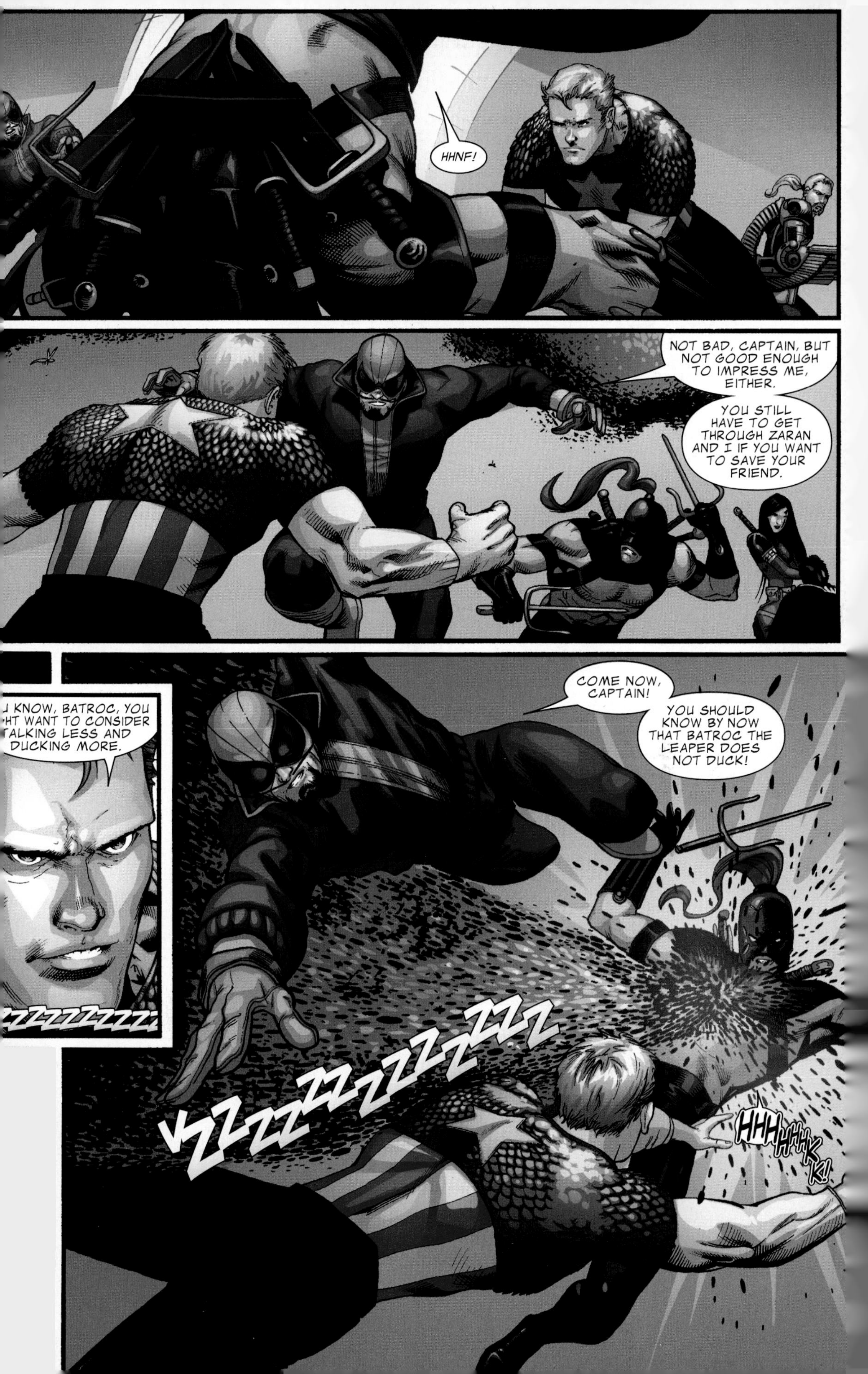
HHNF!
NOT BAD, CAPTAIN, BUT NOT GOOD ENOUGH TO IMPRESS ME, EITHER.
YOU STILL HAVE TO GET THROUGH ZARAN AND I IF YOU WANT TO SAVE YOUR FRIEND.
U KNOW, BATROC, YOU
HT WANT TO CONSIDER
TALKING LESS AND
DUCKING MORE.
ZZZZZZZZZZZ
COME NOW, CAPTAIN!
YOU SHOULD KNOW BY NOW THAT BATROC THE LEAPER DOES NOT DUCK!
VZZZZZZZZZZZZZZ
HHHHHKK!

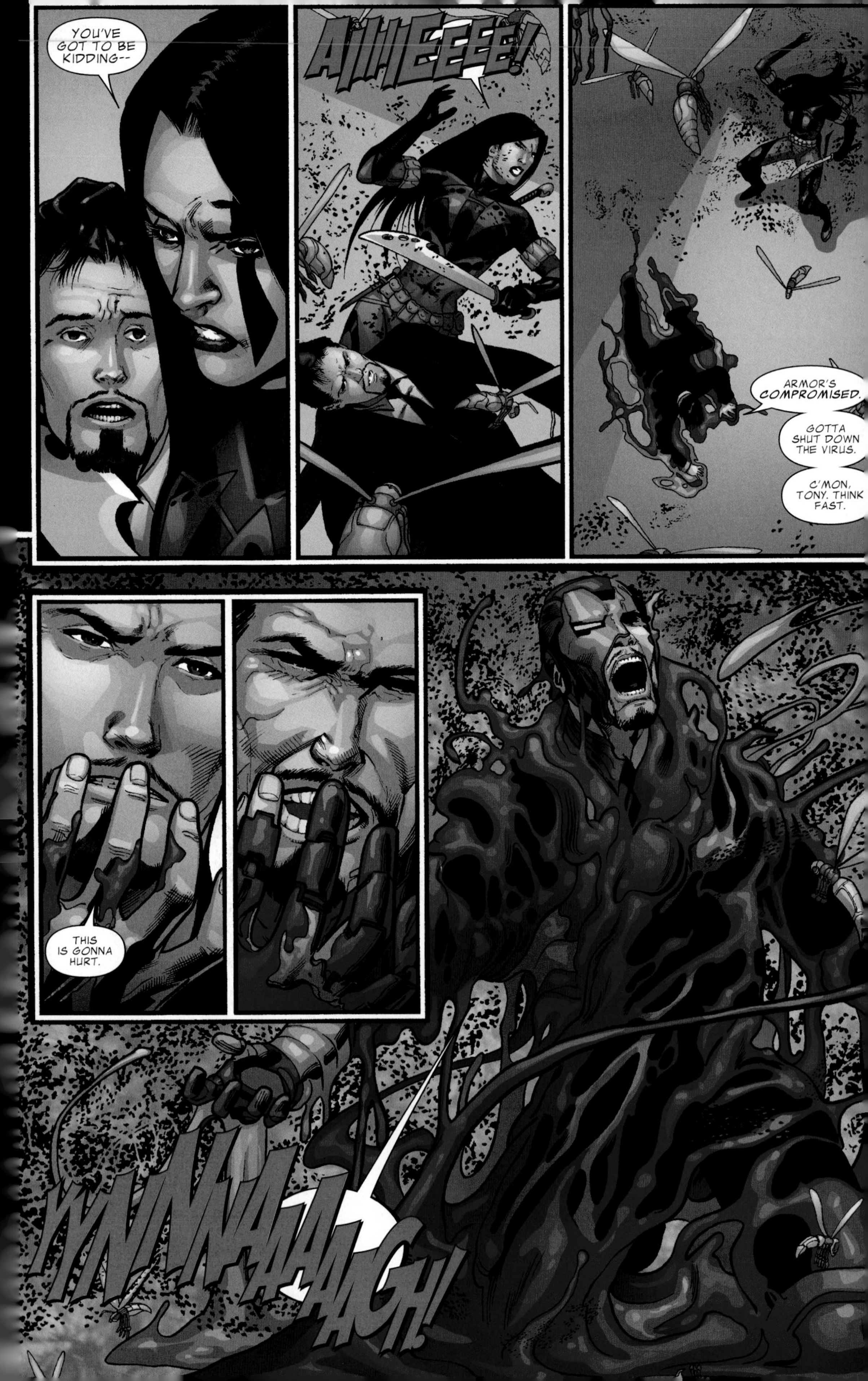
YOU'VE GOT TO BE KIDDING--
AIIIEEEE!
ARMOR'S COMPROMISED.
GOTTA SHUT DOWN THE VIRUS.
C'MON, TONY. THINK FAST.
THIS IS GONNA HURT.
YYNNAAAAGH!

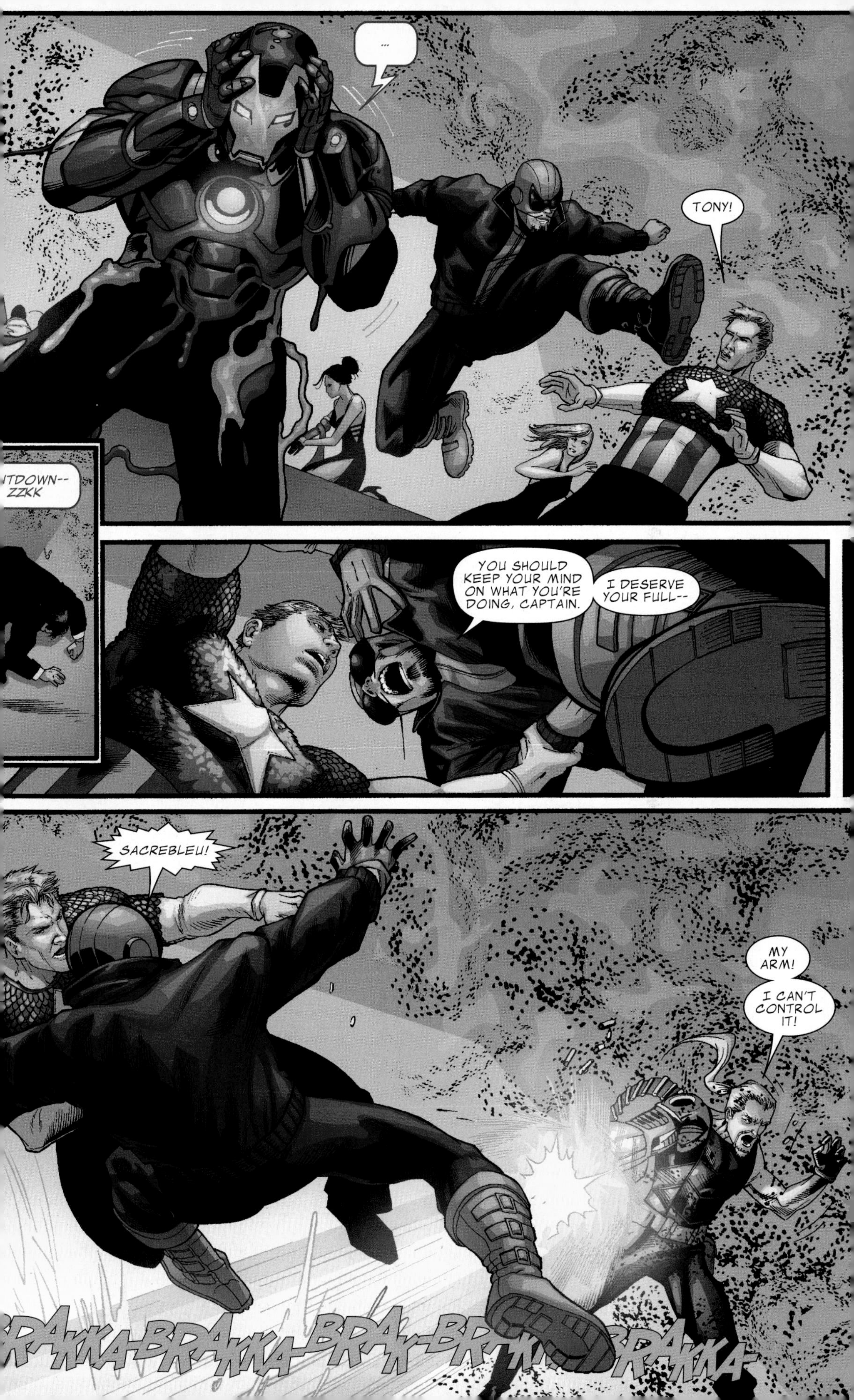
...
TONY!
...TDOWN--
ZZKK
YOU SHOULD KEEP YOUR MIND ON WHAT YOU'RE DOING, CAPTAIN.
I DESERVE YOUR FULL--
SACREBLEU!
MY ARM!
I CAN'T CONTROL IT!
BRAKKA-BRAKKA-BRAK-BR...BRAKKA

GET DOWN!

BRAKKA-BRAKKA-
BRAKKA-BRAKKA-
BRAKKA-
BRAK-
BRAKKA

ALL RIGHT.

I'D SAY THAT WAS A SUFFICIENT *TEST* FOR THE HARVESTER.

NO NEED FOR GOING *GLOBAL* JUST YET. THAT'S A PRIVILEGE RESERVED FOR PAYING CUSTOMERS.

BATROC! WRAP IT UP!

MY...MY ARM...

WITH WHAT WE'RE BEING PAID, RAPIDO, WE'LL BUY YOU A *NEW* ARM!

YOU ALL RIGHT?

DON'T--

NNN

--WORRY ABOUT ME.

ANOTHER COUPLE OF MINUTE AND I WOULD'VE *CHARMED* MY WA OUT OF TROUBLE

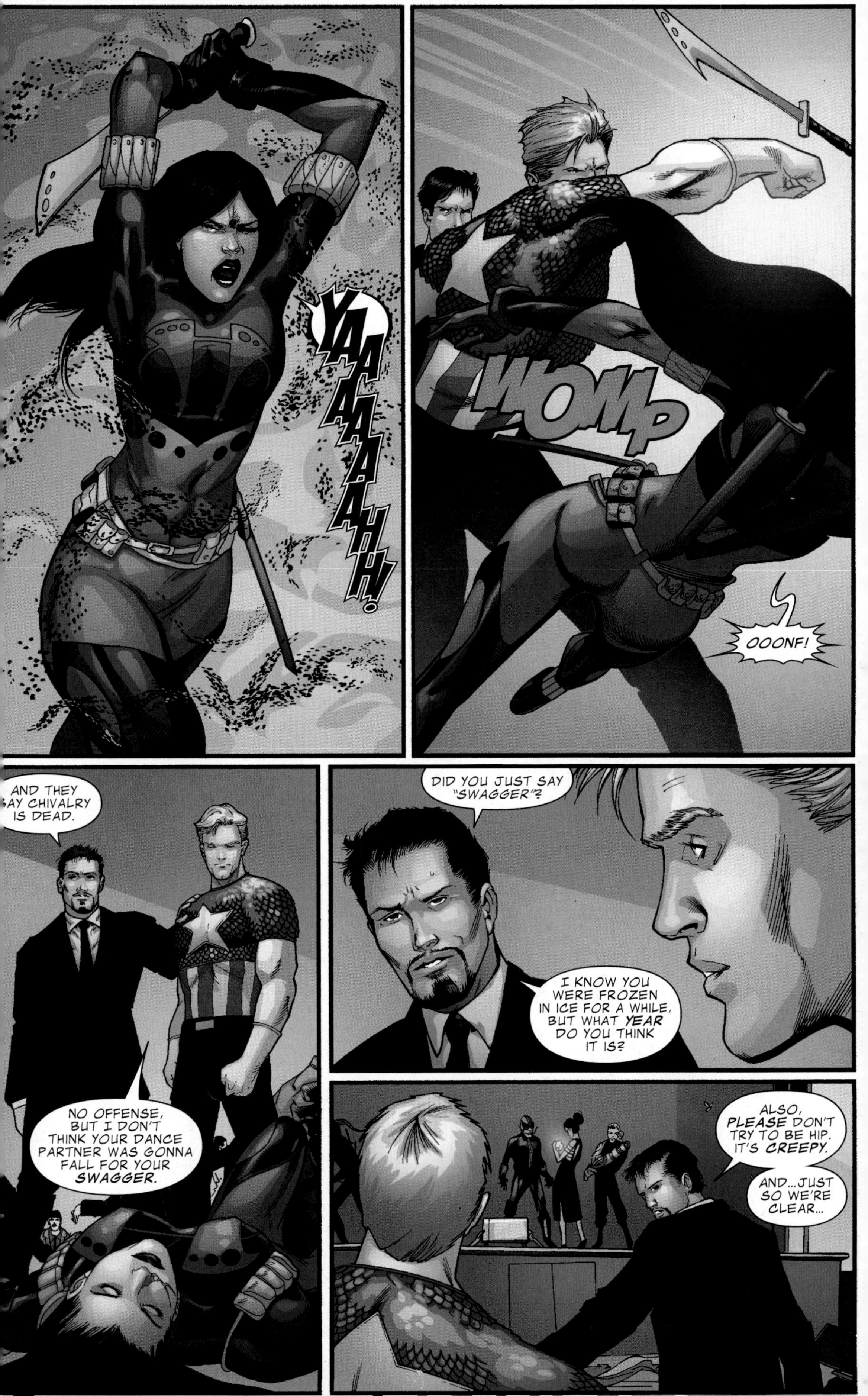
YAAAAAAAHH!
WOMP
OOONF!
AND THEY SAY CHIVALRY IS DEAD.
NO OFFENSE, BUT I DON'T THINK YOUR DANCE PARTNER WAS GONNA FALL FOR YOUR SWAGGER.
DID YOU JUST SAY "SWAGGER"?
I KNOW YOU WERE FROZEN IN ICE FOR A WHILE, BUT WHAT YEAR DO YOU THINK IT IS?
ALSO, PLEASE DON'T TRY TO BE HIP. IT'S CREEPY.
AND...JUST SO WE'RE CLEAR...

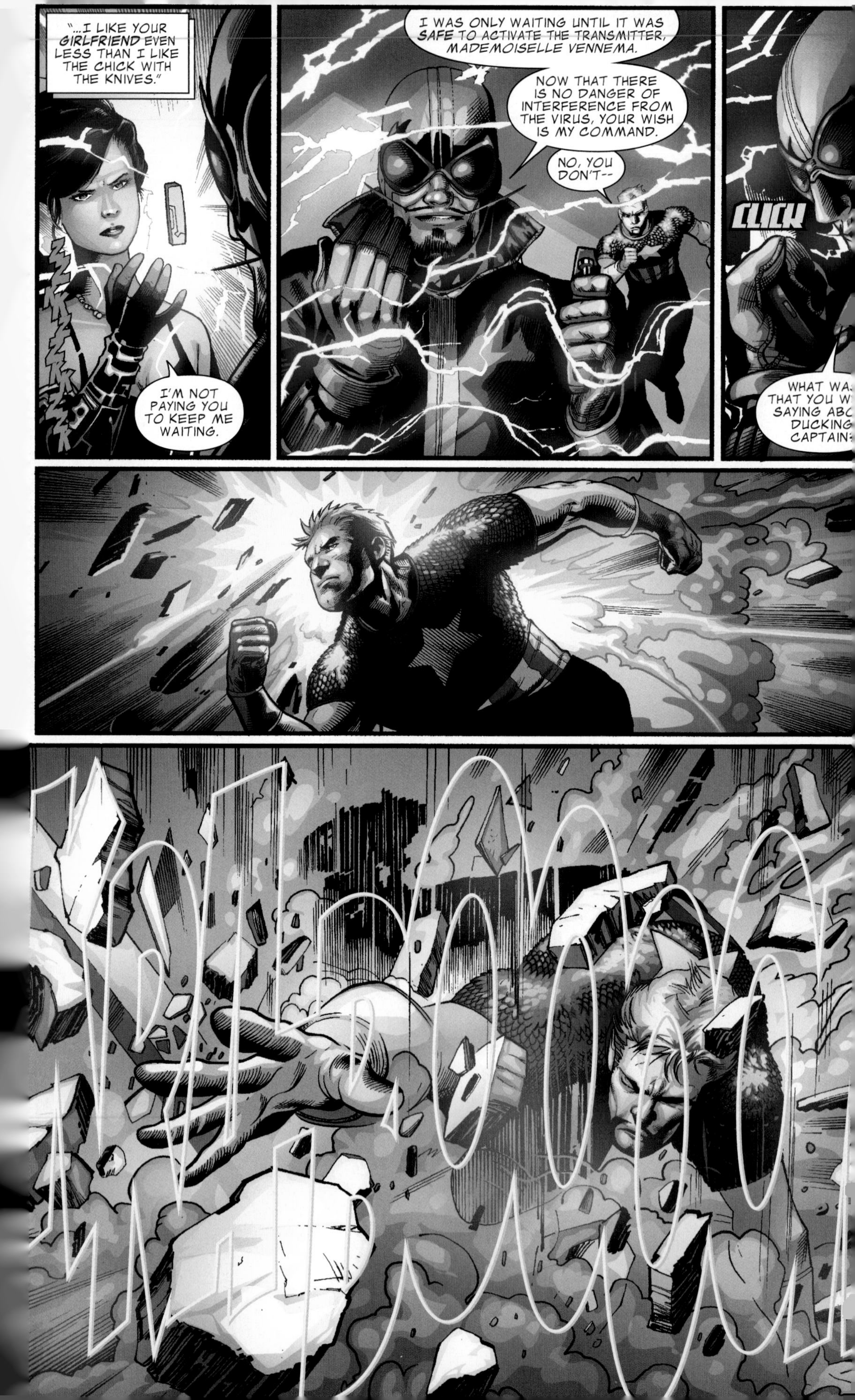
"...I LIKE YOUR GIRLFRIEND EVEN LESS THAN I LIKE THE CHICK WITH THE KNIVES."
I'M NOT PAYING YOU TO KEEP ME WAITING.
I WAS ONLY WAITING UNTIL IT WAS SAFE TO ACTIVATE THE TRANSMITTER, MADEMOISELLE VENNEMA.
NOW THAT THERE IS NO DANGER OF INTERFERENCE FROM THE VIRUS, YOUR WISH IS MY COMMAND.
NO, YOU DON'T--
CLICK
WHAT WA THAT YOU W SAYING ABO DUCKING CAPTAIN

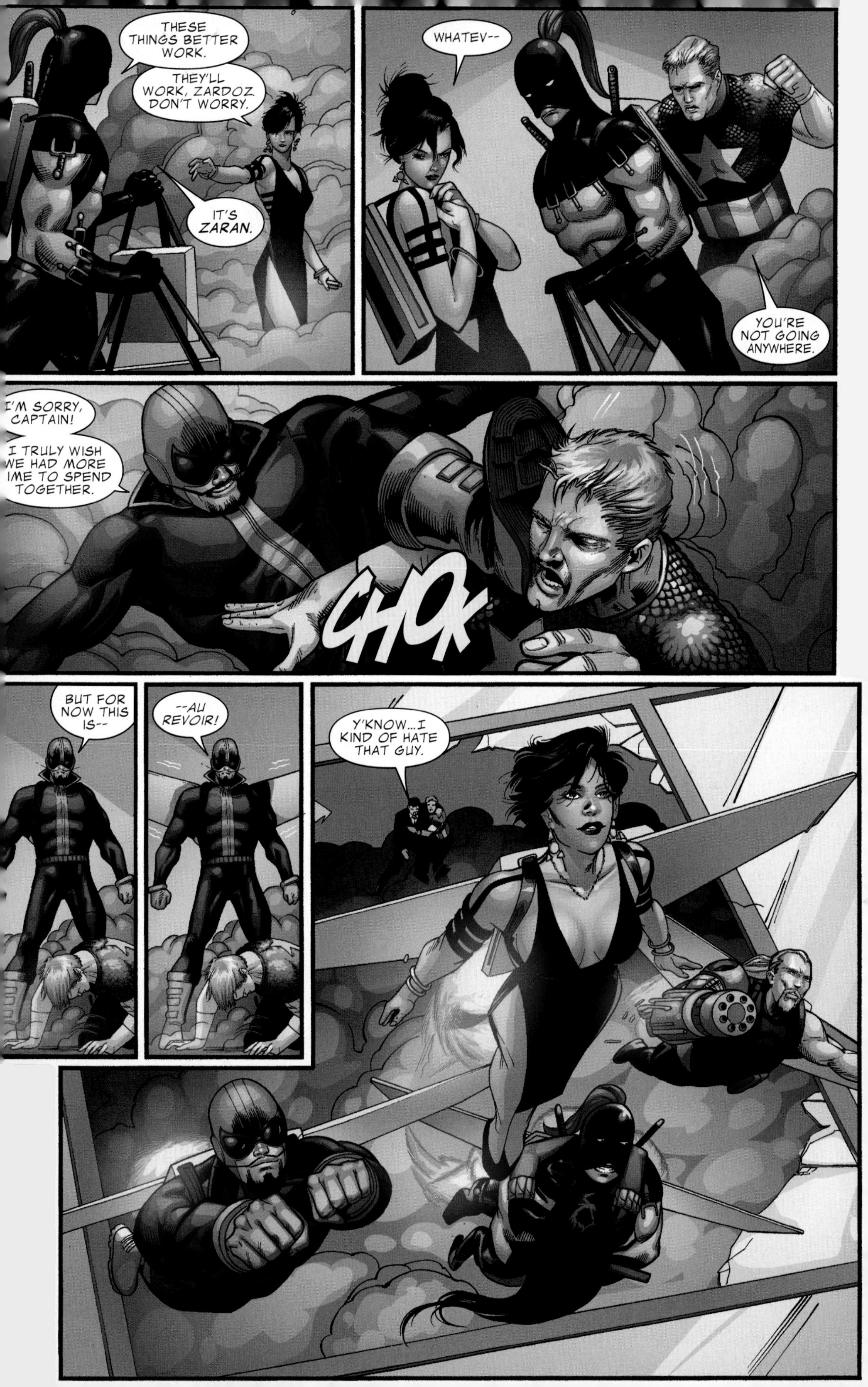
THESE THINGS BETTER WORK.
THEY'LL WORK, ZARDOZ. DON'T WORRY.
IT'S ZARAN.
WHATEV--
YOU'RE NOT GOING ANYWHERE.
I'M SORRY, CAPTAIN!
I TRULY WISH WE HAD MORE TIME TO SPEND TOGETHER.
CHOK
BUT FOR NOW THIS IS--
--AU REVOIR!
Y'KNOW...I KIND OF HATE THAT GUY.

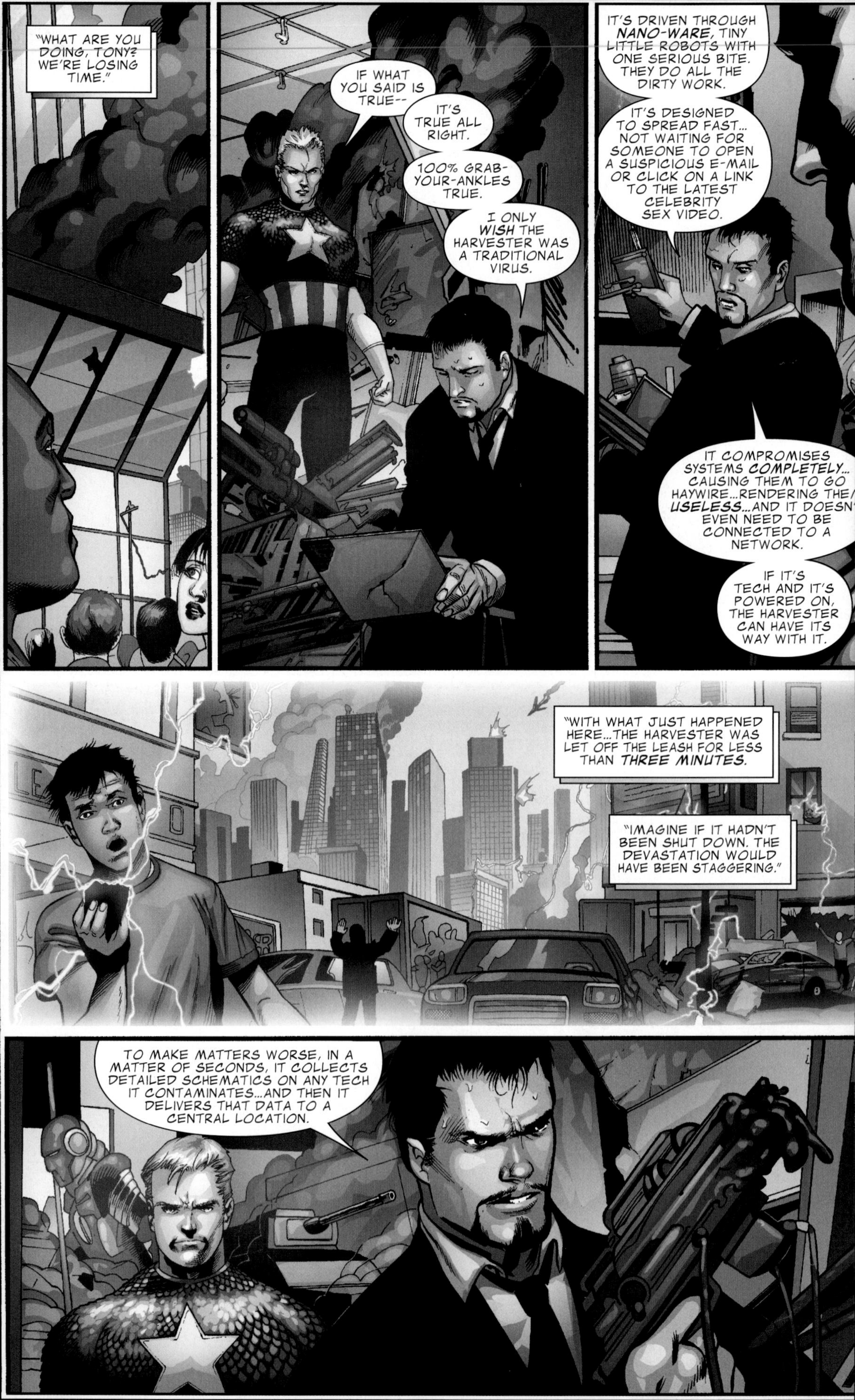
"WHAT ARE YOU DOING, TONY? WE'RE LOSING TIME."
IF WHAT YOU SAID IS TRUE--
IT'S TRUE ALL RIGHT.
100% GRAB-YOUR-ANKLES TRUE.
I ONLY WISH THE HARVESTER WAS A TRADITIONAL VIRUS.
IT'S DRIVEN THROUGH NANO-WARE, TINY LITTLE ROBOTS WITH ONE SERIOUS BITE. THEY DO ALL THE DIRTY WORK.
IT'S DESIGNED TO SPREAD FAST... NOT WAITING FOR SOMEONE TO OPEN A SUSPICIOUS E-MAIL OR CLICK ON A LINK TO THE LATEST CELEBRITY SEX VIDEO.
IT COMPROMISES SYSTEMS COMPLETELY... CAUSING THEM TO GO HAYWIRE...RENDERING THEM USELESS...AND IT DOESN'T EVEN NEED TO BE CONNECTED TO A NETWORK.
IF IT'S TECH AND IT'S POWERED ON, THE HARVESTER CAN HAVE ITS WAY WITH IT.
"WITH WHAT JUST HAPPENED HERE...THE HARVESTER WAS LET OFF THE LEASH FOR LESS THAN THREE MINUTES.
"IMAGINE IF IT HADN'T BEEN SHUT DOWN. THE DEVASTATION WOULD HAVE BEEN STAGGERING."
TO MAKE MATTERS WORSE, IN A MATTER OF SECONDS, IT COLLECTS DETAILED SCHEMATICS ON ANY TECH IT CONTAMINATES...AND THEN IT DELIVERS THAT DATA TO A CENTRAL LOCATION.

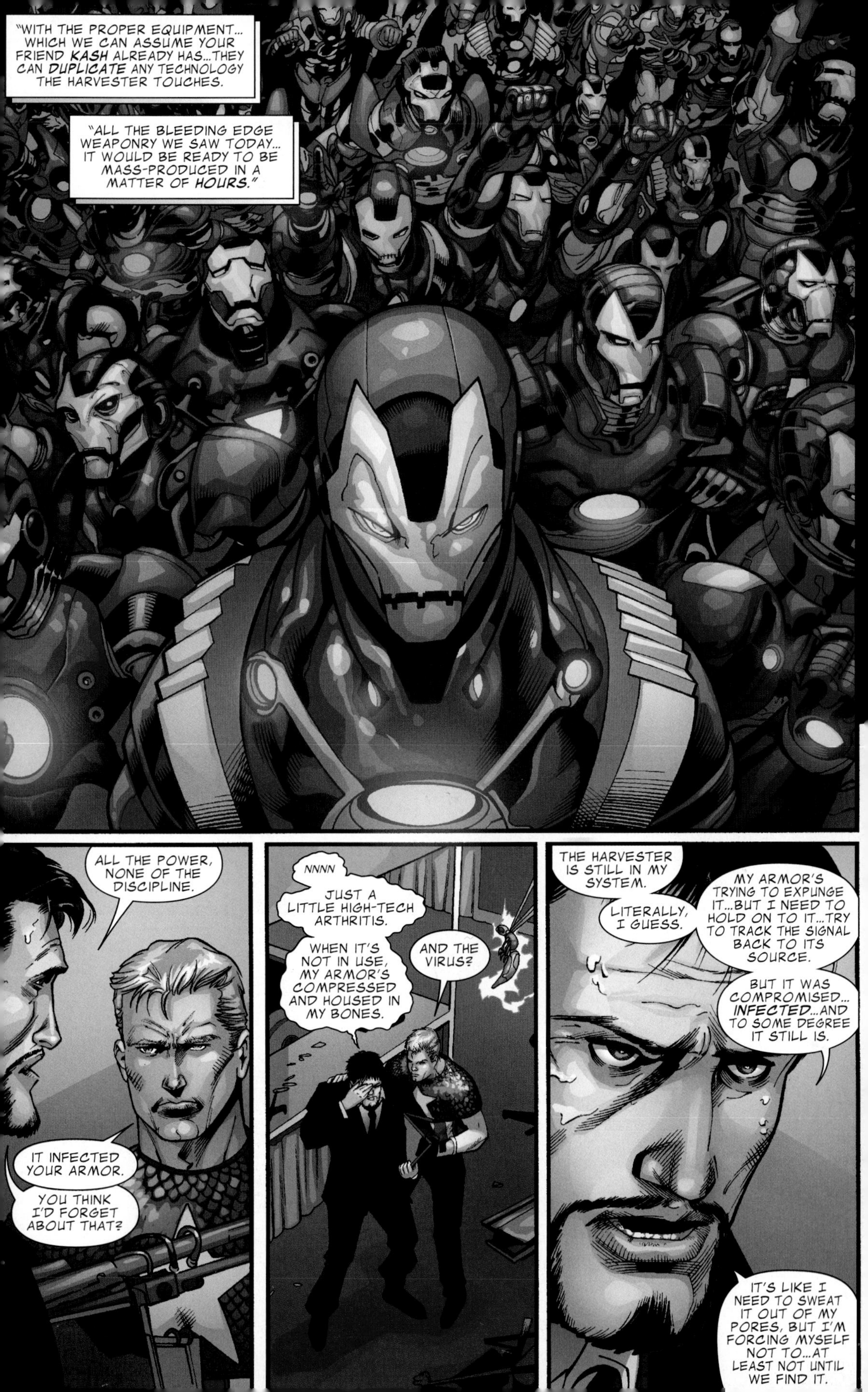
"WITH THE PROPER EQUIPMENT... WHICH WE CAN ASSUME YOUR FRIEND KASH ALREADY HAS...THEY CAN DUPLICATE ANY TECHNOLOGY THE HARVESTER TOUCHES.
"ALL THE BLEEDING EDGE WEAPONRY WE SAW TODAY... IT WOULD BE READY TO BE MASS-PRODUCED IN A MATTER OF HOURS."
ALL THE POWER, NONE OF THE DISCIPLINE.
IT INFECTED YOUR ARMOR.
YOU THINK I'D FORGET ABOUT THAT?
NNNN
JUST A LITTLE HIGH-TECH ARTHRITIS.
WHEN IT'S NOT IN USE, MY ARMOR'S COMPRESSED AND HOUSED IN MY BONES.
AND THE VIRUS?
THE HARVESTER IS STILL IN MY SYSTEM.
LITERALLY, I GUESS.
MY ARMOR'S TRYING TO EXPUNGE IT...BUT I NEED TO HOLD ON TO IT...TRY TO TRACK THE SIGNAL BACK TO ITS SOURCE.
BUT IT WAS COMPROMISED... INFECTED...AND TO SOME DEGREE IT STILL IS.
IT'S LIKE I NEED TO SWEAT IT OUT OF MY PORES, BUT I'M FORCING MYSELF NOT TO...AT LEAST NOT UNTIL WE FIND IT.

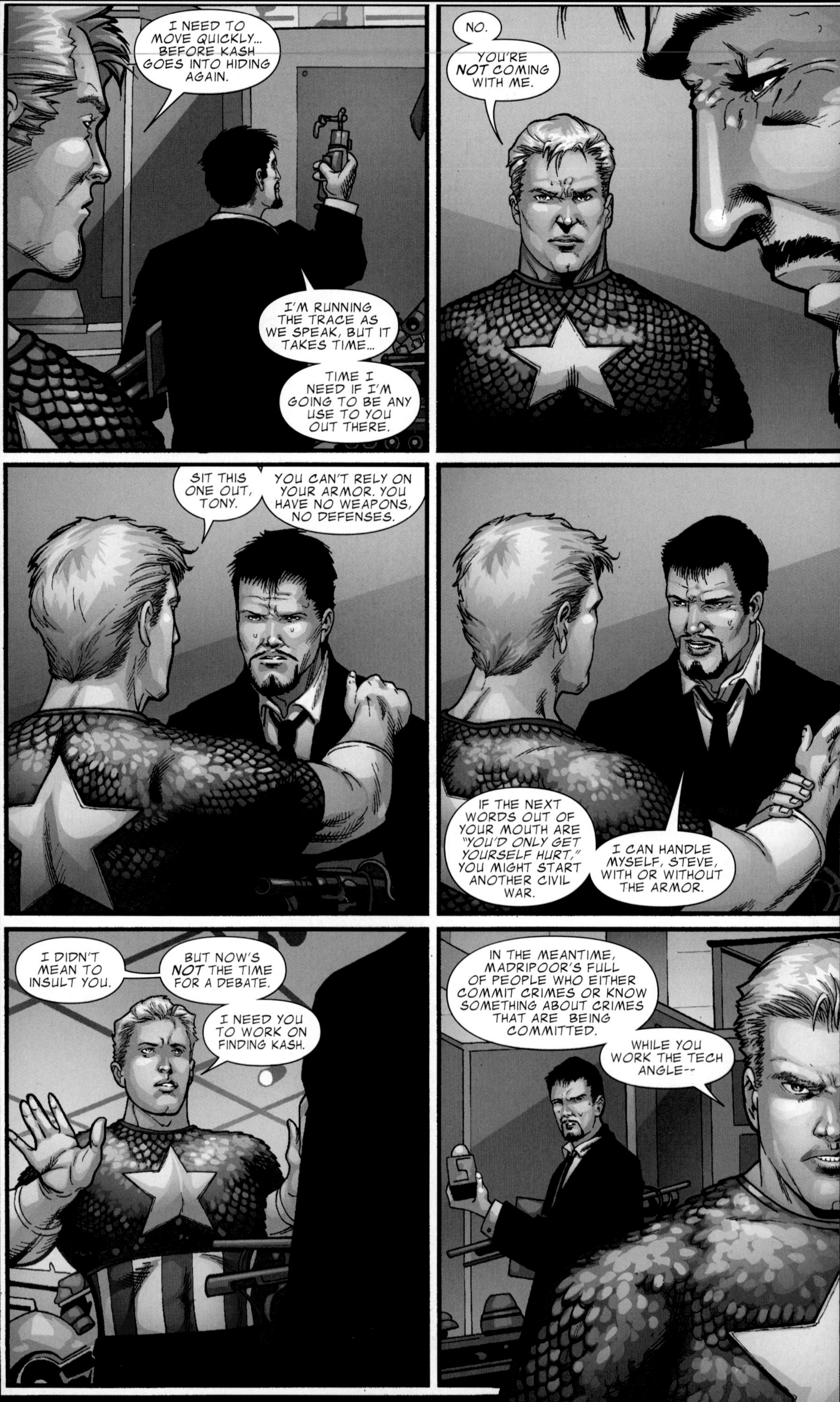
I NEED TO MOVE QUICKLY... BEFORE KASH GOES INTO HIDING AGAIN.
I'M RUNNING THE TRACE AS WE SPEAK, BUT IT TAKES TIME...
TIME I NEED IF I'M GOING TO BE ANY USE TO YOU OUT THERE.
NO.
YOU'RE *NOT* COMING WITH ME.
SIT THIS ONE OUT, TONY.
YOU CAN'T RELY ON YOUR ARMOR. YOU HAVE NO WEAPONS, NO DEFENSES.
IF THE NEXT WORDS OUT OF YOUR MOUTH ARE *"YOU'D ONLY GET YOURSELF HURT,"* YOU MIGHT START ANOTHER CIVIL WAR.
I CAN HANDLE MYSELF, STEVE, WITH OR WITHOUT THE ARMOR.
I DIDN'T MEAN TO INSULT YOU.
BUT NOW'S *NOT* THE TIME FOR A DEBATE.
I NEED YOU TO WORK ON FINDING KASH.
IN THE MEANTIME, MADRIPOOR'S FULL OF PEOPLE WHO EITHER COMMIT CRIMES OR KNOW SOMETHING ABOUT CRIMES THAT ARE BEING COMMITTED.
WHILE YOU WORK THE TECH ANGLE--

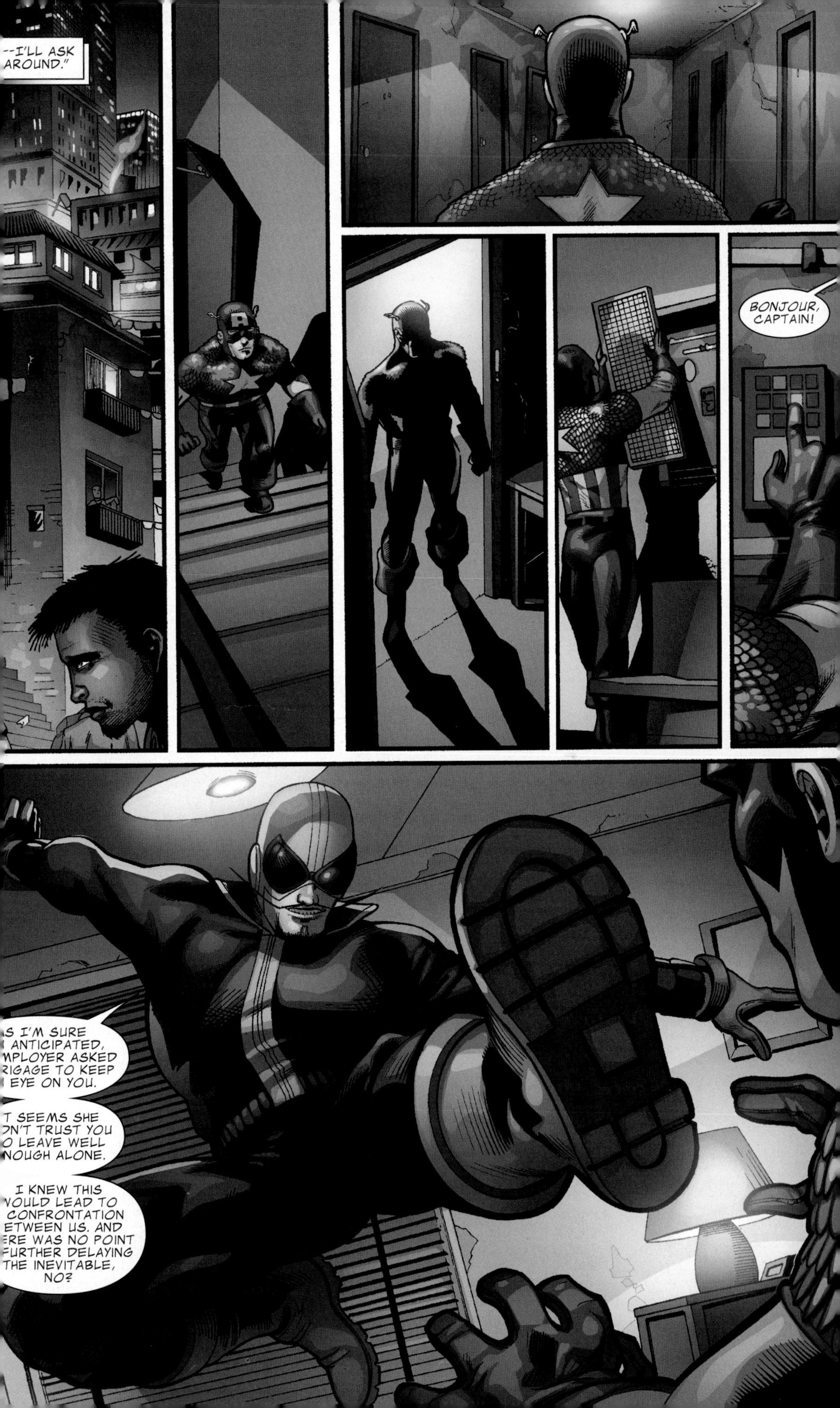
--I'LL ASK AROUND."
BONJOUR, CAPTAIN!
S I'M SURE ANTICIPATED, MPLOYER ASKED RIGAGE TO KEEP EYE ON YOU.
T SEEMS SHE ON'T TRUST YOU O LEAVE WELL NOUGH ALONE.
I KNEW THIS VOULD LEAD TO CONFRONTATION ETWEEN US. AND ERE WAS NO POINT FURTHER DELAYING THE INEVITABLE, NO?

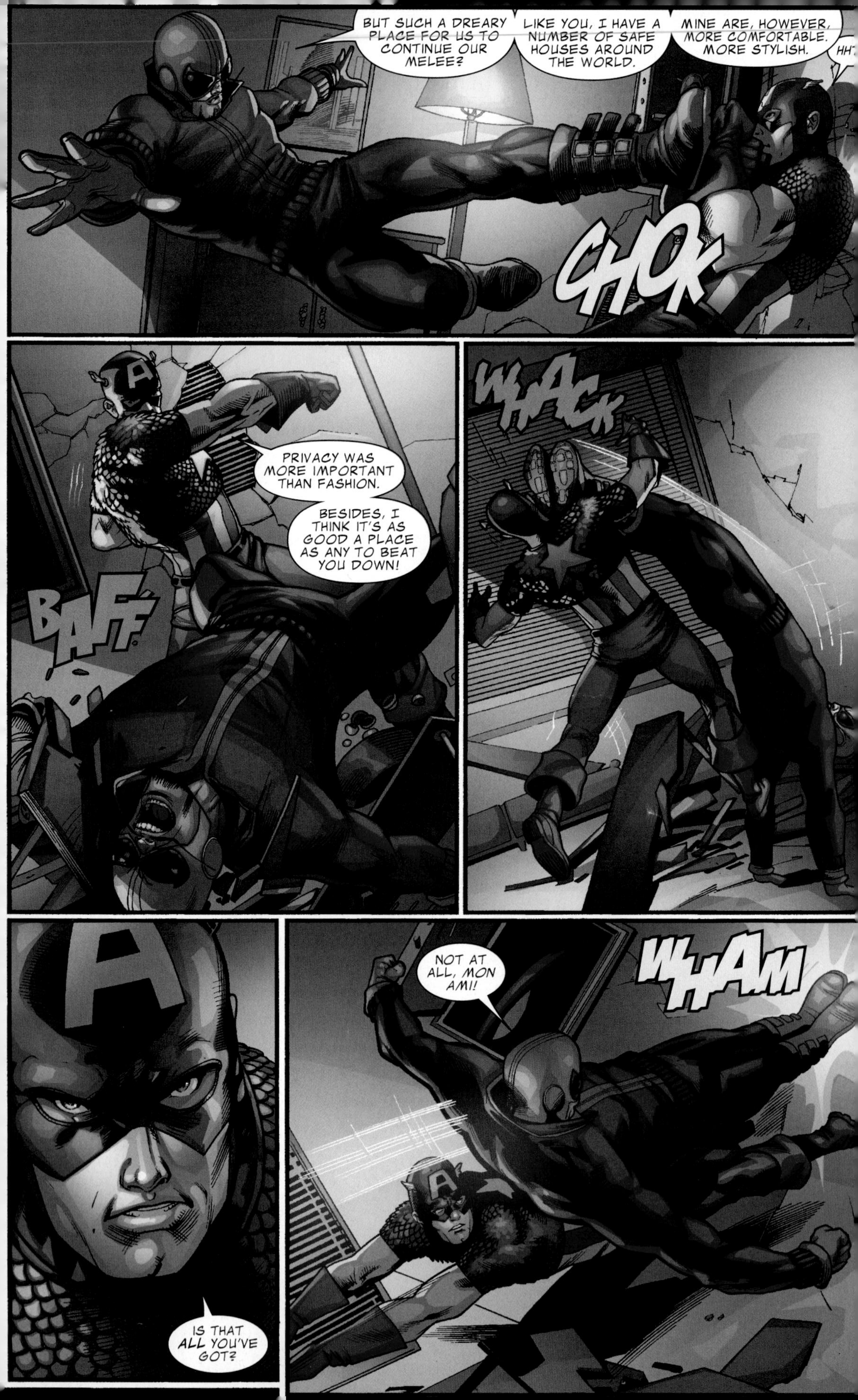

BUT SUCH A DREARY PLACE FOR US TO CONTINUE OUR MELEE?
LIKE YOU, I HAVE A NUMBER OF SAFE HOUSES AROUND THE WORLD.
MINE ARE, HOWEVER, MORE COMFORTABLE. MORE STYLISH.
CHOK
PRIVACY WAS MORE IMPORTANT THAN FASHION.
BESIDES, I THINK IT'S AS GOOD A PLACE AS ANY TO BEAT YOU DOWN!
BAFF
WHACK
IS THAT ALL YOU'VE GOT?
NOT AT ALL, MON AMI!
WHAM

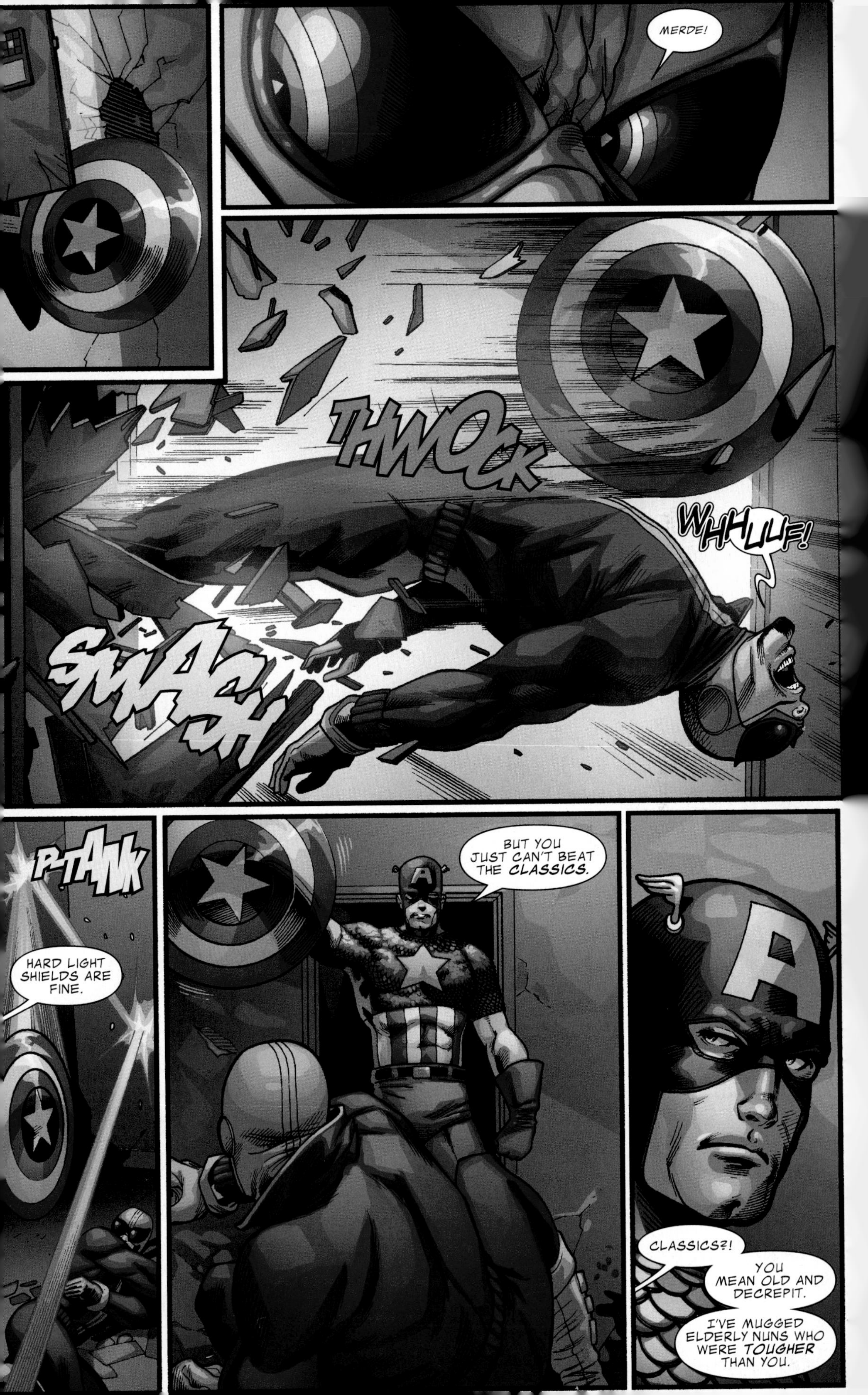
MERDE!
THWOCK
WHHUUF!
SMASH
P-TANK
HARD LIGHT SHIELDS ARE FINE.
BUT YOU JUST CAN'T BEAT THE CLASSICS.
CLASSICS?!
YOU MEAN OLD AND DECREPIT.
I'VE MUGGED ELDERLY NUNS WHO WERE TOUGHER THAN YOU.

STILL, YOUR SHIELD-THROWING HAND WILL MAKE A NICE TROPHY.

I'M GONNA HANG IT FROM MY REAR-VIEW MIRROR.

YOUNG LADY, IF YOU'VE GOT THE **BRASS** TO BACK UP THOSE TOUGH WORDS, I SUGGEST YOU STOP TALKING AND START FIGHTING.

HOW'S **THIS** FOR BRASS?

KA-TANG

SHHHKKKK

AAAGH!

IT WOULD PLEASE ME TO ACCEPT YOUR SURRENDER NOW, CAPTAIN!

YOU'RE BADLY OUTNUMBERED! YOU CANNOT WIN THIS FIGHT!

UUUNF!

KR-KRAK

WHA--

YOU GUYS MIND BACKIN' OFF OF MY PARTNER?

WA-CH-OOM!

PAFF

P-POP

POW

PAFF

PAFF

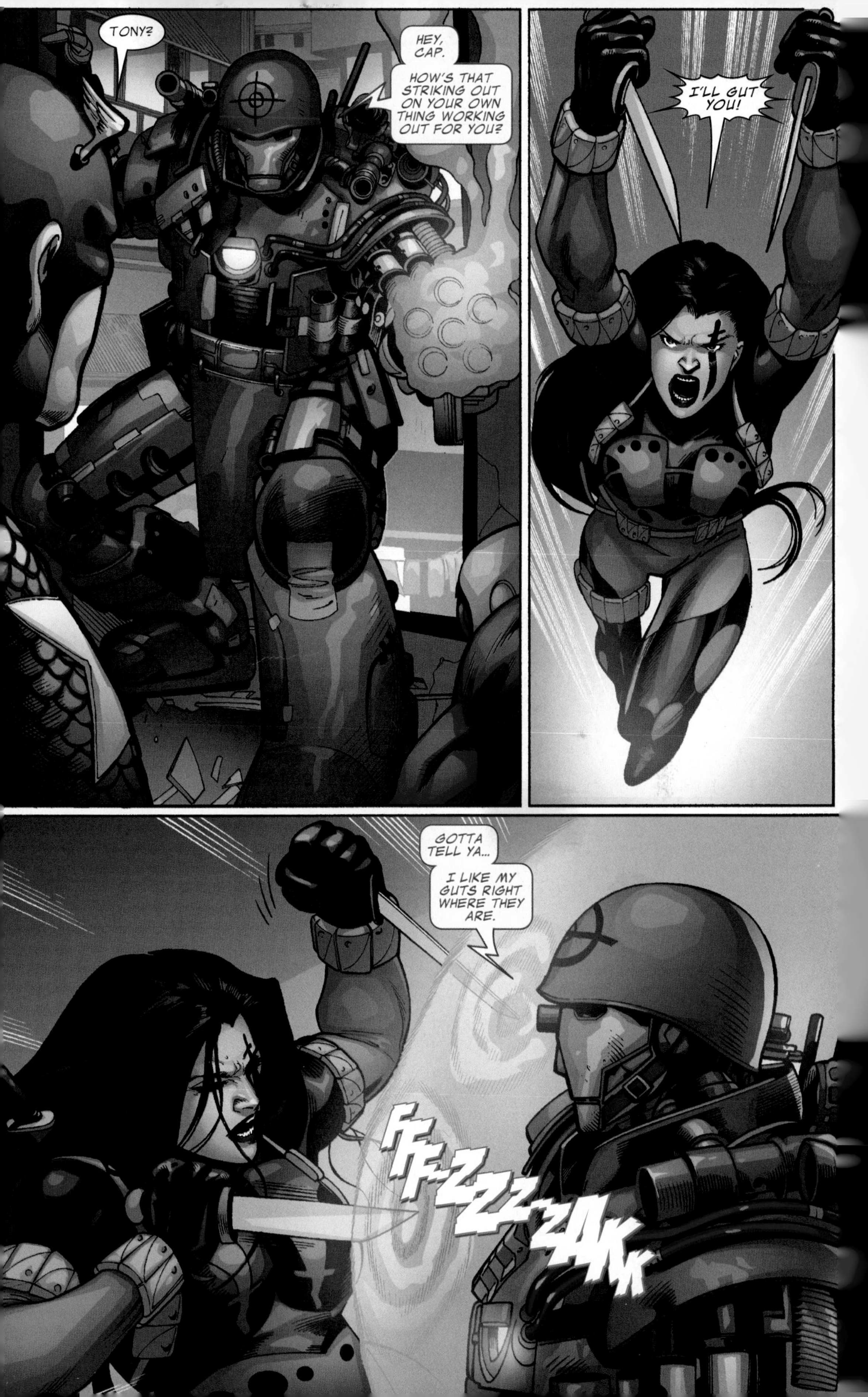
TONY?
HEY, CAP.
HOW'S THAT STRIKING OUT ON YOUR OWN THING WORKING OUT FOR YOU?
I'LL GUT YOU!
GOTTA TELL YA...
I LIKE MY GUTS RIGHT WHERE THEY ARE.
FFF-ZZZZ-ZAKK

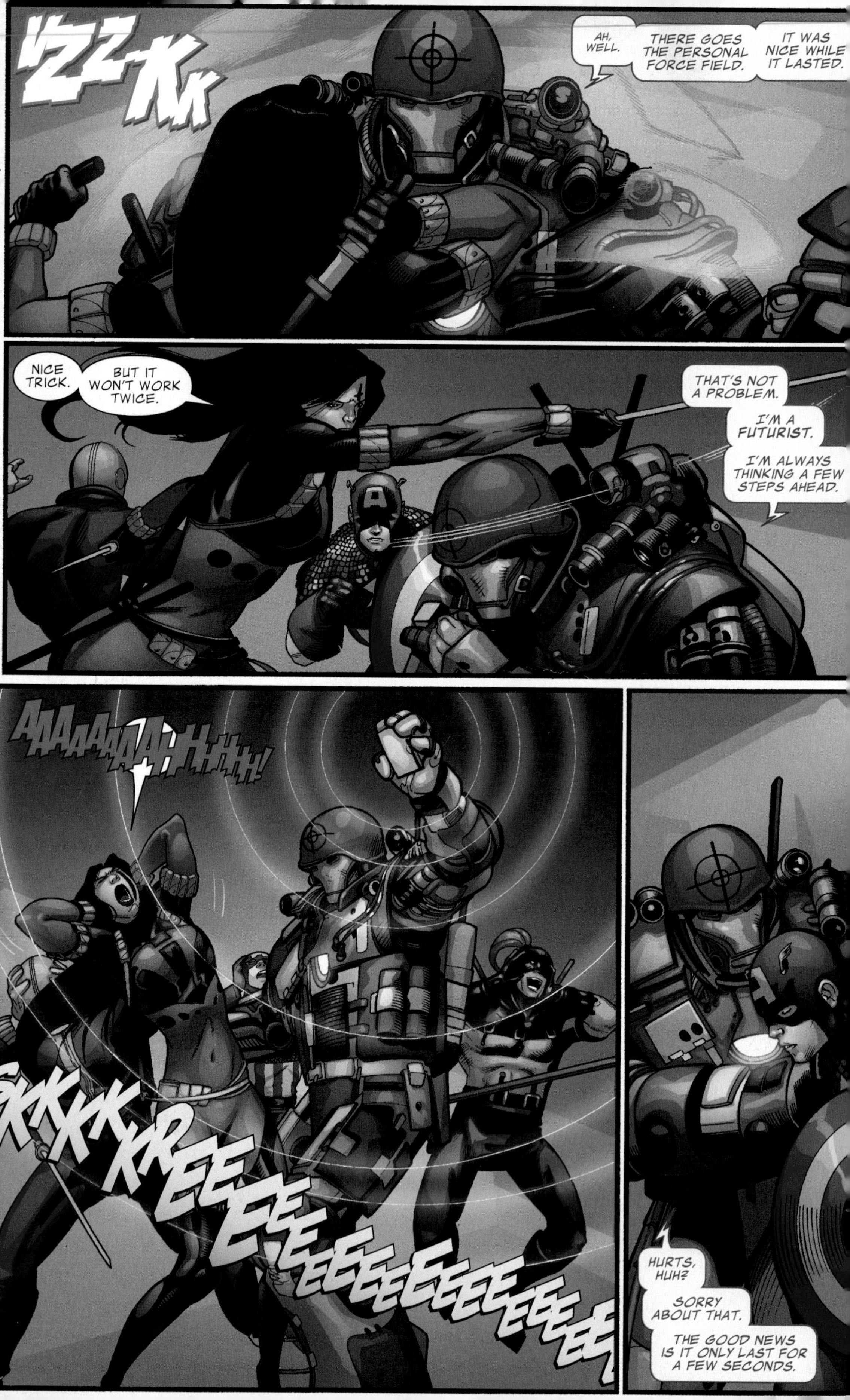
VZZ-KK
AH, WELL.
THERE GOES THE PERSONAL FORCE FIELD.
IT WAS NICE WHILE IT LASTED.
NICE TRICK.
BUT IT WON'T WORK TWICE.
THAT'S NOT A PROBLEM.
I'M A FUTURIST.
I'M ALWAYS THINKING A FEW STEPS AHEAD.
AAAAAAAHHHHH!
SKKKKKREEEEEEEEEEEEEEEEEEEE
HURTS, HUH?
SORRY ABOUT THAT.
THE GOOD NEWS IS IT ONLY LAST FOR A FEW SECONDS.

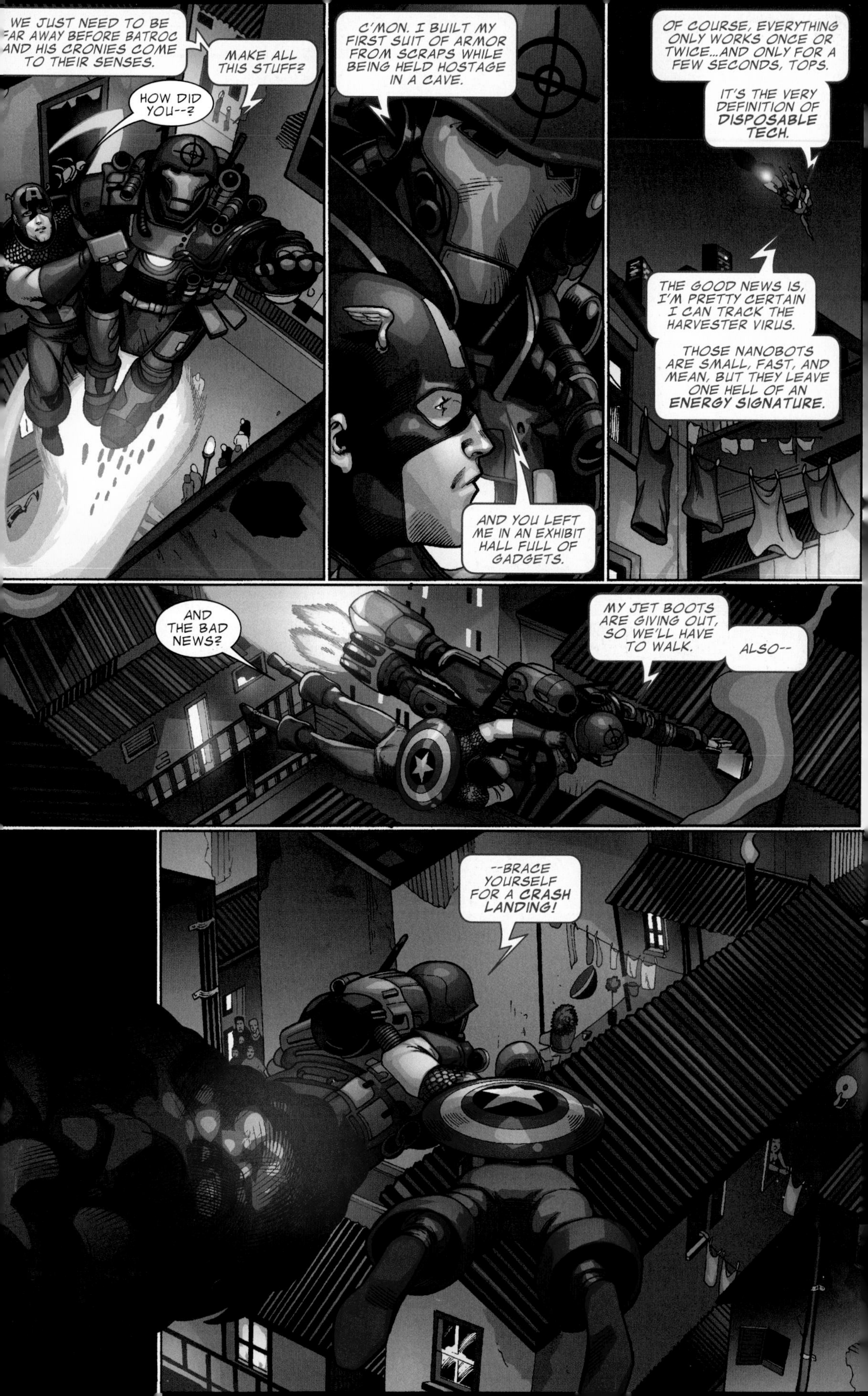
WE JUST NEED TO BE FAR AWAY BEFORE BATROC AND HIS CRONIES COME TO THEIR SENSES.
HOW DID YOU--?
MAKE ALL THIS STUFF?
C'MON. I BUILT MY FIRST SUIT OF ARMOR FROM SCRAPS WHILE BEING HELD HOSTAGE IN A CAVE.
AND YOU LEFT ME IN AN EXHIBIT HALL FULL OF GADGETS.
OF COURSE, EVERYTHING ONLY WORKS ONCE OR TWICE...AND ONLY FOR A FEW SECONDS, TOPS.
IT'S THE VERY DEFINITION OF DISPOSABLE TECH.
THE GOOD NEWS IS, I'M PRETTY CERTAIN I CAN TRACK THE HARVESTER VIRUS.
THOSE NANOBOTS ARE SMALL, FAST, AND MEAN, BUT THEY LEAVE ONE HELL OF AN ENERGY SIGNATURE.
AND THE BAD NEWS?
MY JET BOOTS ARE GIVING OUT, SO WE'LL HAVE TO WALK.
ALSO--
--BRACE YOURSELF FOR A CRASH LANDING!

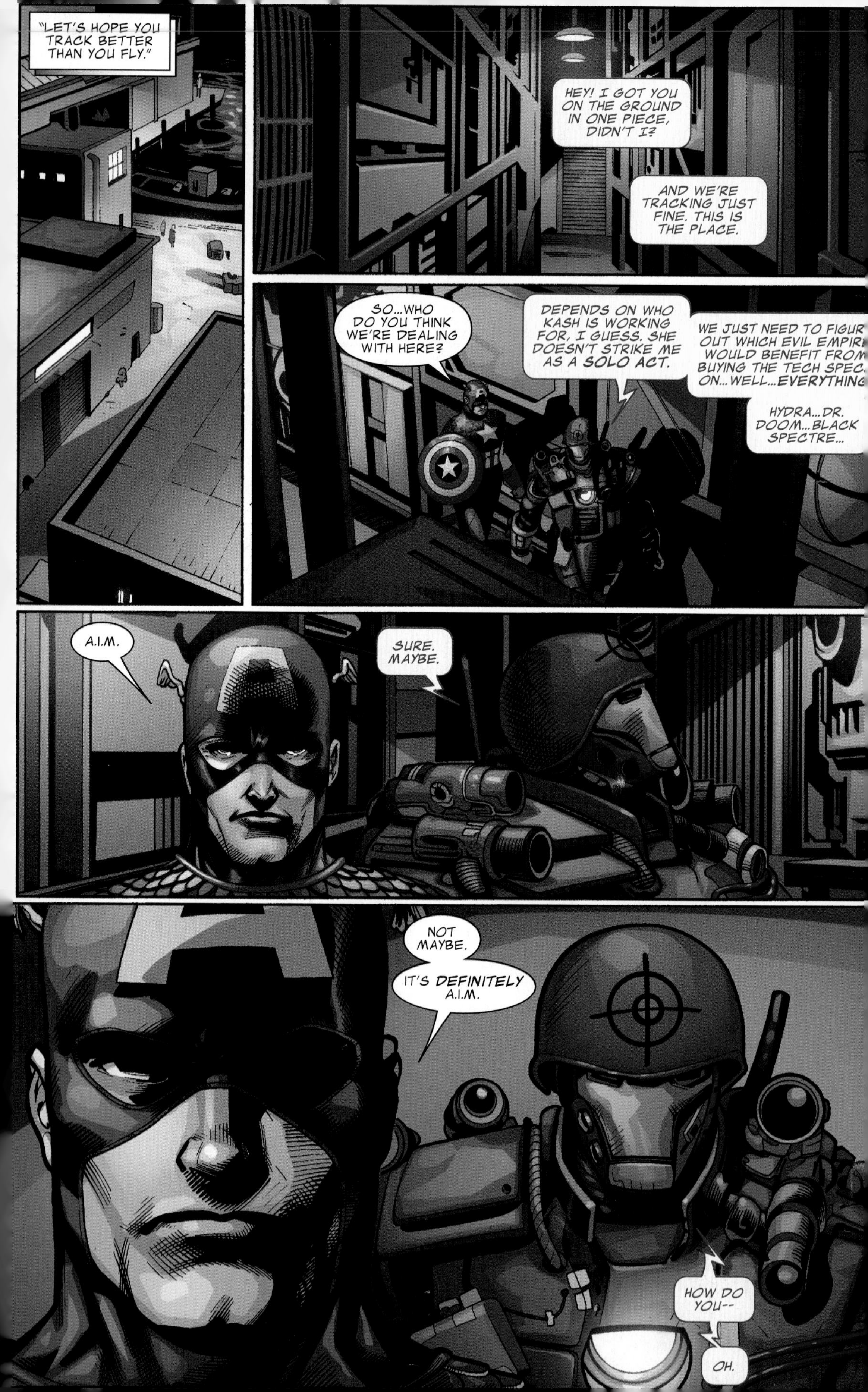
"LET'S HOPE YOU TRACK BETTER THAN YOU FLY."
HEY! I GOT YOU ON THE GROUND IN ONE PIECE, DIDN'T I?
AND WE'RE TRACKING JUST FINE. THIS IS THE PLACE.
SO...WHO DO YOU THINK WE'RE DEALING WITH HERE?
DEPENDS ON WHO KASH IS WORKING FOR, I GUESS. SHE DOESN'T STRIKE ME AS A SOLO ACT.
WE JUST NEED TO FIGUR OUT WHICH EVIL EMPIR WOULD BENEFIT FROM BUYING THE TECH SPEC ON...WELL...EVERYTHING
HYDRA...DR. DOOM...BLACK SPECTRE...
A.I.M.
SURE. MAYBE.
NOT MAYBE.
IT'S DEFINITELY A.I.M.
HOW DO YOU--
OH.

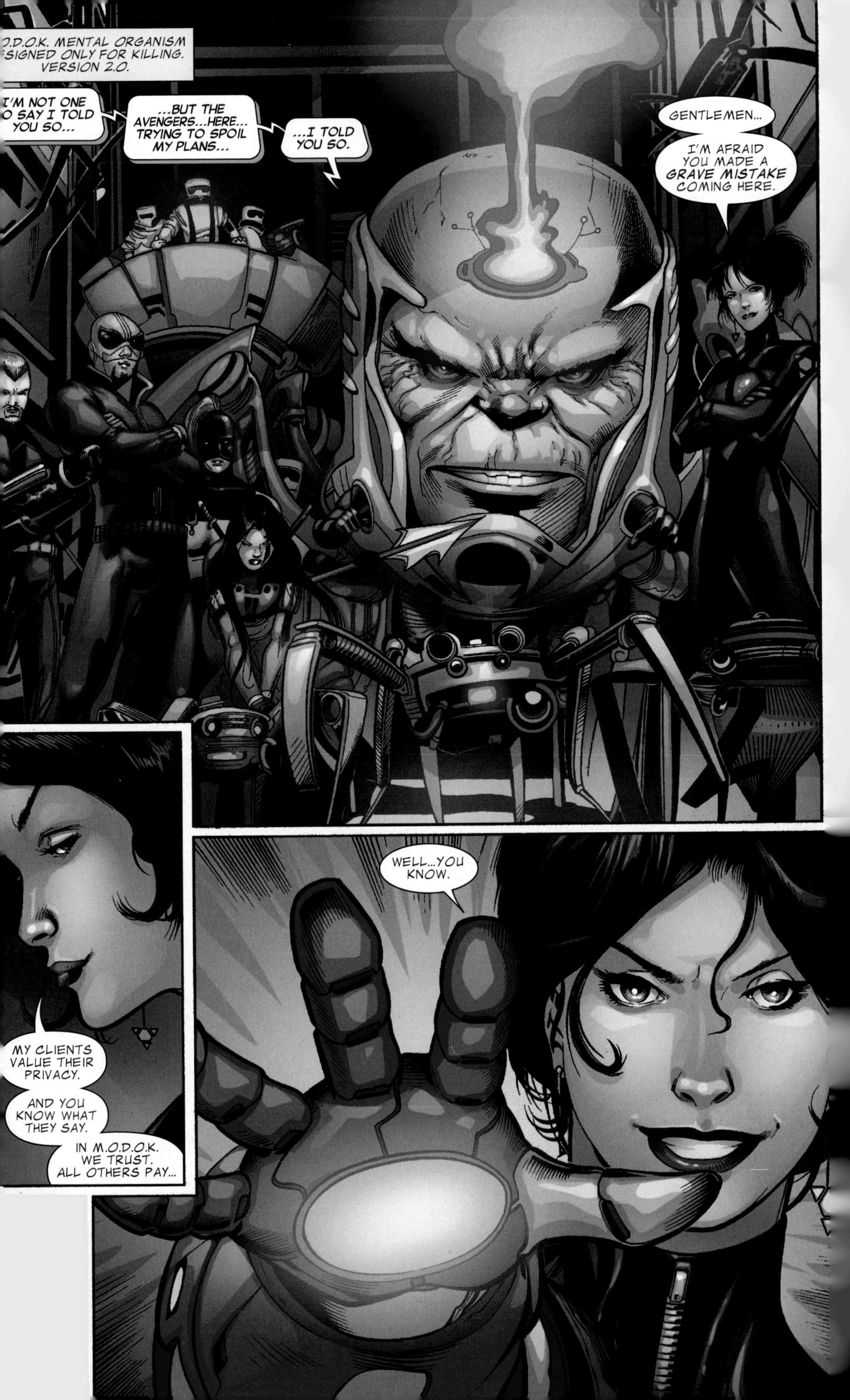

.O.D.O.K. MENTAL ORGANISM
ESIGNED ONLY FOR KILLING.
VERSION 2.0.
I'M NOT ONE
O SAY I TOLD
YOU SO...
...BUT THE AVENGERS...HERE... TRYING TO SPOIL MY PLANS...
...I TOLD YOU SO.
GENTLEMEN...
I'M AFRAID YOU MADE A GRAVE MISTAKE COMING HERE.
MY CLIENTS VALUE THEIR PRIVACY.
AND YOU KNOW WHAT THEY SAY.
IN M.O.D.O.K. WE TRUST. ALL OTHERS PAY...
WELL...YOU KNOW.

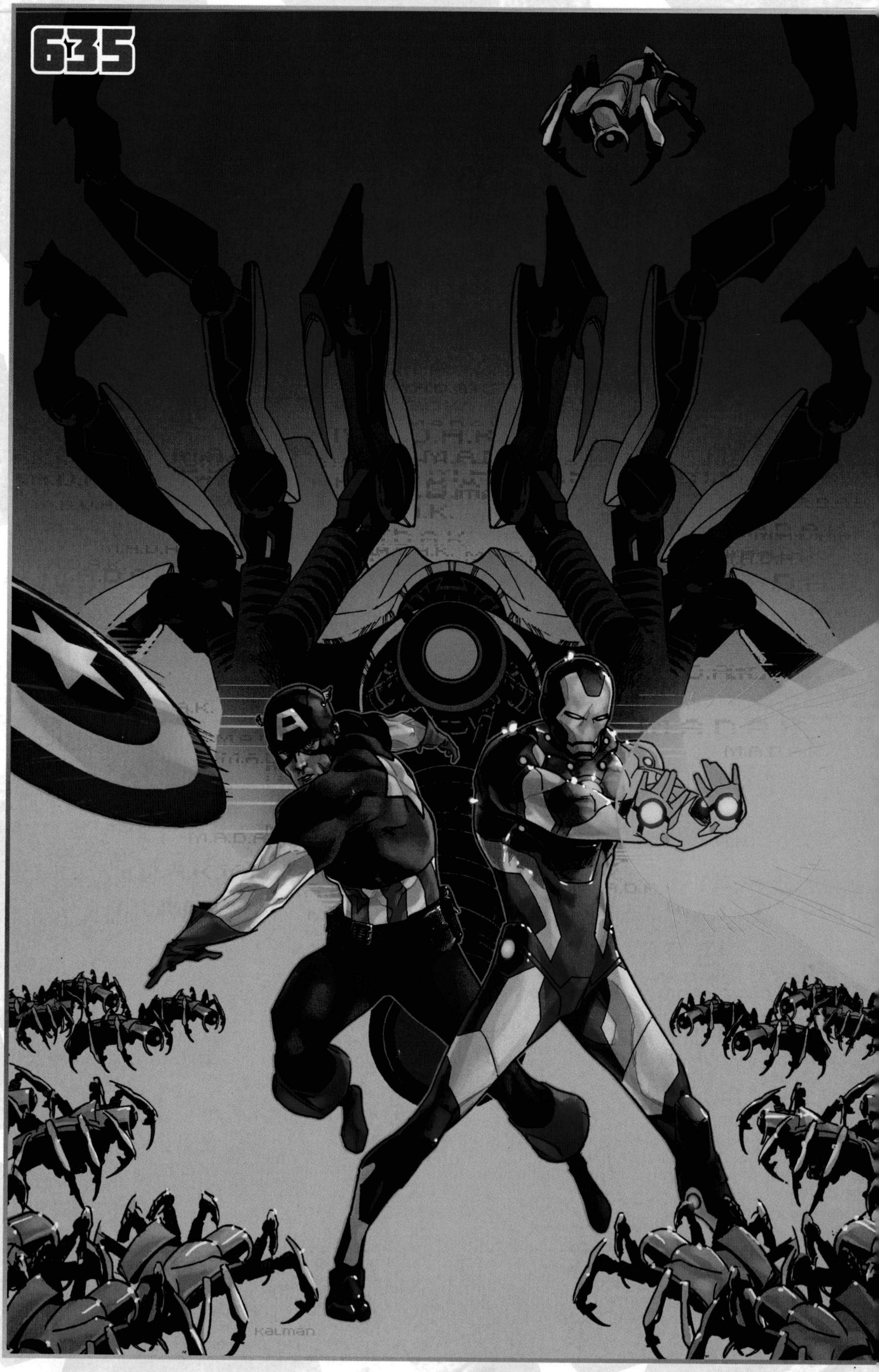
635
KALMAN

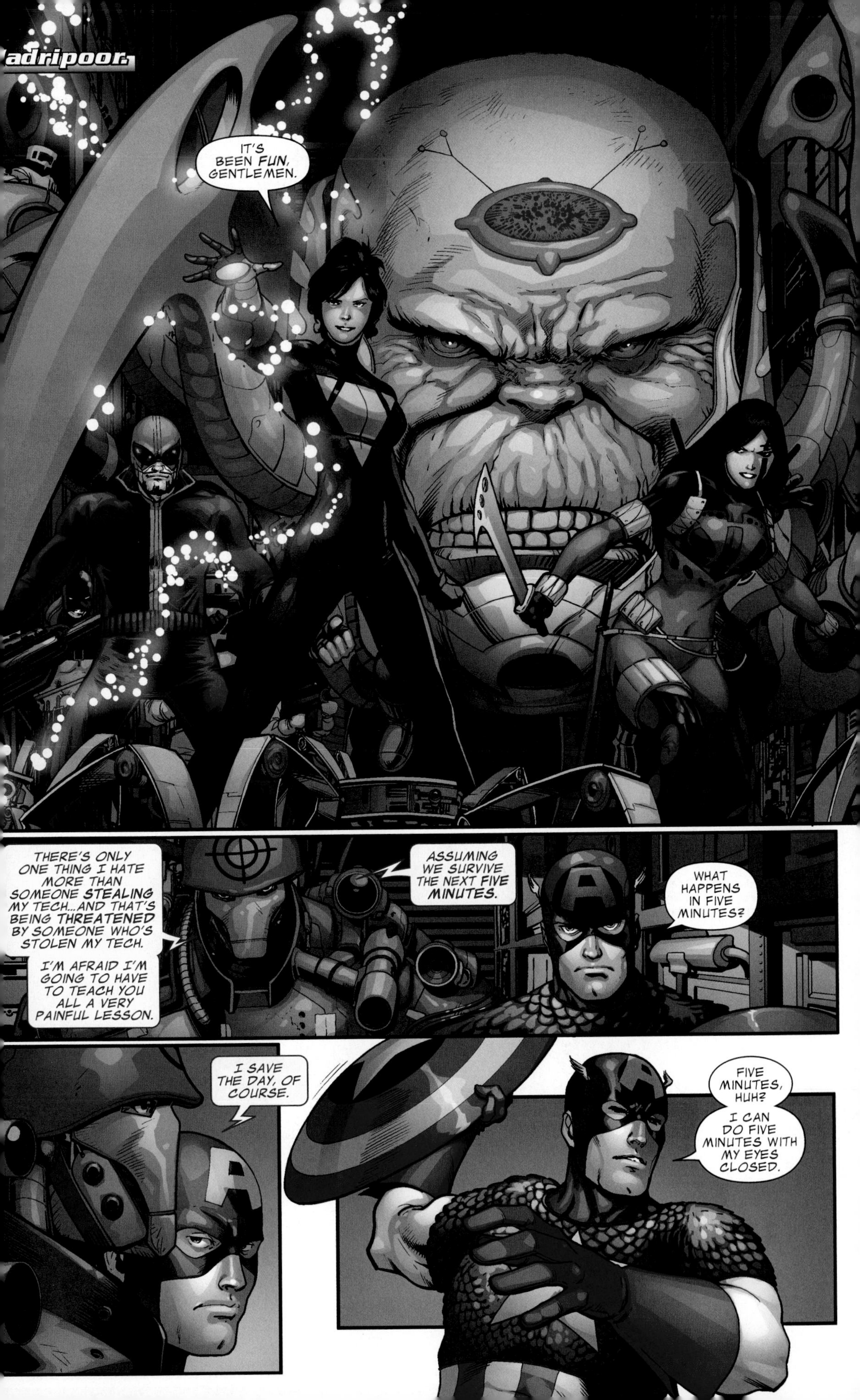
adripoor.
IT'S BEEN FUN, GENTLEMEN.
THERE'S ONLY ONE THING I HATE MORE THAN SOMEONE STEALING MY TECH...AND THAT'S BEING THREATENED BY SOMEONE WHO'S STOLEN MY TECH.
I'M AFRAID I'M GOING TO HAVE TO TEACH YOU ALL A VERY PAINFUL LESSON.
ASSUMING WE SURVIVE THE NEXT FIVE MINUTES.
WHAT HAPPENS IN FIVE MINUTES?
I SAVE THE DAY, OF COURSE.
FIVE MINUTES, HUH?
I CAN DO FIVE MINUTES WITH MY EYES CLOSED.

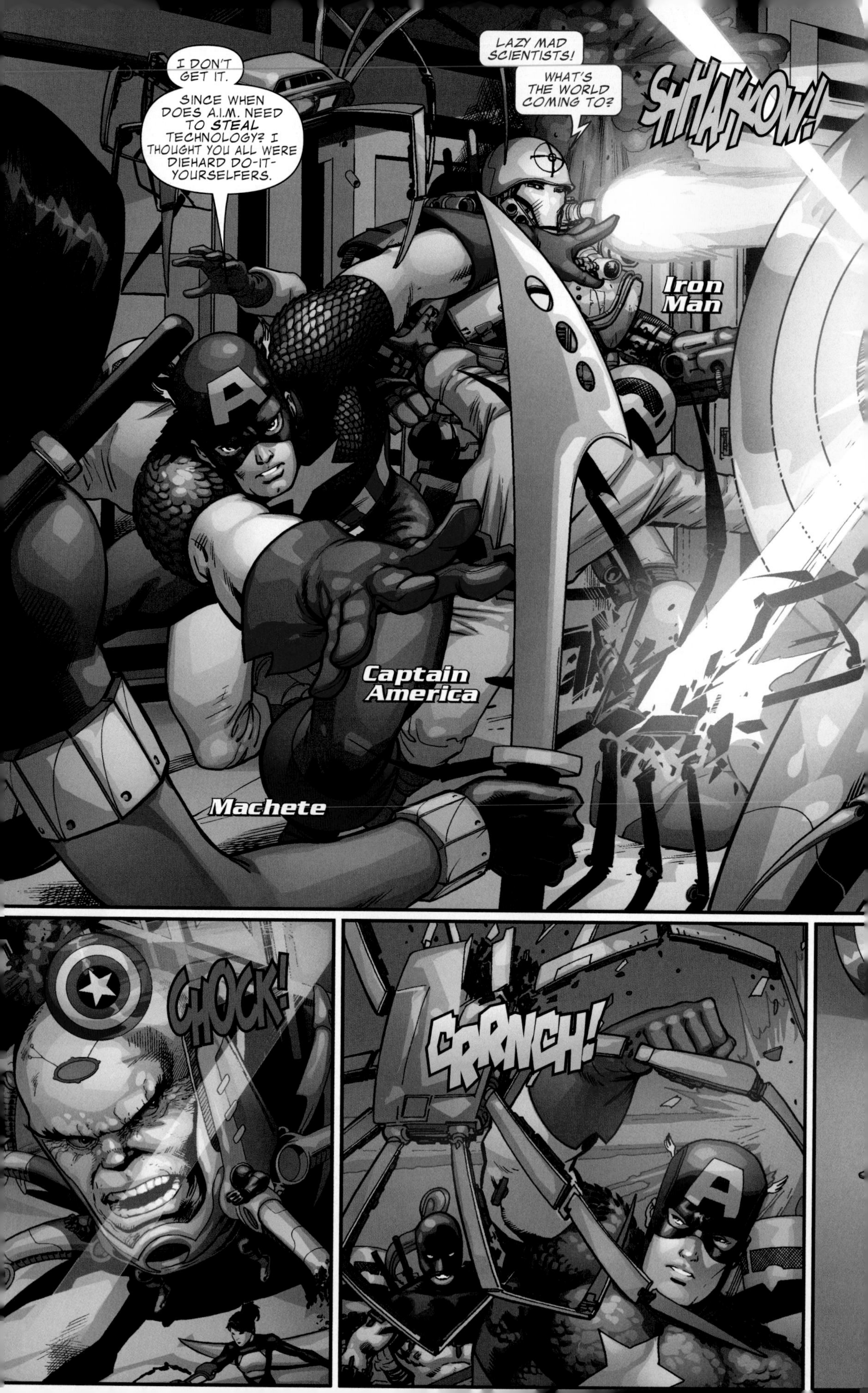

I DON'T GET IT.
SINCE WHEN DOES A.I.M. NEED TO STEAL TECHNOLOGY? I THOUGHT YOU ALL WERE DIEHARD DO-IT-YOURSELFERS.
LAZY MAD SCIENTISTS!
WHAT'S THE WORLD COMING TO?
SHHAKKOW!
Iron Man
Captain America
Machete
CHOCK!
CRRNCH!

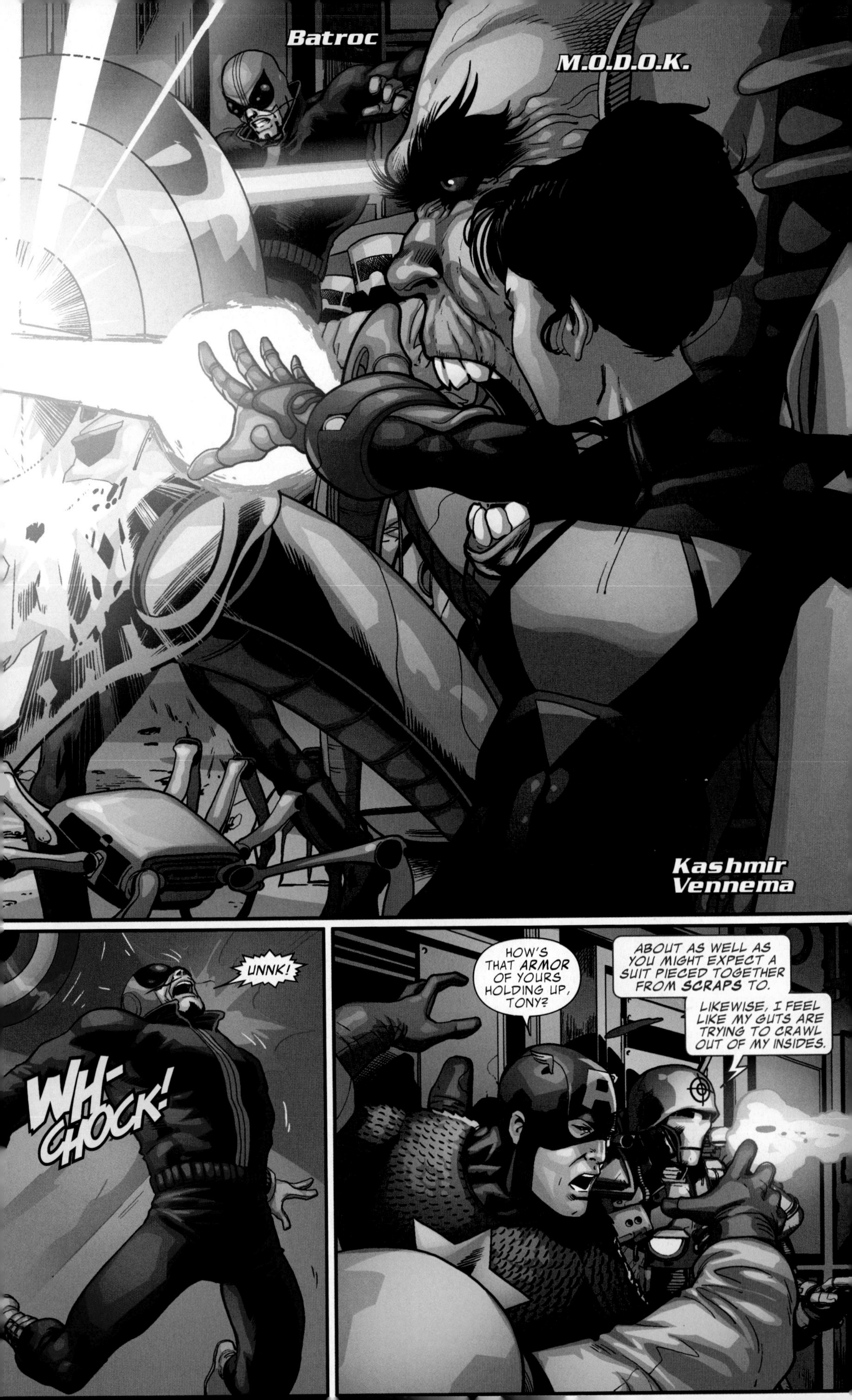
Batroc
M.O.D.O.K.
Kashmir Vennema
UNNK!
WH-CHOCK!
HOW'S THAT ARMOR OF YOURS HOLDING UP, TONY?
ABOUT AS WELL AS YOU MIGHT EXPECT A SUIT PIECED TOGETHER FROM SCRAPS TO.
LIKEWISE, I FEEL LIKE MY GUTS ARE TRYING TO CRAWL OUT OF MY INSIDES.

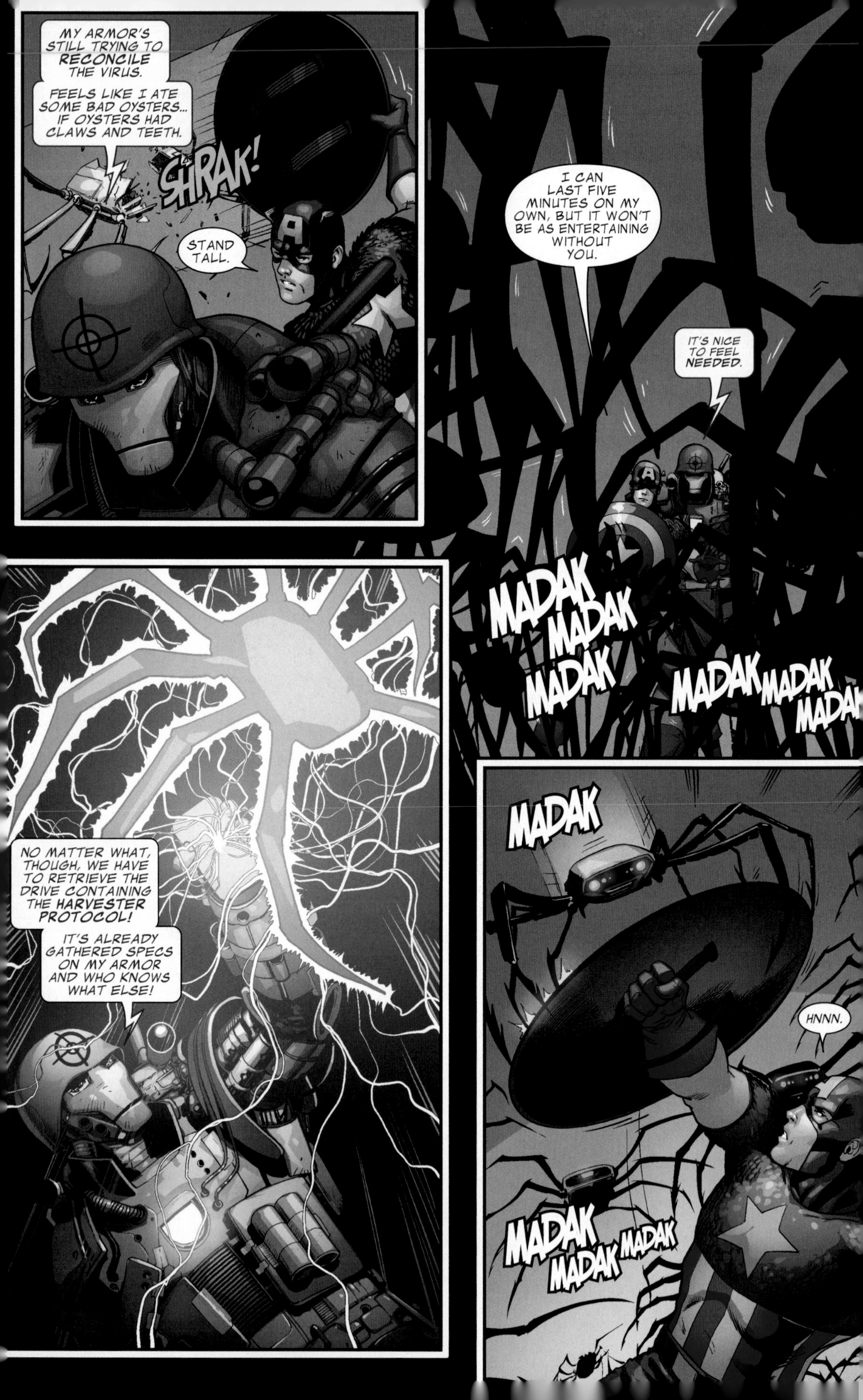
MY ARMOR'S STILL TRYING TO RECONCILE THE VIRUS.
FEELS LIKE I ATE SOME BAD OYSTERS... IF OYSTERS HAD CLAWS AND TEETH.
SHRAK!
STAND TALL.
I CAN LAST FIVE MINUTES ON MY OWN, BUT IT WON'T BE AS ENTERTAINING WITHOUT YOU.
IT'S NICE TO FEEL NEEDED.
MADAK MADAK MADAK
MADAK MADAK MADAK
NO MATTER WHAT, THOUGH, WE HAVE TO RETRIEVE THE DRIVE CONTAINING THE HARVESTER PROTOCOL!
IT'S ALREADY GATHERED SPECS ON MY ARMOR AND WHO KNOWS WHAT ELSE!
MADAK
HNNN.
MADAK MADAK MADAK

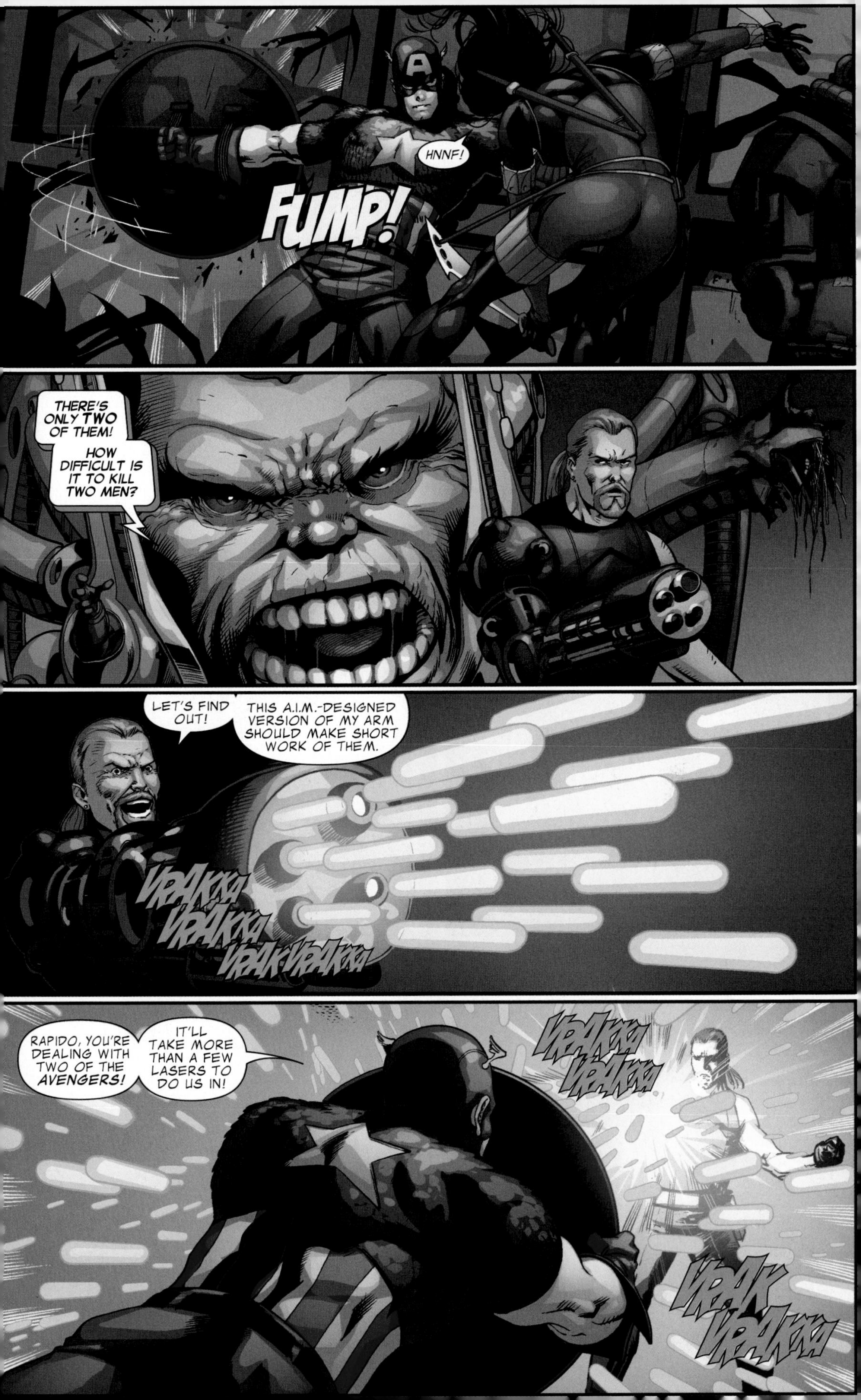
HNNF!
FUMP!
THERE'S ONLY TWO OF THEM!
HOW DIFFICULT IS IT TO KILL TWO MEN?
LET'S FIND OUT!
THIS A.I.M.-DESIGNED VERSION OF MY ARM SHOULD MAKE SHORT WORK OF THEM.
VRAKKA VRAKKA VRAK-VRAKKA
RAPIDO, YOU'RE DEALING WITH TWO OF THE AVENGERS!
IT'LL TAKE MORE THAN A FEW LASERS TO DO US IN!
VRAKKA VRAKKA
VRAK VRAKKA

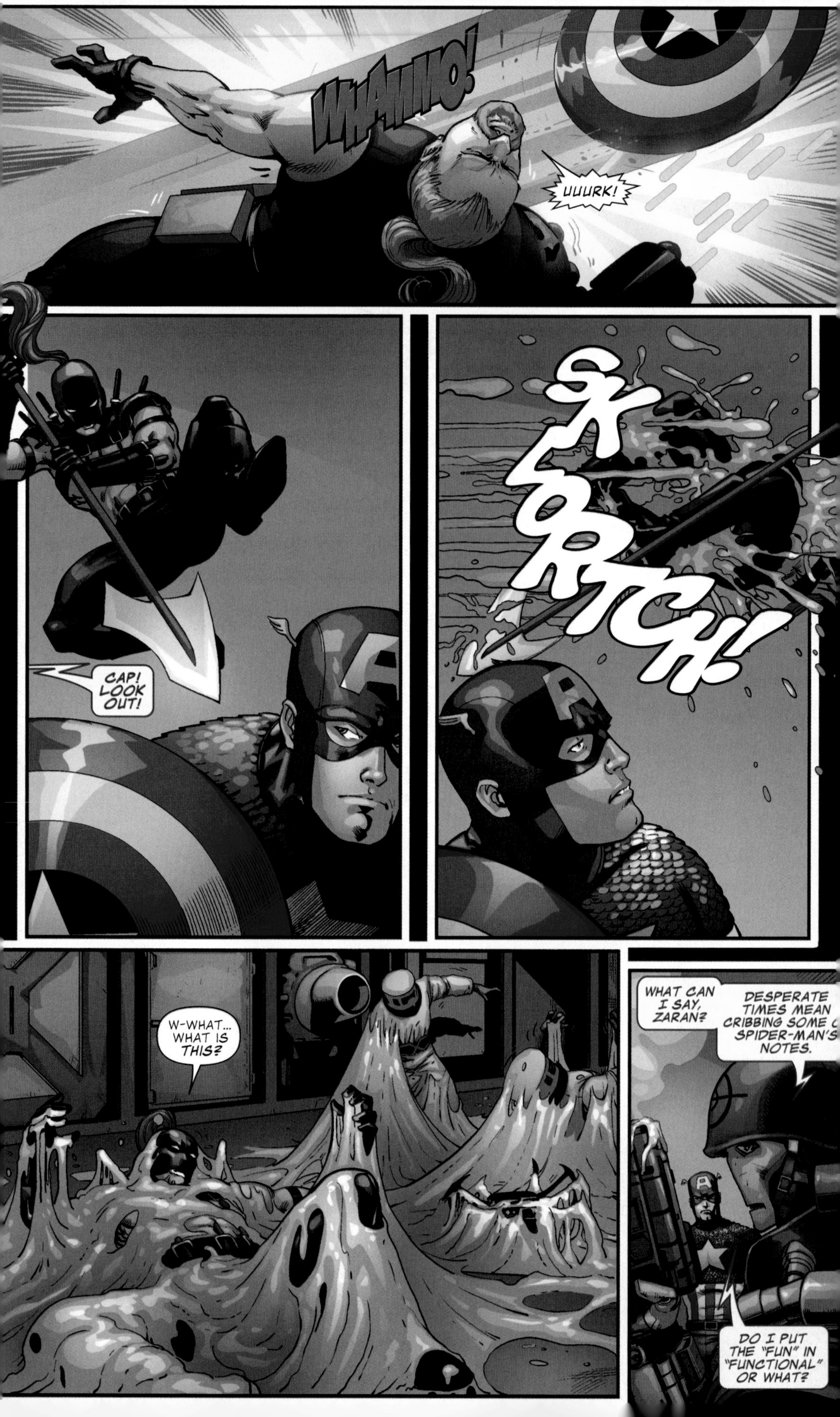
WHAMMO!
UUURK!
CAP! LOOK OUT!
SKLORTCH!
W-WHAT... WHAT IS THIS?
WHAT CAN I SAY, ZARAN?
DESPERATE TIMES MEAN CRIBBING SOME OF SPIDER-MAN'S NOTES.
DO I PUT THE "FUN" IN "FUNCTIONAL" OR WHAT?

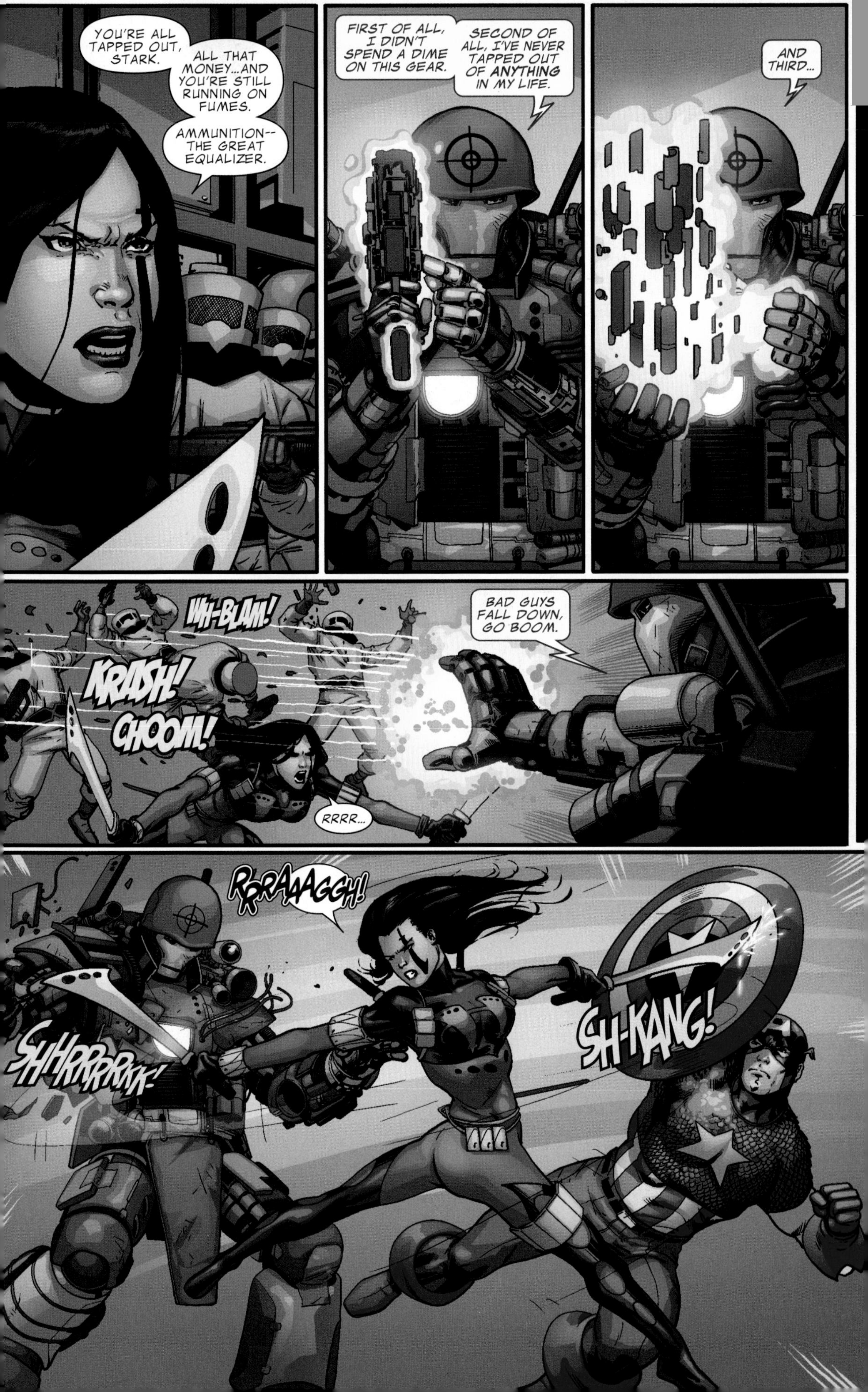
YOU'RE ALL TAPPED OUT, STARK.
ALL THAT MONEY...AND YOU'RE STILL RUNNING ON FUMES.
AMMUNITION--THE GREAT EQUALIZER.
FIRST OF ALL, I DIDN'T SPEND A DIME ON THIS GEAR.
SECOND OF ALL, I'VE NEVER TAPPED OUT OF ANYTHING IN MY LIFE.
AND THIRD...
WH-BLAM!
KRASH!
CHOOM!
BAD GUYS FALL DOWN, GO BOOM.
RRRR...
RRRRAAAGGH!
SHHRRRRKK!
SH-KANG!

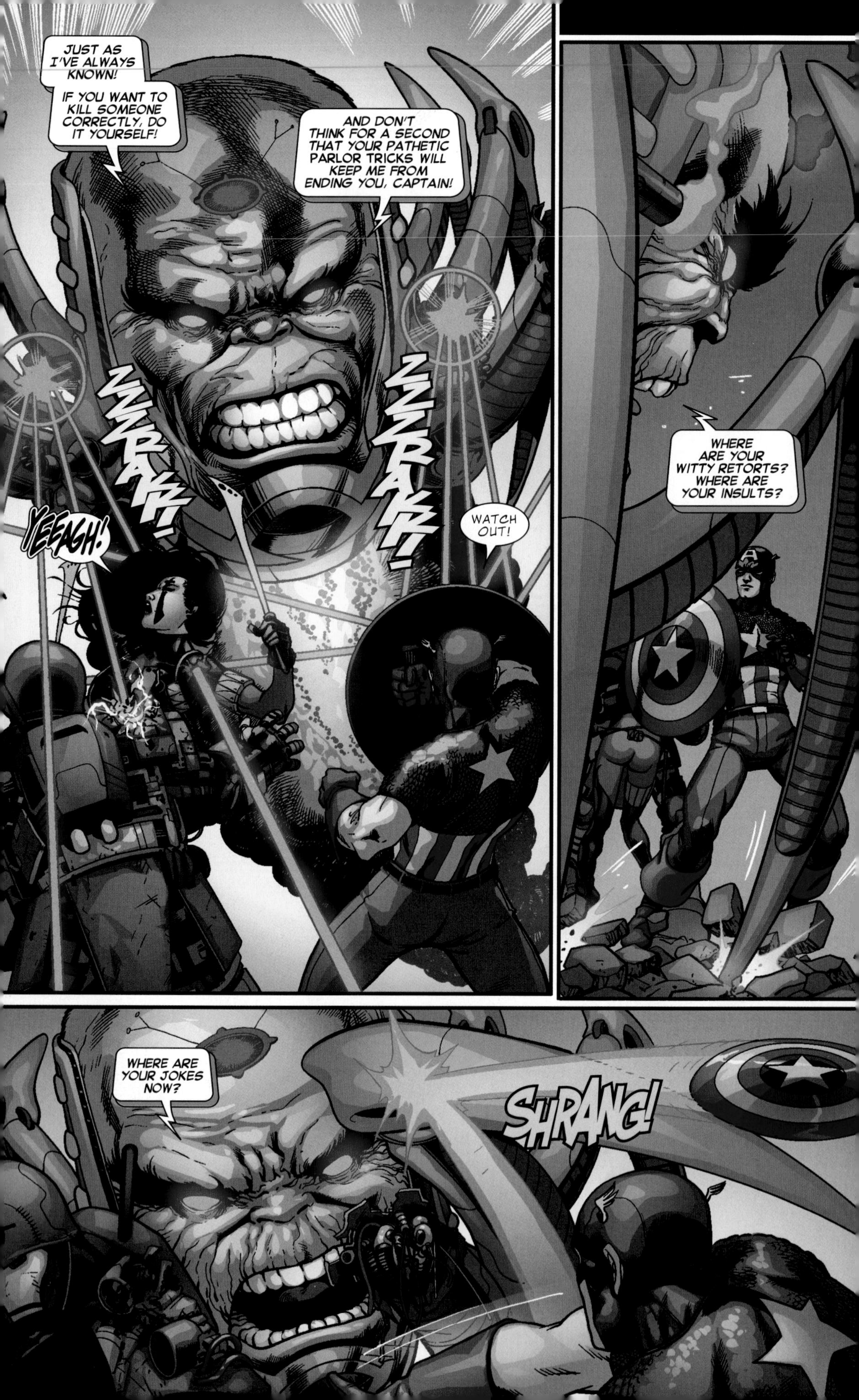
JUST AS I'VE ALWAYS KNOWN!
IF YOU WANT TO KILL SOMEONE CORRECTLY, DO IT YOURSELF!
AND DON'T THINK FOR A SECOND THAT YOUR PATHETIC PARLOR TRICKS WILL KEEP ME FROM ENDING YOU, CAPTAIN!
ZZZRAKK!
ZZZRAKK!
YEEAGH!
WATCH OUT!
WHERE ARE YOUR WITTY RETORTS? WHERE ARE YOUR INSULTS?
WHERE ARE YOUR JOKES NOW?
SHRANG!

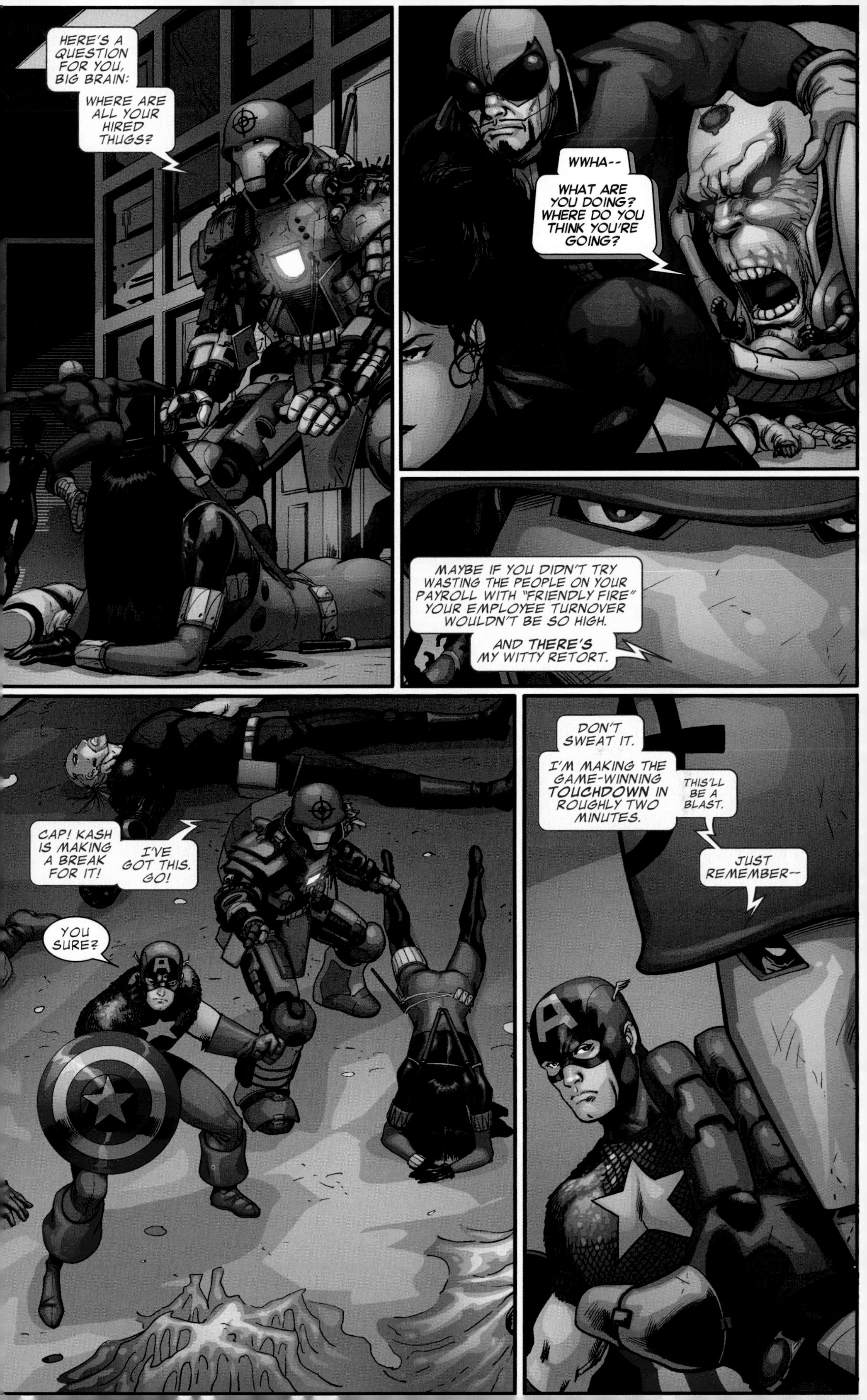
HERE'S A QUESTION FOR YOU, BIG BRAIN:
WHERE ARE ALL YOUR HIRED THUGS?
WWHA--
WHAT ARE YOU DOING? WHERE DO YOU THINK YOU'RE GOING?
MAYBE IF YOU DIDN'T TRY WASTING THE PEOPLE ON YOUR PAYROLL WITH "FRIENDLY FIRE" YOUR EMPLOYEE TURNOVER WOULDN'T BE SO HIGH.
AND THERE'S MY WITTY RETORT.
CAP! KASH IS MAKING A BREAK FOR IT!
I'VE GOT THIS. GO!
YOU SURE?
DON'T SWEAT IT.
I'M MAKING THE GAME-WINNING TOUCHDOWN IN ROUGHLY TWO MINUTES.
THIS'LL BE A BLAST.
JUST REMEMBER--

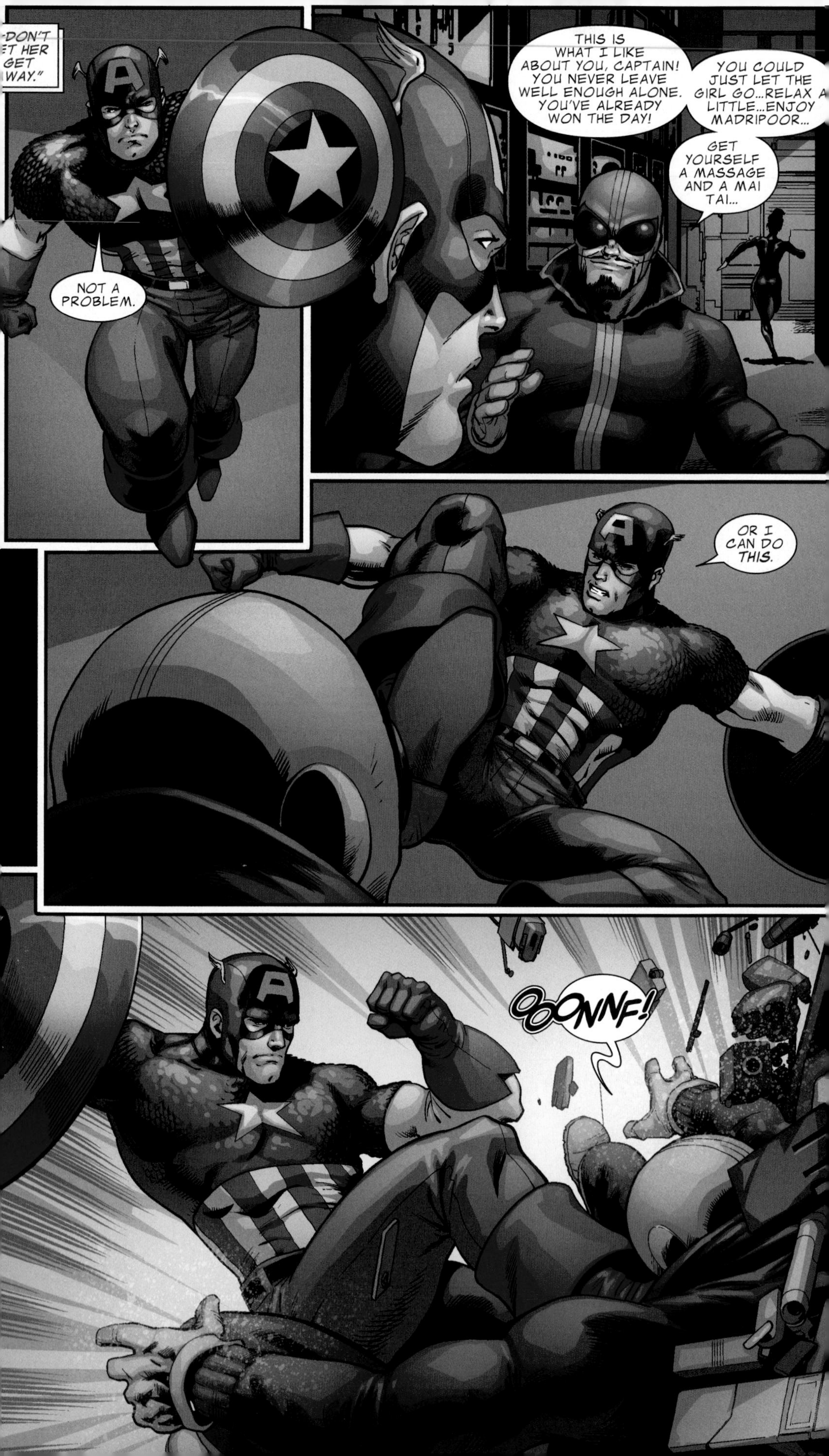
"-DON'T ET HER GET WAY."
NOT A PROBLEM.
THIS IS WHAT I LIKE ABOUT YOU, CAPTAIN! YOU NEVER LEAVE WELL ENOUGH ALONE. YOU'VE ALREADY WON THE DAY!
YOU COULD JUST LET THE GIRL GO...RELAX A LITTLE...ENJOY MADRIPOOR...
GET YOURSELF A MASSAGE AND A MAI TAI...
OR I CAN DO THIS.
OOOONNF!

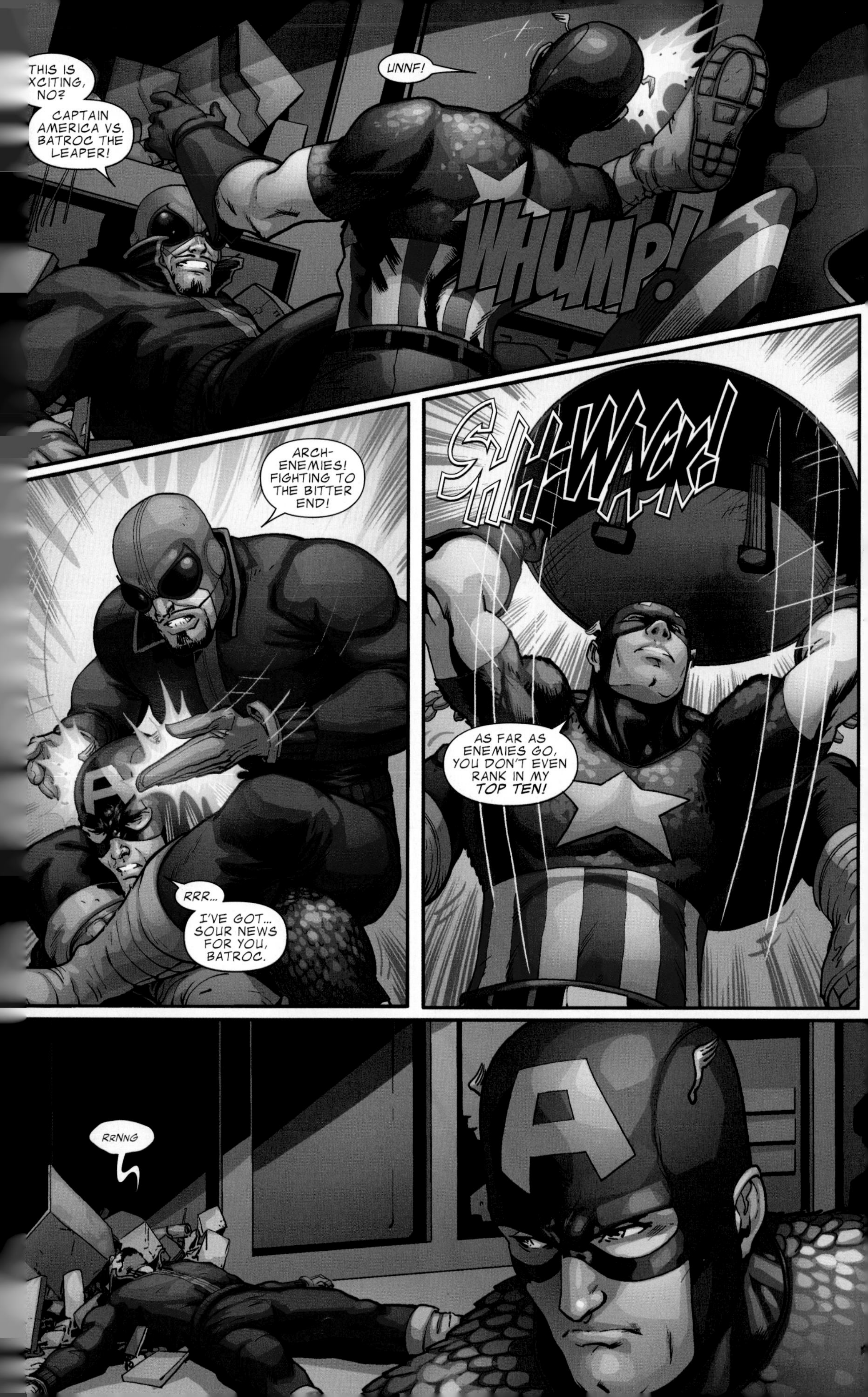
THIS IS XCITING, NO?
CAPTAIN AMERICA VS. BATROC THE LEAPER!
UNNF!
WHUMP!
ARCH-ENEMIES! FIGHTING TO THE BITTER END!
RRR... I'VE GOT... SOUR NEWS FOR YOU, BATROC.
SHH-WACK!
AS FAR AS ENEMIES GO, YOU DON'T EVEN RANK IN MY *TOP TEN!*
RRNNG

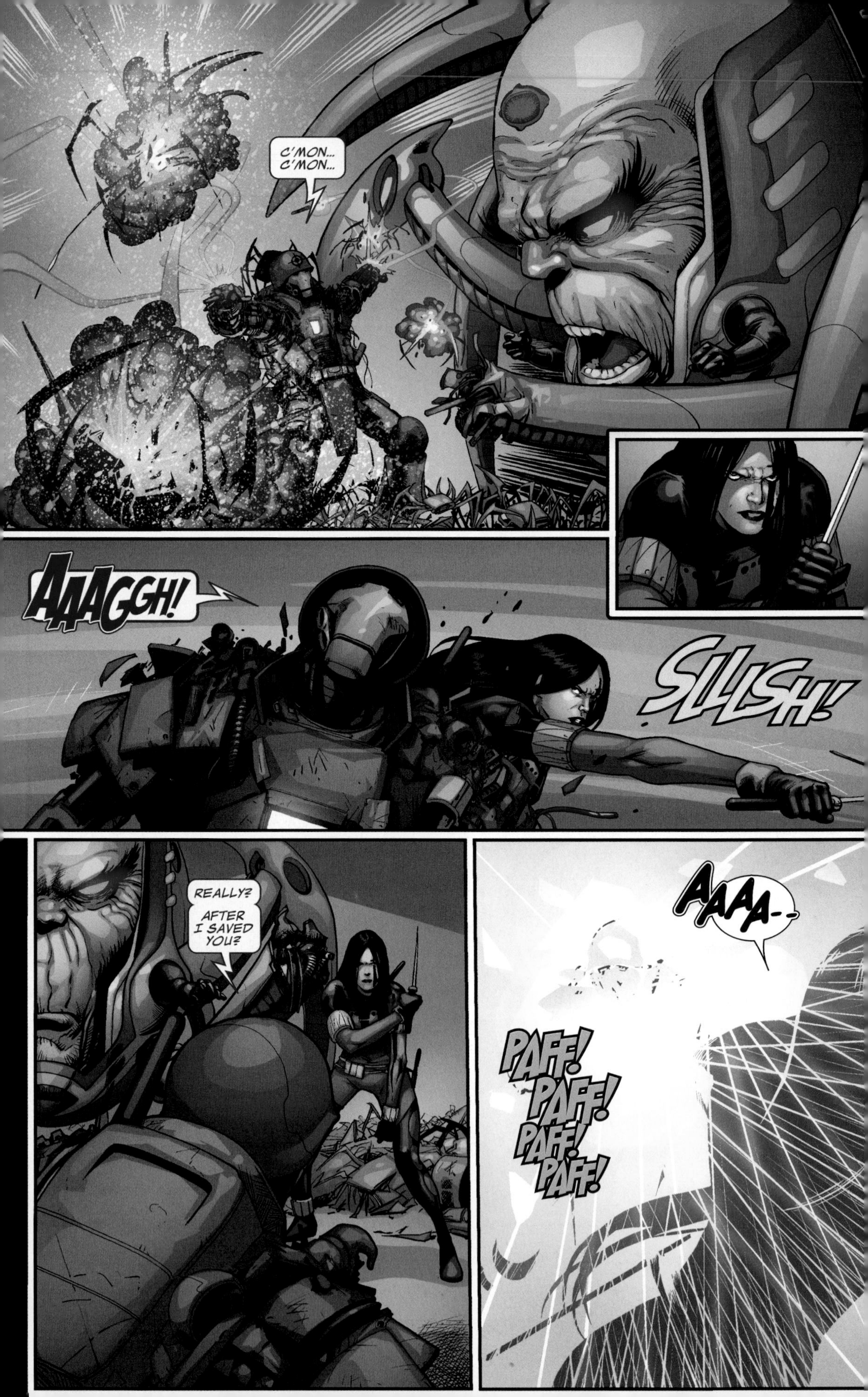
C'MON... C'MON...
AAAGGH!
SLLLSH!
REALLY? AFTER I SAVED YOU?
AAAA--
PAFF! PAFF! PAFF! PAFF!

STROBE EFFECT. I LIKE TO THINK IT WAS MY OWN DAZZLING PERSONALITY THAT INSPIRED THAT ONE.

OOOFF!

YOU SHOULD PAY LESS ATTENTION TO THE WOMAN, STARK...

...AND MORE ATTENTION TO THE SOURCE OF YOUR ANNIHILATION!

IT MIGHT HAVE BEEN A GOOD IDEA FOR YOU TO SIT THIS ONE OUT, DON'T YOU THINK?

YOU'RE NO HERO.

WITHOUT YOUR ARMOR... YOUR REAL ARMOR... YOU'RE NOTHING BUT A WEAK MAN PLAYING DRESS-UP.

YOU'RE RIGHT ABOUT ONE THING, M.O.D.O.K.

THIS PIECEMEAL ARMOR IS ALL RIGHT.

BUT IT'S NOTHING COMPARED TO THE REAL DEAL.

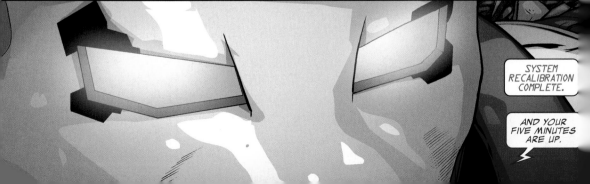

SYSTEM RECALIBRATION COMPLETE.

AND YOUR FIVE MINUTES ARE UP.

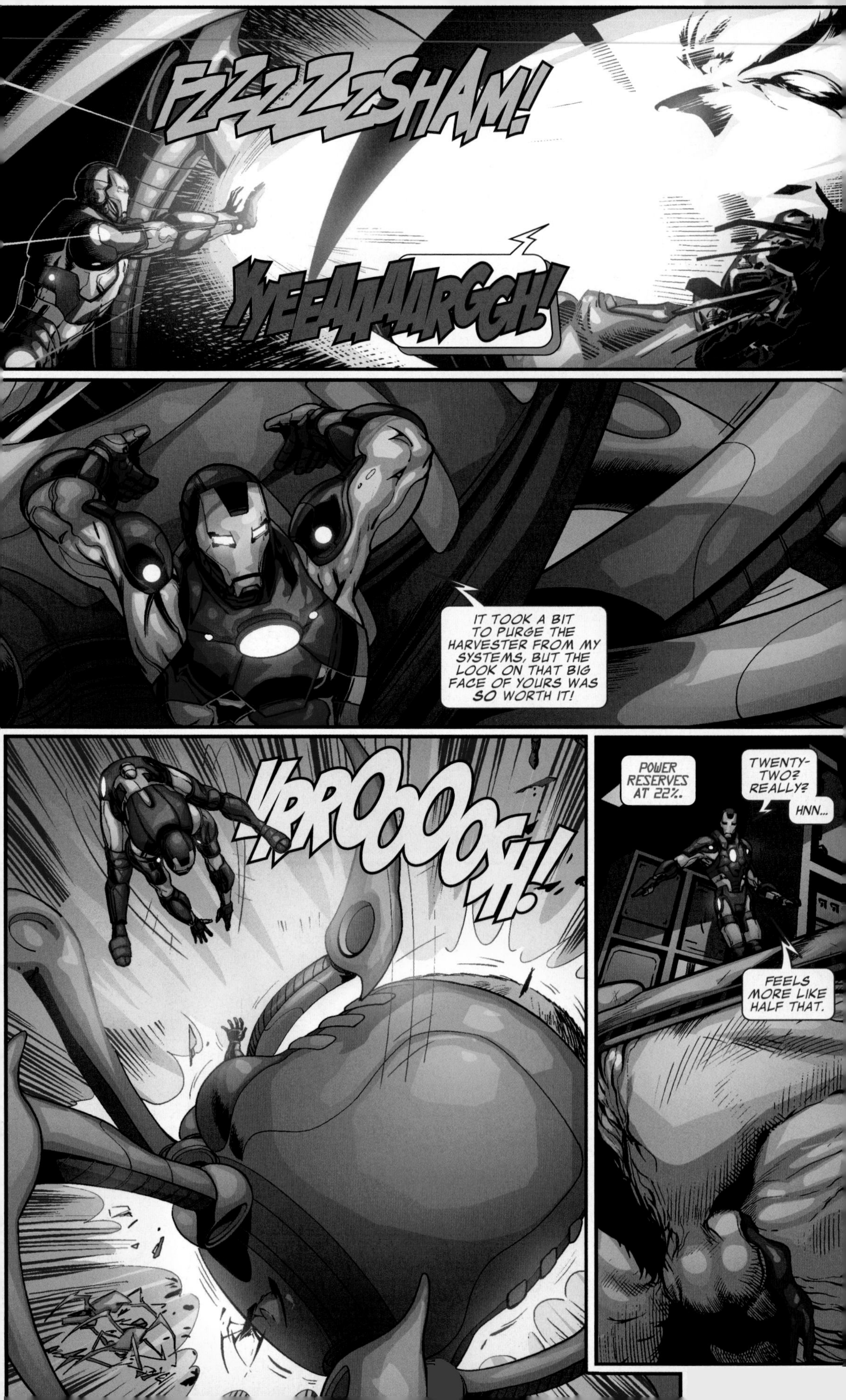
FZZZZZSHAM!
YYEEAAAARGGH!
IT TOOK A BIT TO PURGE THE HARVESTER FROM MY SYSTEMS, BUT THE LOOK ON THAT BIG FACE OF YOURS WAS SO WORTH IT!
VRROOOOOSH!
POWER RESERVES AT 22%.
TWENTY-TWO? REALLY?
HNN...
FEELS MORE LIKE HALF THAT.

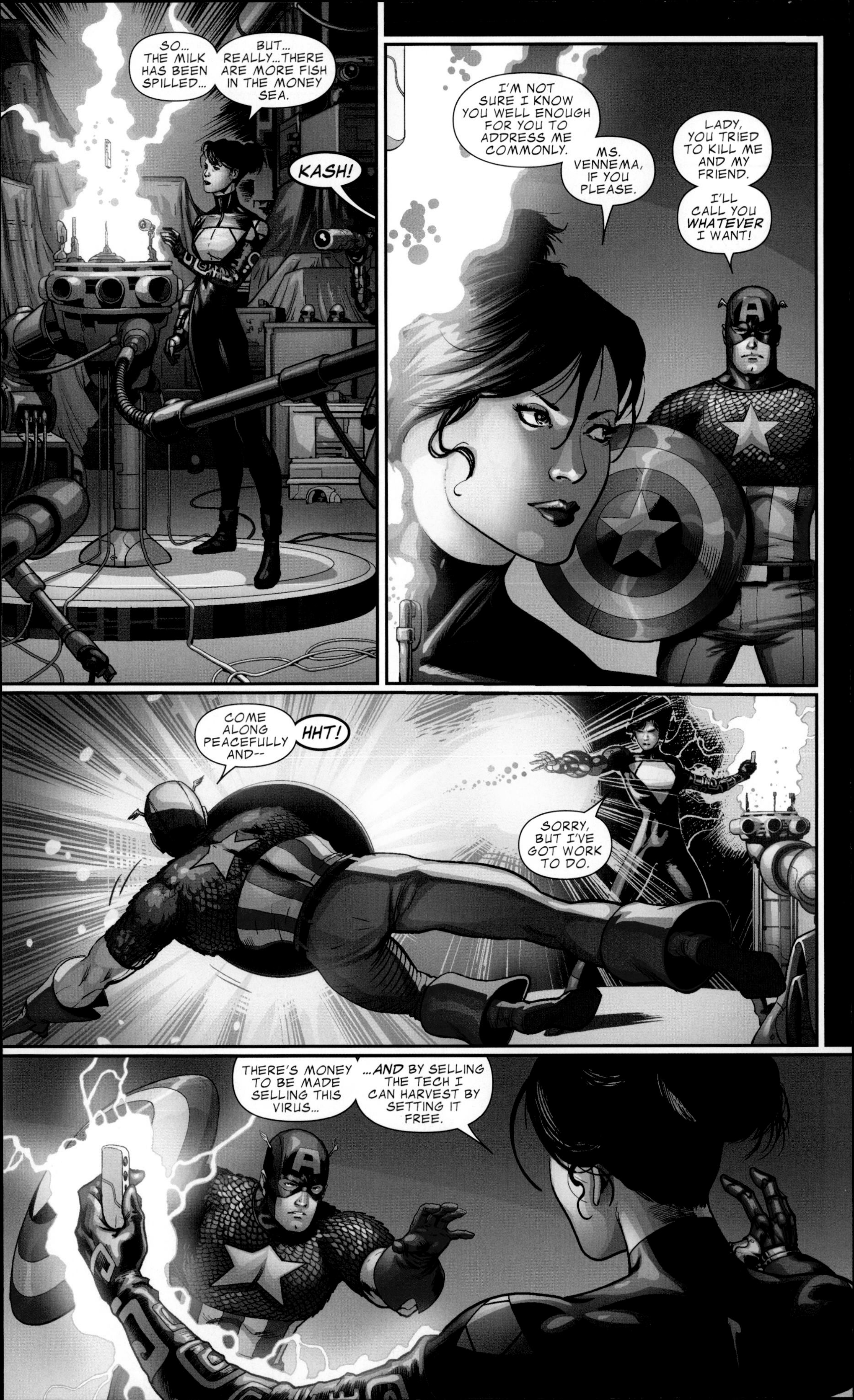
SO... THE MILK HAS BEEN SPILLED...
BUT... REALLY...THERE ARE MORE FISH IN THE MONEY SEA.
KASH!
I'M NOT SURE I KNOW YOU WELL ENOUGH FOR YOU TO ADDRESS ME COMMONLY.
MS. VENNEMA, IF YOU PLEASE.
LADY, YOU TRIED TO KILL ME AND MY FRIEND.
I'LL CALL YOU WHATEVER I WANT!
COME ALONG PEACEFULLY AND--
HHT!
SORRY, BUT I'VE GOT WORK TO DO.
THERE'S MONEY TO BE MADE SELLING THIS VIRUS...
...AND BY SELLING THE TECH I CAN HARVEST BY SETTING IT FREE.

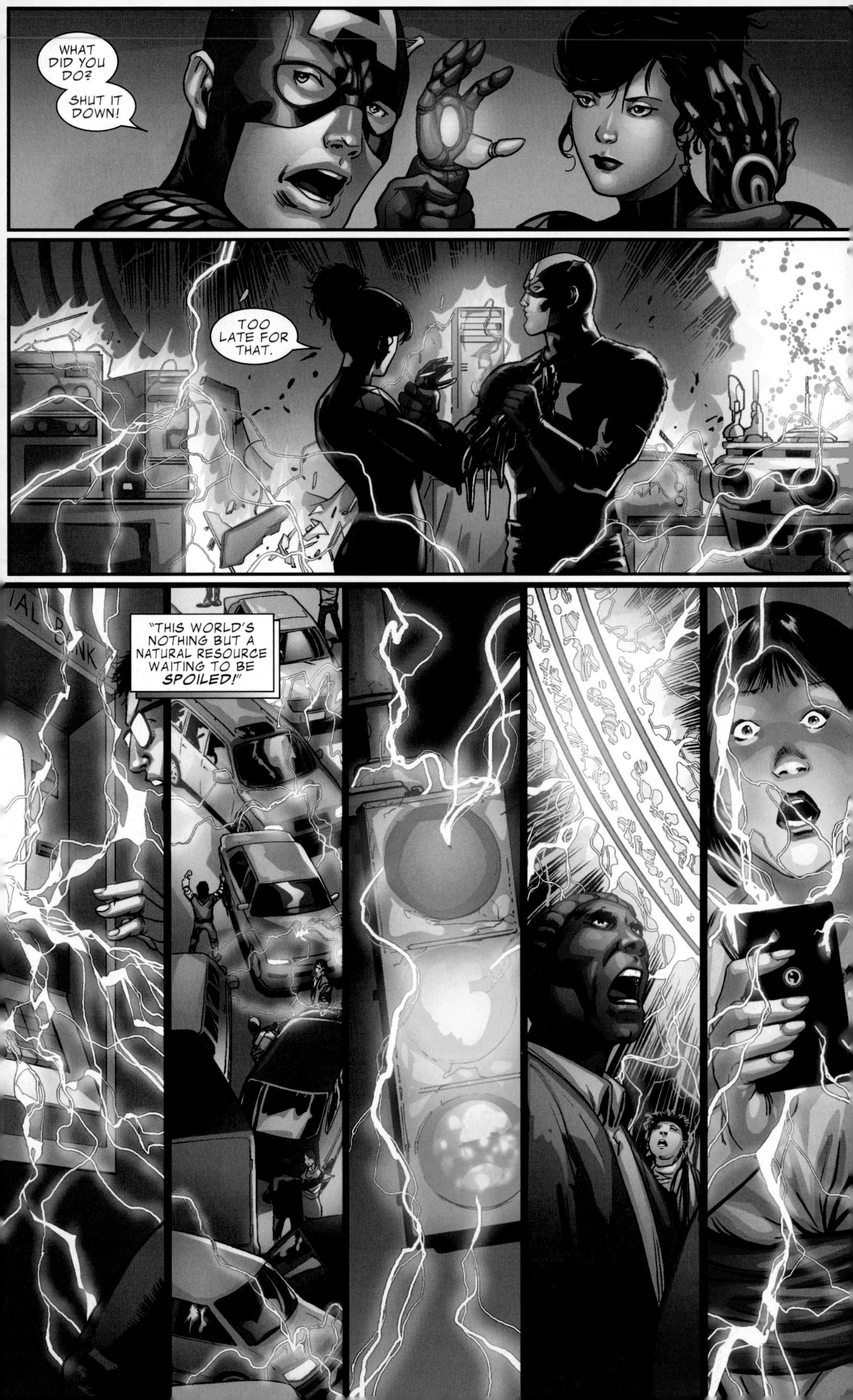
WHAT DID YOU DO?
SHUT IT DOWN!
TOO LATE FOR THAT.
"THIS WORLD'S NOTHING BUT A NATURAL RESOURCE WAITING TO BE SPOILED!"

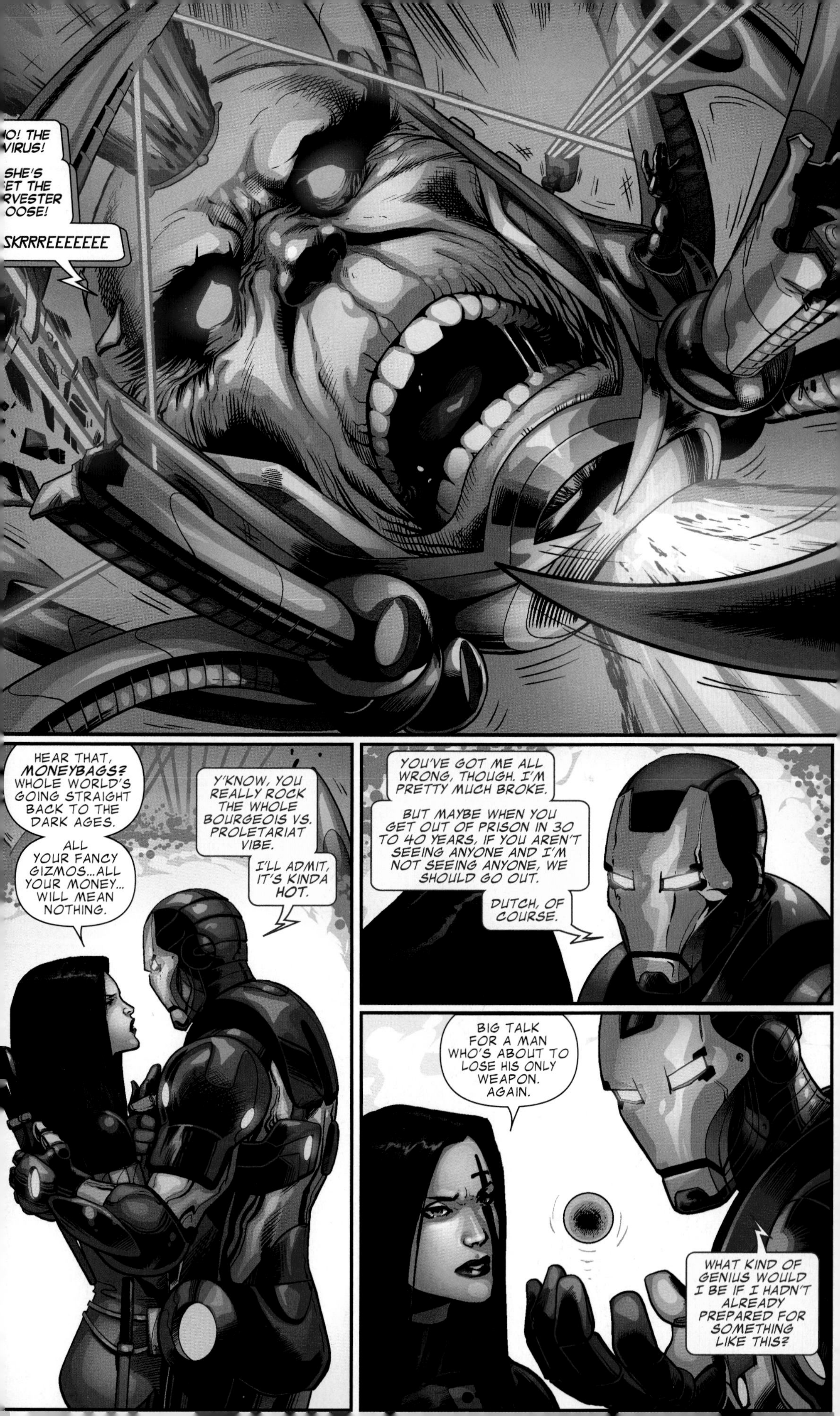
O! THE VIRUS!
SHE'S ET THE RVESTER OOSE!
SKRRREEEEEEE
HEAR THAT, MONEYBAGS? WHOLE WORLD'S GOING STRAIGHT BACK TO THE DARK AGES.
ALL YOUR FANCY GIZMOS...ALL YOUR MONEY... WILL MEAN NOTHING.
Y'KNOW, YOU REALLY ROCK THE WHOLE BOURGEOIS VS. PROLETARIAT VIBE.
I'LL ADMIT, IT'S KINDA HOT.
YOU'VE GOT ME ALL WRONG, THOUGH. I'M PRETTY MUCH BROKE.
BUT MAYBE WHEN YOU GET OUT OF PRISON IN 30 TO 40 YEARS, IF YOU AREN'T SEEING ANYONE AND I'M NOT SEEING ANYONE, WE SHOULD GO OUT.
DUTCH, OF COURSE.
BIG TALK FOR A MAN WHO'S ABOUT TO LOSE HIS ONLY WEAPON. AGAIN.
WHAT KIND OF GENIUS WOULD I BE IF I HADN'T ALREADY PREPARED FOR SOMETHING LIKE THIS?

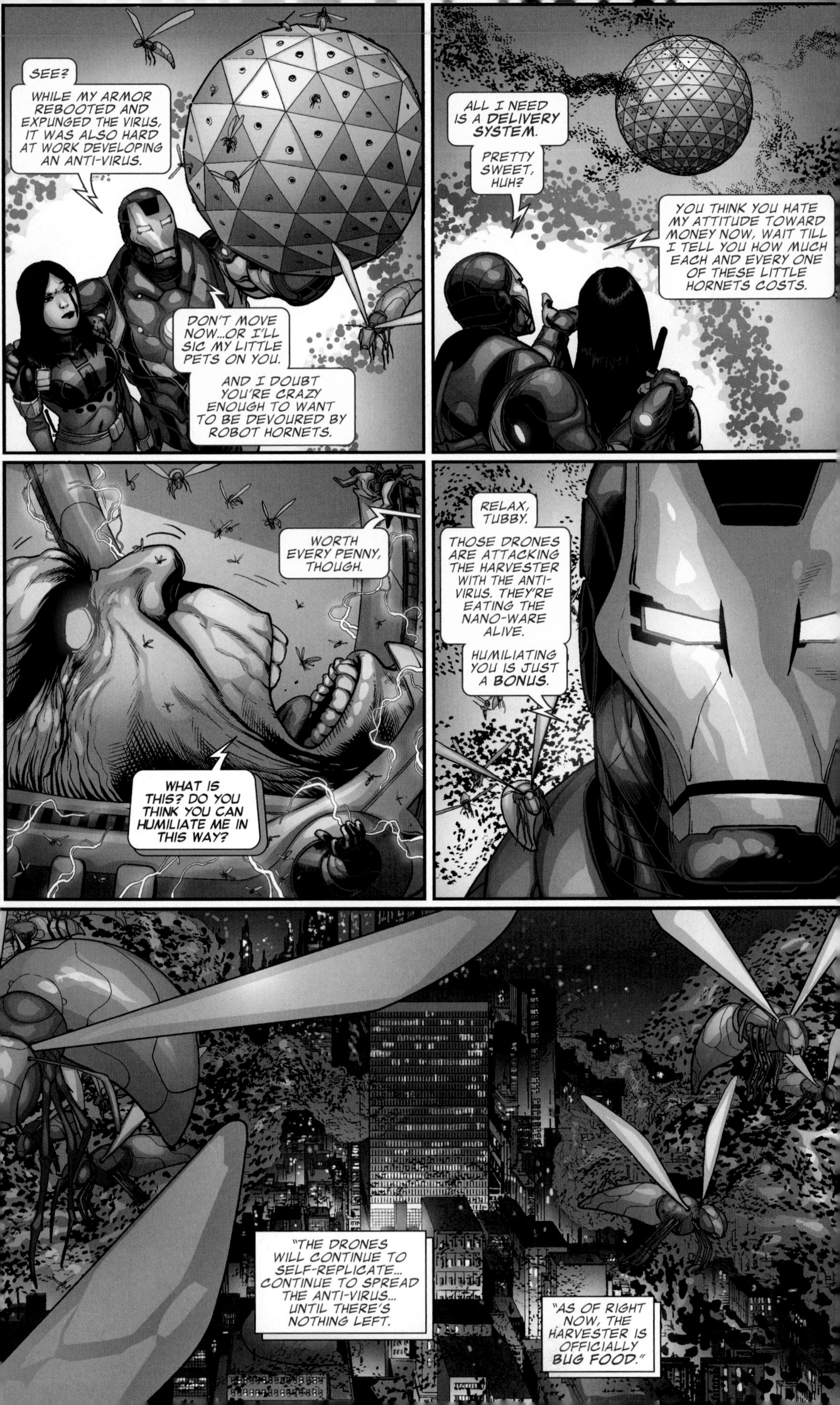
SEE?
WHILE MY ARMOR REBOOTED AND EXPUNGED THE VIRUS, IT WAS ALSO HARD AT WORK DEVELOPING AN ANTI-VIRUS.
DON'T MOVE NOW...OR I'LL SIC MY LITTLE PETS ON YOU.
AND I DOUBT YOU'RE CRAZY ENOUGH TO WANT TO BE DEVOURED BY ROBOT HORNETS.
ALL I NEED IS A DELIVERY SYSTEM.
PRETTY SWEET, HUH?
YOU THINK YOU HATE MY ATTITUDE TOWARD MONEY NOW, WAIT TILL I TELL YOU HOW MUCH EACH AND EVERY ONE OF THESE LITTLE HORNETS COSTS.
WORTH EVERY PENNY, THOUGH.
WHAT IS THIS? DO YOU THINK YOU CAN HUMILIATE ME IN THIS WAY?
RELAX, TUBBY.
THOSE DRONES ARE ATTACKING THE HARVESTER WITH THE ANTI-VIRUS. THEY'RE EATING THE NANO-WARE ALIVE.
HUMILIATING YOU IS JUST A BONUS.
"THE DRONES WILL CONTINUE TO SELF-REPLICATE... CONTINUE TO SPREAD THE ANTI-VIRUS... UNTIL THERE'S NOTHING LEFT.
"AS OF RIGHT NOW, THE HARVESTER IS OFFICIALLY BUG FOOD."

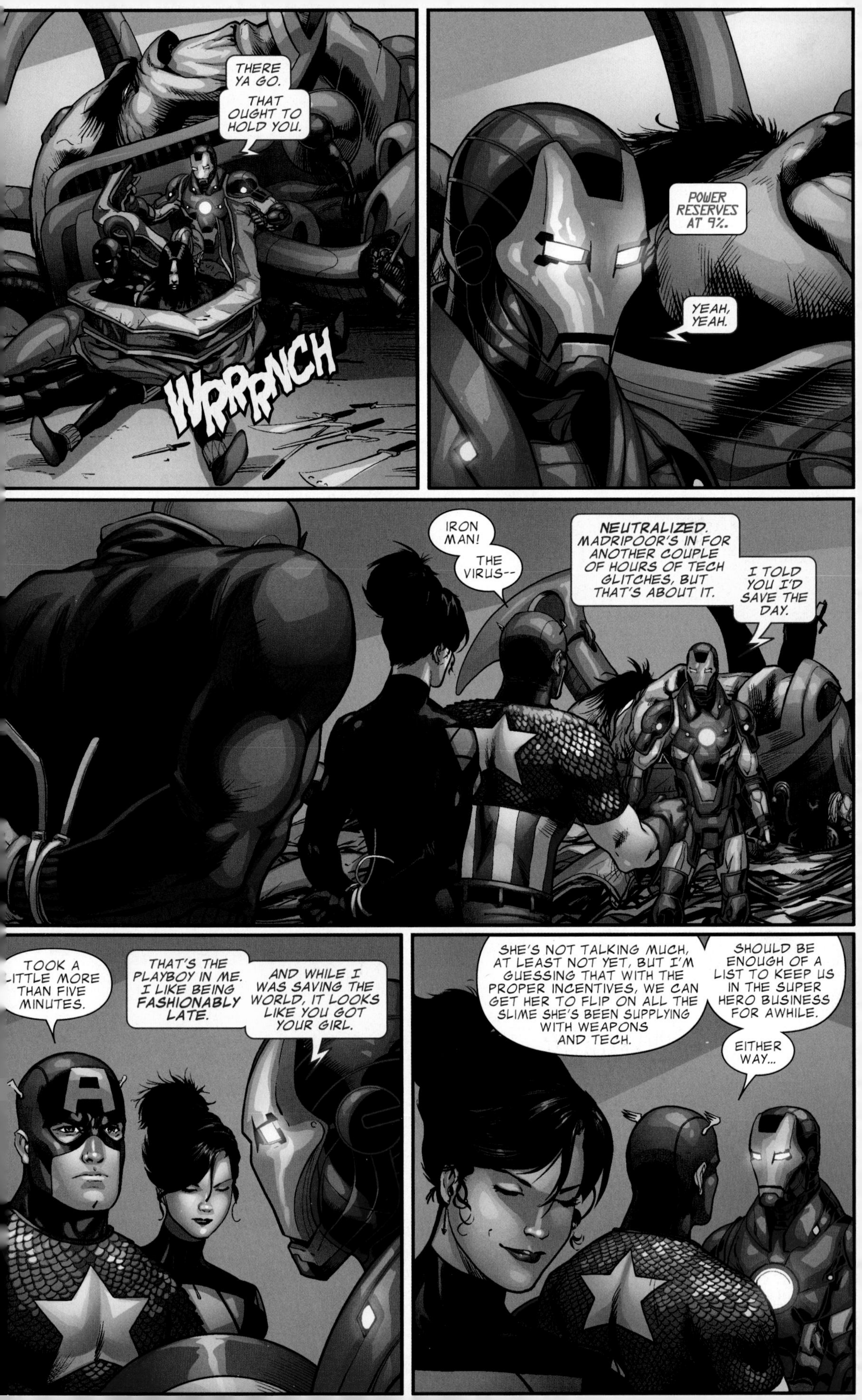
THERE YA GO. THAT OUGHT TO HOLD YOU.
WRRRNCH
POWER RESERVES AT 9%.
YEAH, YEAH.
IRON MAN! THE VIRUS--
NEUTRALIZED. MADRIPOOR'S IN FOR ANOTHER COUPLE OF HOURS OF TECH GLITCHES, BUT THAT'S ABOUT IT.
I TOLD YOU I'D SAVE THE DAY.
TOOK A LITTLE MORE THAN FIVE MINUTES.
THAT'S THE PLAYBOY IN ME. I LIKE BEING FASHIONABLY LATE.
AND WHILE I WAS SAVING THE WORLD, IT LOOKS LIKE YOU GOT YOUR GIRL.
SHE'S NOT TALKING MUCH, AT LEAST NOT YET, BUT I'M GUESSING THAT WITH THE PROPER INCENTIVES, WE CAN GET HER TO FLIP ON ALL THE SLIME SHE'S BEEN SUPPLYING WITH WEAPONS AND TECH.
SHOULD BE ENOUGH OF A LIST TO KEEP US IN THE SUPER HERO BUSINESS FOR AWHILE.
EITHER WAY...

"...IT LOOKS LIKE KASHMIR VENNEMA IS EFFECTIVELY OUT OF BUSINESS."

OPERATIVE 12 HAS NOT REPORTED IN SINCE HER LAST TRANSMISSION.

I THINK WE'D BE SAFE IN ASSUMING SHE'S BEEN APPREHENDED.

IF THAT'S THE CASE, IT'S HER OWN FAULT.

SHE SHOULD HAVE GONE WITH ONE OF OUR SECURITY DETAILS INSTEAD OF HIRING LOCALLY.

I WARNED HER TIME AND AGAIN THAT HER RECKLESSNESS WOULD NEGATIVELY IMPACT THE BOTTOM LINE AT SOME POINT.

THIS WOULD HAVE BEEN A WIN FOR US. NOW WE'VE LOST THE HARVESTER AND OUR REPUTATION'S BEEN DAMAGED.

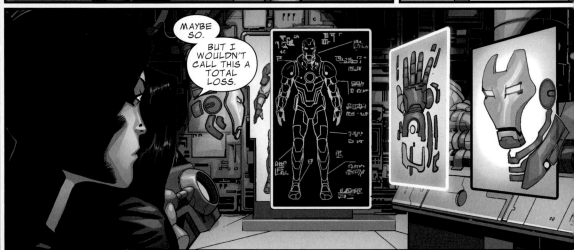

MAYBE SO.

BUT I WOULDN'T CALL THIS A TOTAL LOSS.

"WE'RE STILL IN THE BLACK.

"AND THAT'S NOT TOO SHABBY IN THIS ECONOMIC CLIMATE."

The End.

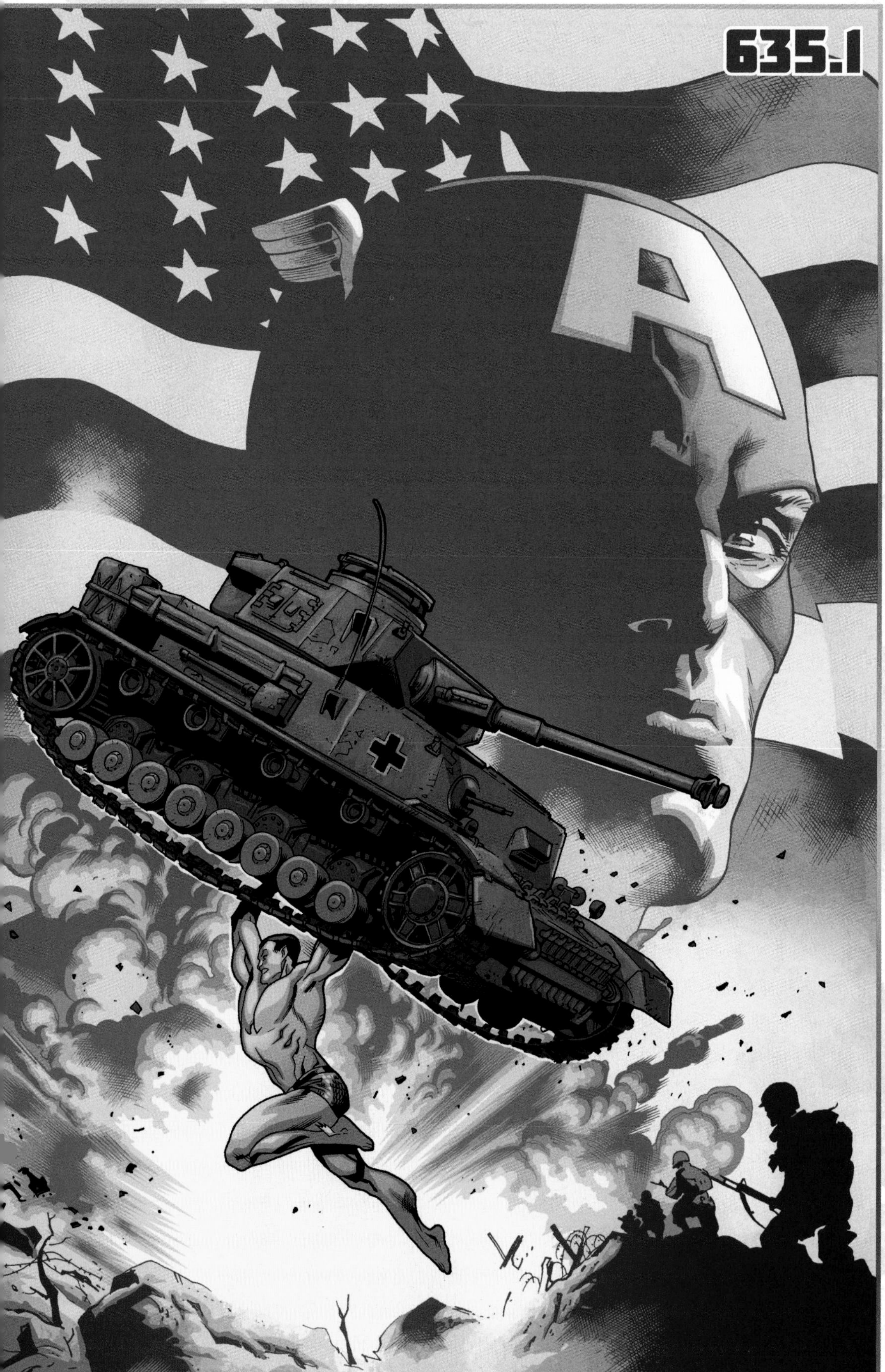
635.1

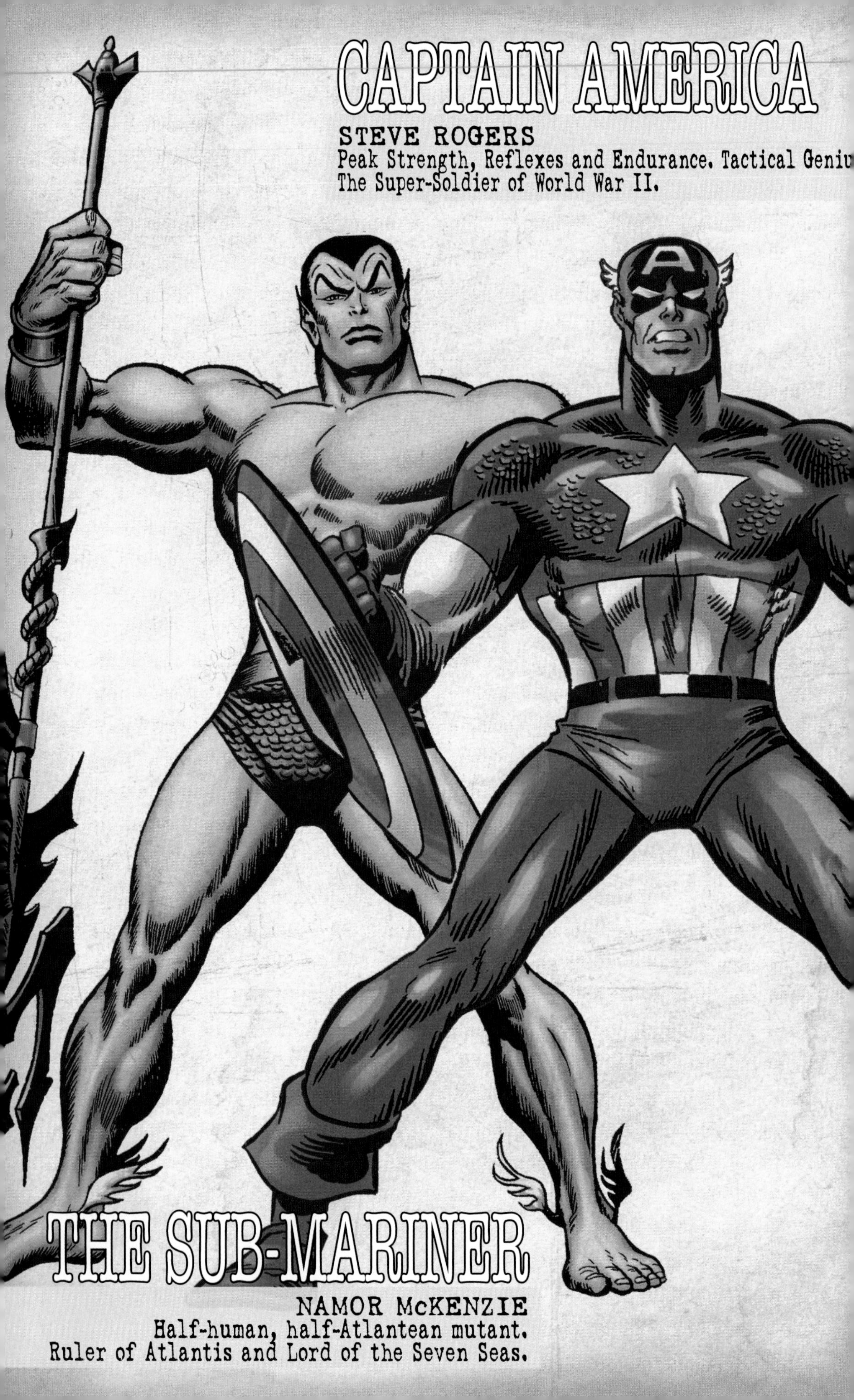
CAPTAIN AMERICA
STEVE ROGERS
Peak Strength, Reflexes and Endurance. Tactical Geniu
The Super-Soldier of World War II.
THE SUB-MARINER
NAMOR McKENZIE
Half-human, half-Atlantean mutant.
Ruler of Atlantis and Lord of the Seven Seas.

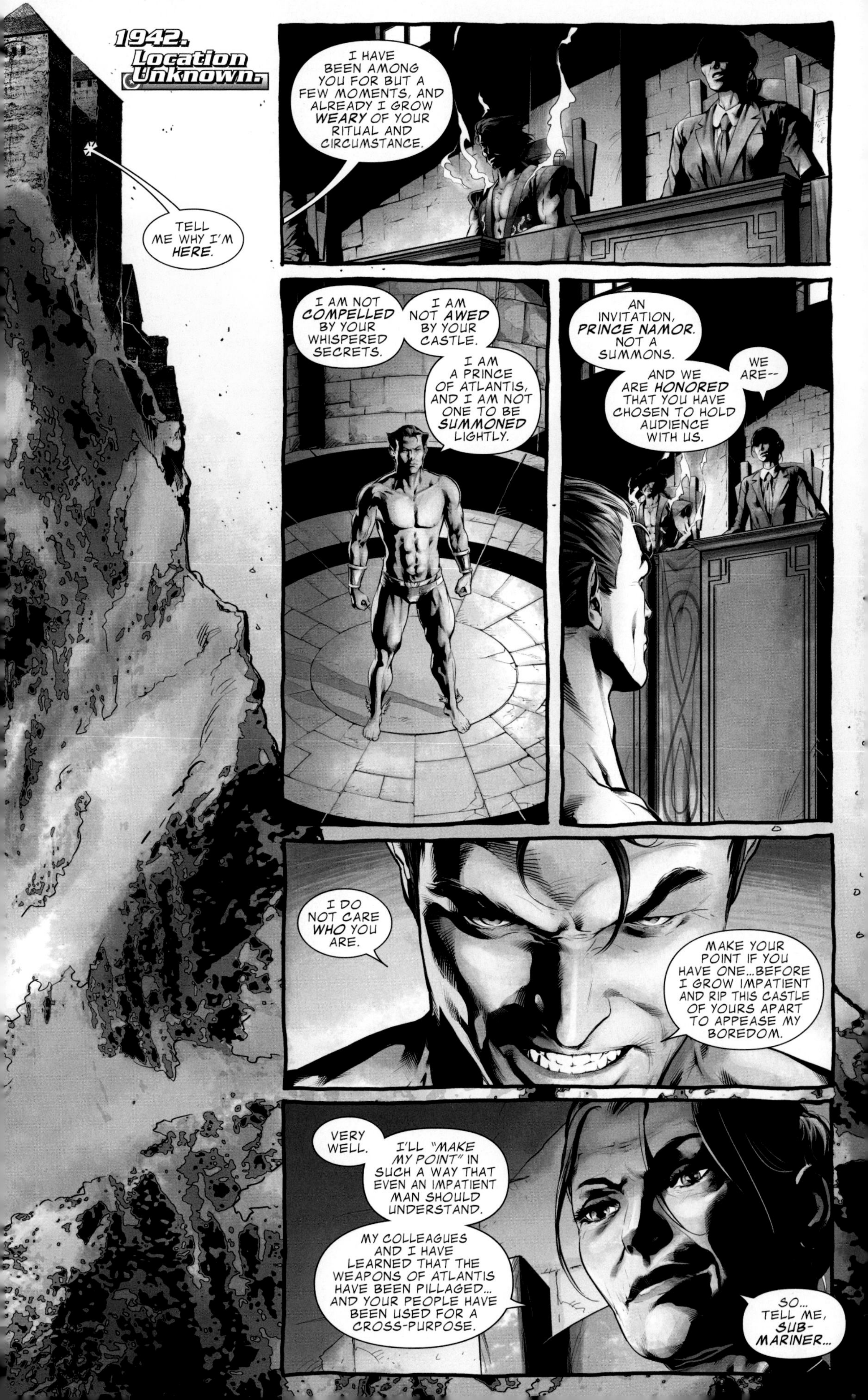
1942. Location Unknown.
TELL ME WHY I'M *HERE*.
I HAVE BEEN AMONG YOU FOR BUT A FEW MOMENTS, AND ALREADY I GROW *WEARY* OF YOUR RITUAL AND CIRCUMSTANCE.
I AM NOT *COMPELLED* BY YOUR WHISPERED SECRETS.
I AM NOT *AWED* BY YOUR CASTLE.
I AM A PRINCE OF ATLANTIS, AND I AM NOT ONE TO BE *SUMMONED* LIGHTLY.
AN INVITATION, *PRINCE NAMOR*. NOT A SUMMONS.
AND WE ARE *HONORED* THAT YOU HAVE CHOSEN TO HOLD AUDIENCE WITH US.
WE ARE--
I DO NOT CARE *WHO* YOU ARE.
MAKE YOUR POINT IF YOU HAVE ONE...BEFORE I GROW IMPATIENT AND RIP THIS CASTLE OF YOURS APART TO APPEASE MY BOREDOM.
VERY WELL.
I'LL *"MAKE MY POINT"* IN SUCH A WAY THAT EVEN AN IMPATIENT MAN SHOULD UNDERSTAND.
MY COLLEAGUES AND I HAVE LEARNED THAT THE WEAPONS OF ATLANTIS HAVE BEEN PILLAGED... AND YOUR PEOPLE HAVE BEEN USED FOR A CROSS-PURPOSE.
SO... TELL ME, *SUB-MARINER*...

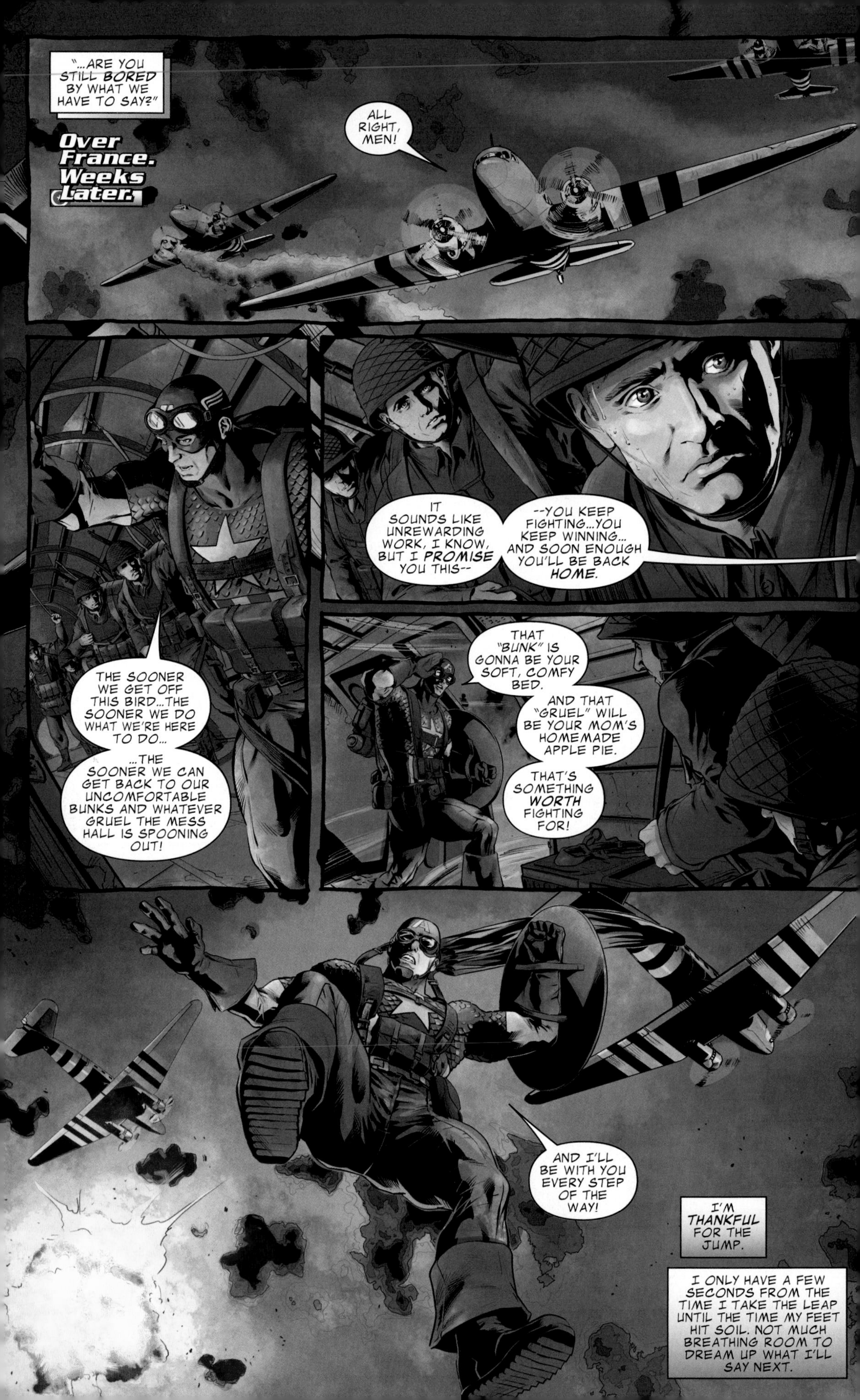

"...ARE YOU STILL BORED BY WHAT WE HAVE TO SAY?"
Over France. Weeks Later.
ALL RIGHT, MEN!
THE SOONER WE GET OFF THIS BIRD...THE SOONER WE DO WHAT WE'RE HERE TO DO...
...THE SOONER WE CAN GET BACK TO OUR UNCOMFORTABLE BUNKS AND WHATEVER GRUEL THE MESS HALL IS SPOONING OUT!
IT SOUNDS LIKE UNREWARDING WORK, I KNOW, BUT I PROMISE YOU THIS--
--YOU KEEP FIGHTING...YOU KEEP WINNING... AND SOON ENOUGH YOU'LL BE BACK HOME.
THAT "BUNK" IS GONNA BE YOUR SOFT, COMFY BED.
AND THAT "GRUEL" WILL BE YOUR MOM'S HOMEMADE APPLE PIE.
THAT'S SOMETHING WORTH FIGHTING FOR!
AND I'LL BE WITH YOU EVERY STEP OF THE WAY!
I'M THANKFUL FOR THE JUMP.
I ONLY HAVE A FEW SECONDS FROM THE TIME I TAKE THE LEAP UNTIL THE TIME MY FEET HIT SOIL. NOT MUCH BREATHING ROOM TO DREAM UP WHAT I'LL SAY NEXT.

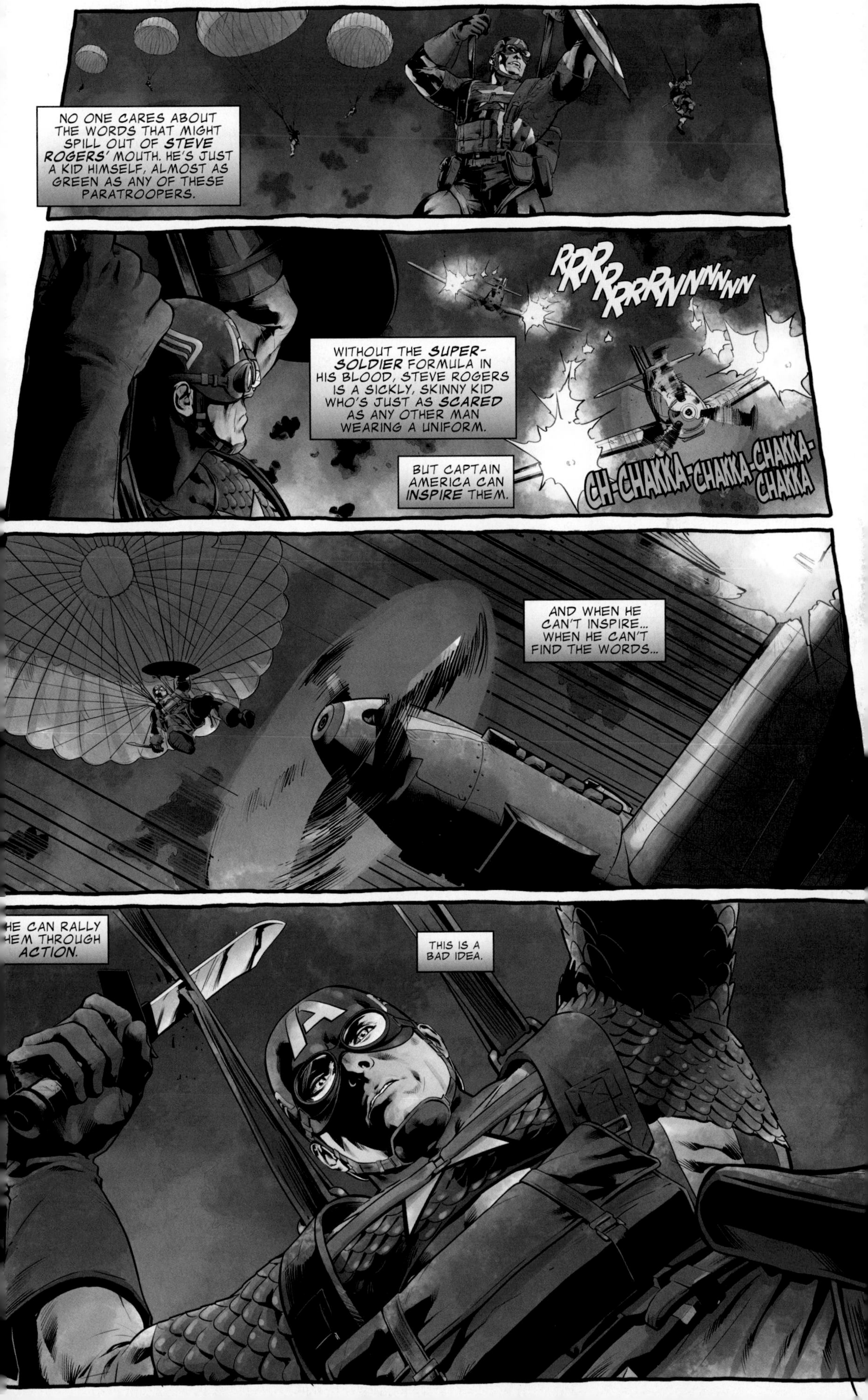
NO ONE CARES ABOUT THE WORDS THAT MIGHT SPILL OUT OF STEVE ROGERS' MOUTH. HE'S JUST A KID HIMSELF, ALMOST AS GREEN AS ANY OF THESE PARATROOPERS.
RRRRRRRNNNNNN
WITHOUT THE SUPER-SOLDIER FORMULA IN HIS BLOOD, STEVE ROGERS IS A SICKLY, SKINNY KID WHO'S JUST AS SCARED AS ANY OTHER MAN WEARING A UNIFORM.
BUT CAPTAIN AMERICA CAN INSPIRE THEM.
CH-CHAKKA-CHAKKA-CHAKKA-CHAKKA
AND WHEN HE CAN'T INSPIRE... WHEN HE CAN'T FIND THE WORDS...
HE CAN RALLY THEM THROUGH ACTION.
THIS IS A BAD IDEA.

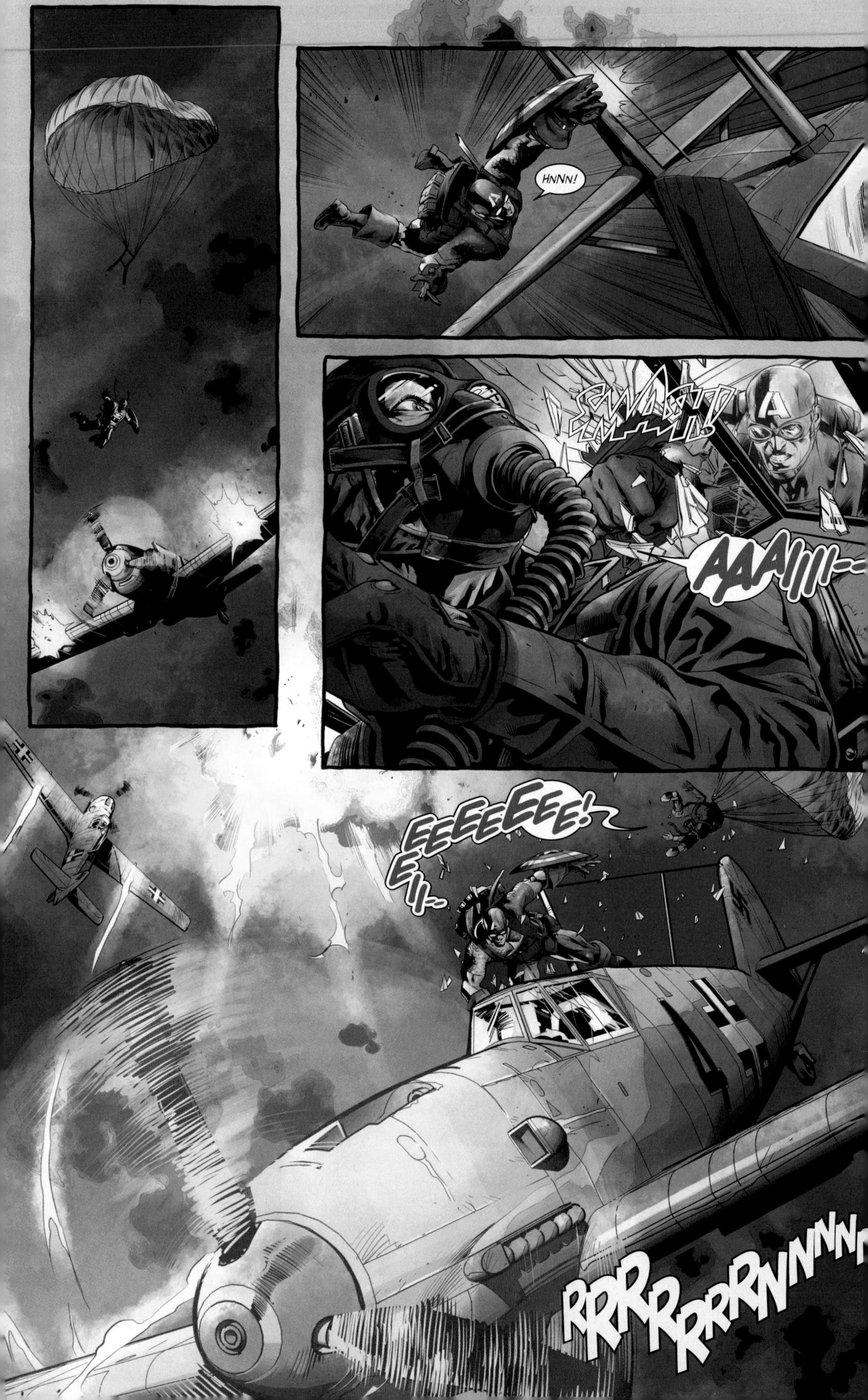
HNNN!
SMASH!
AAAIIII--
EEEEEEEEE!
Eııı-
RRRRRRRRNNNNN

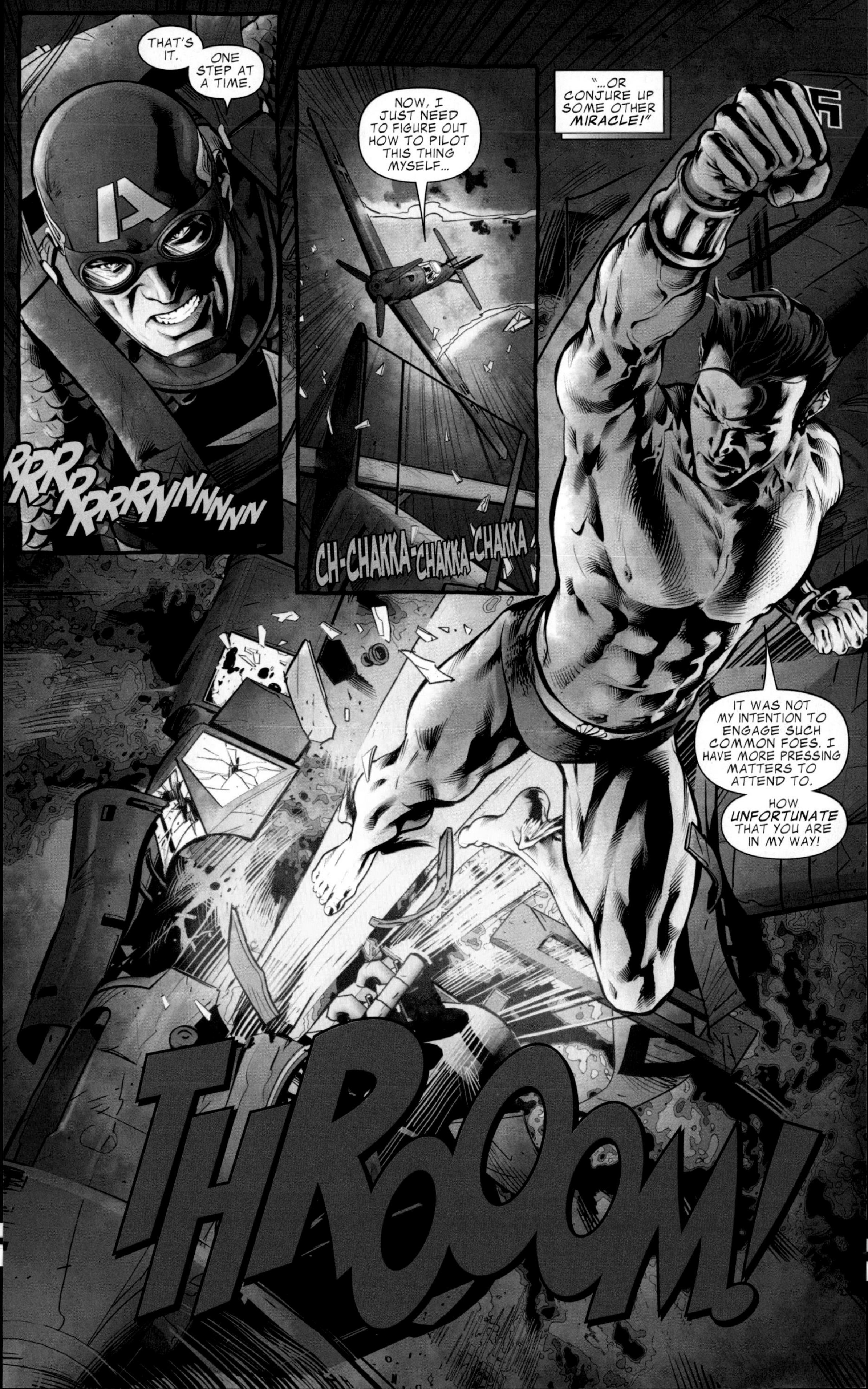
THAT'S IT.
ONE STEP AT A TIME.
RRRRRRRRNNNNNN
NOW, I JUST NEED TO FIGURE OUT HOW TO PILOT THIS THING MYSELF...
CH-CHAKKA-CHAKKA-CHAKKA
"...OR CONJURE UP SOME OTHER MIRACLE!"
IT WAS NOT MY INTENTION TO ENGAGE SUCH COMMON FOES. I HAVE MORE PRESSING MATTERS TO ATTEND TO.
HOW UNFORTUNATE THAT YOU ARE IN MY WAY!
THROOM!

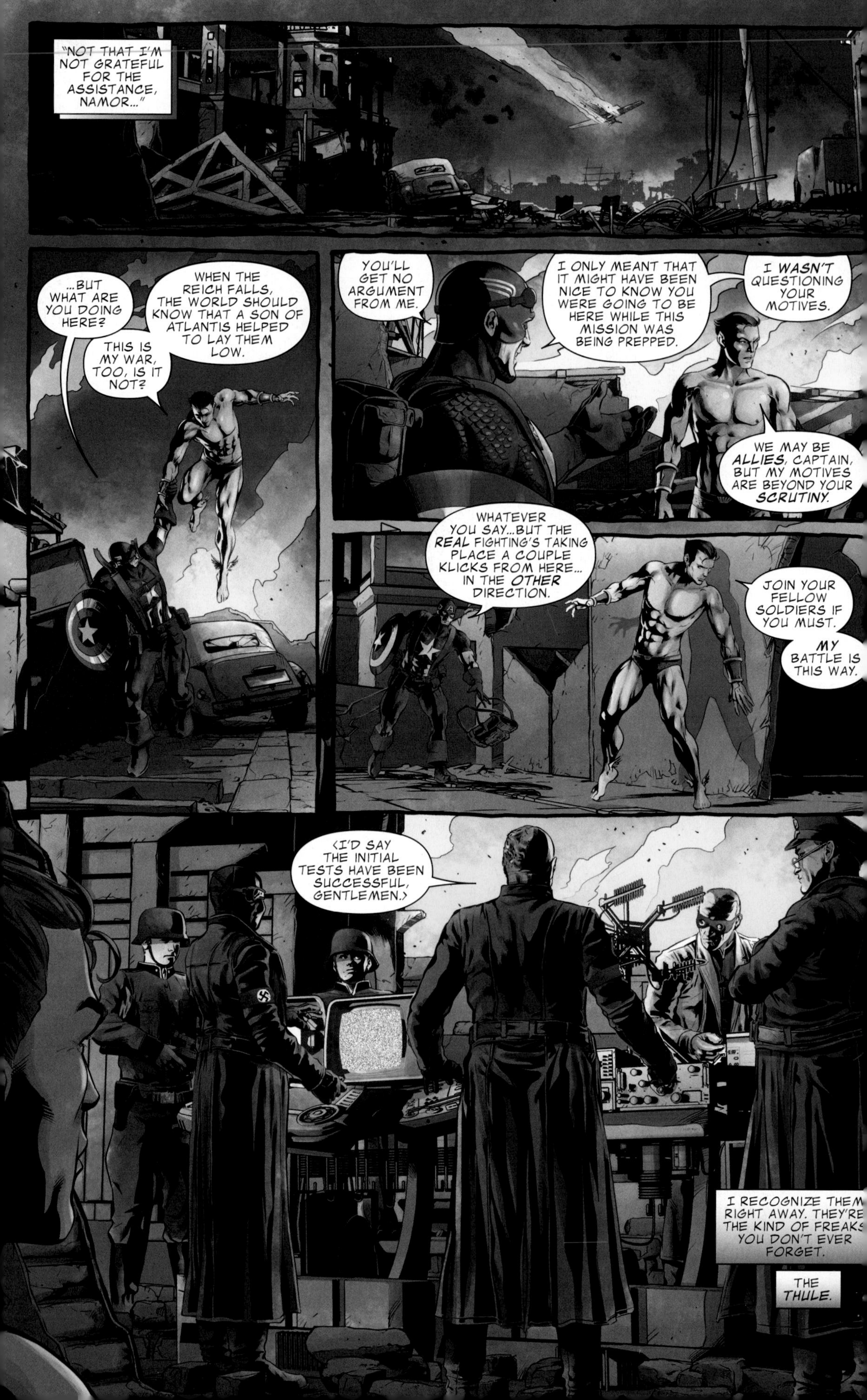
"NOT THAT I'M NOT GRATEFUL FOR THE ASSISTANCE, NAMOR..."
...BUT WHAT ARE YOU DOING HERE?
THIS IS MY WAR, TOO, IS IT NOT?
WHEN THE REICH FALLS, THE WORLD SHOULD KNOW THAT A SON OF ATLANTIS HELPED TO LAY THEM LOW.
YOU'LL GET NO ARGUMENT FROM ME.
I ONLY MEANT THAT IT MIGHT HAVE BEEN NICE TO KNOW YOU WERE GOING TO BE HERE WHILE THIS MISSION WAS BEING PREPPED.
I WASN'T QUESTIONING YOUR MOTIVES.
WE MAY BE ALLIES, CAPTAIN, BUT MY MOTIVES ARE BEYOND YOUR SCRUTINY.
WHATEVER YOU SAY...BUT THE REAL FIGHTING'S TAKING PLACE A COUPLE KLICKS FROM HERE... IN THE OTHER DIRECTION.
JOIN YOUR FELLOW SOLDIERS IF YOU MUST.
MY BATTLE IS THIS WAY.
<I'D SAY THE INITIAL TESTS HAVE BEEN SUCCESSFUL, GENTLEMEN.>
I RECOGNIZE THEM RIGHT AWAY. THEY'RE THE KIND OF FREAKS YOU DON'T EVER FORGET.
THE THULE.

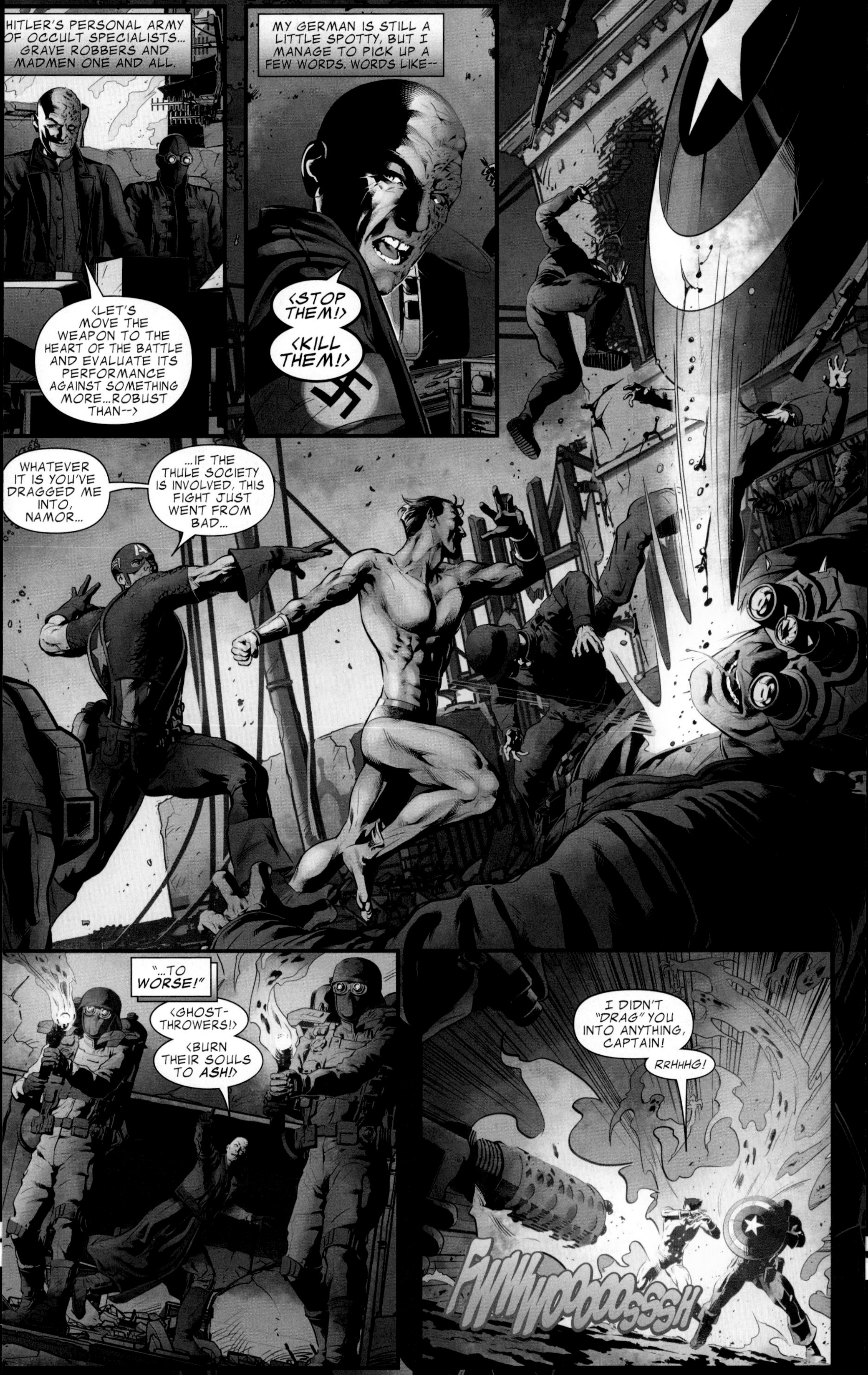
HITLER'S PERSONAL ARMY OF OCCULT SPECIALISTS... GRAVE ROBBERS AND MADMEN ONE AND ALL.
<LET'S MOVE THE WEAPON TO THE HEART OF THE BATTLE AND EVALUATE ITS PERFORMANCE AGAINST SOMETHING MORE...ROBUST THAN-->
MY GERMAN IS STILL A LITTLE SPOTTY, BUT I MANAGE TO PICK UP A FEW WORDS. WORDS LIKE--
<STOP THEM!>
<KILL THEM!>
WHATEVER IT IS YOU'VE DRAGGED ME INTO, NAMOR...
...IF THE THULE SOCIETY IS INVOLVED, THIS FIGHT JUST WENT FROM BAD...
"...TO WORSE!"
<GHOST-THROWERS!>
<BURN THEIR SOULS TO ASH!>
I DIDN'T "DRAG" YOU INTO ANYTHING, CAPTAIN!
RRHHHG!
FWHHHOOOOOSSSH

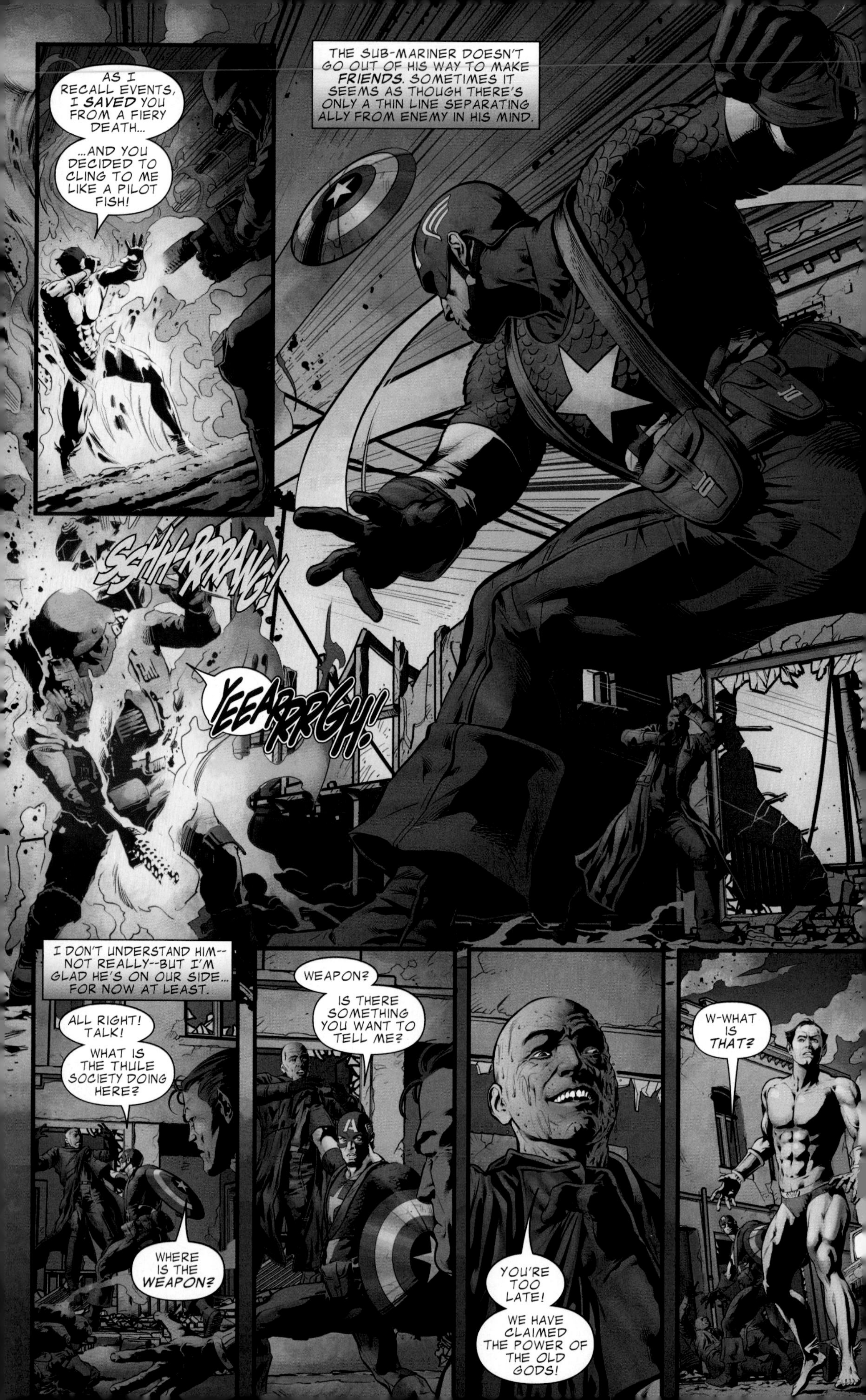
AS I RECALL EVENTS, I **SAVED** YOU FROM A FIERY DEATH...
...AND YOU DECIDED TO CLING TO ME LIKE A PILOT FISH!
THE SUB-MARINER DOESN'T GO OUT OF HIS WAY TO MAKE **FRIENDS**. SOMETIMES IT SEEMS AS THOUGH THERE'S ONLY A THIN LINE SEPARATING ALLY FROM ENEMY IN HIS MIND.
SSHH-RRRANG!
YEEARRRGH!
I DON'T UNDERSTAND HIM--NOT REALLY--BUT I'M GLAD HE'S ON OUR SIDE... FOR NOW AT LEAST.
ALL RIGHT! TALK!
WHAT IS THE THULE SOCIETY DOING HERE?
WHERE IS THE **WEAPON**?
WEAPON?
IS THERE SOMETHING YOU WANT TO TELL ME?
YOU'RE TOO LATE!
WE HAVE CLAIMED THE POWER OF THE OLD GODS!
W-WHAT IS **THAT**?

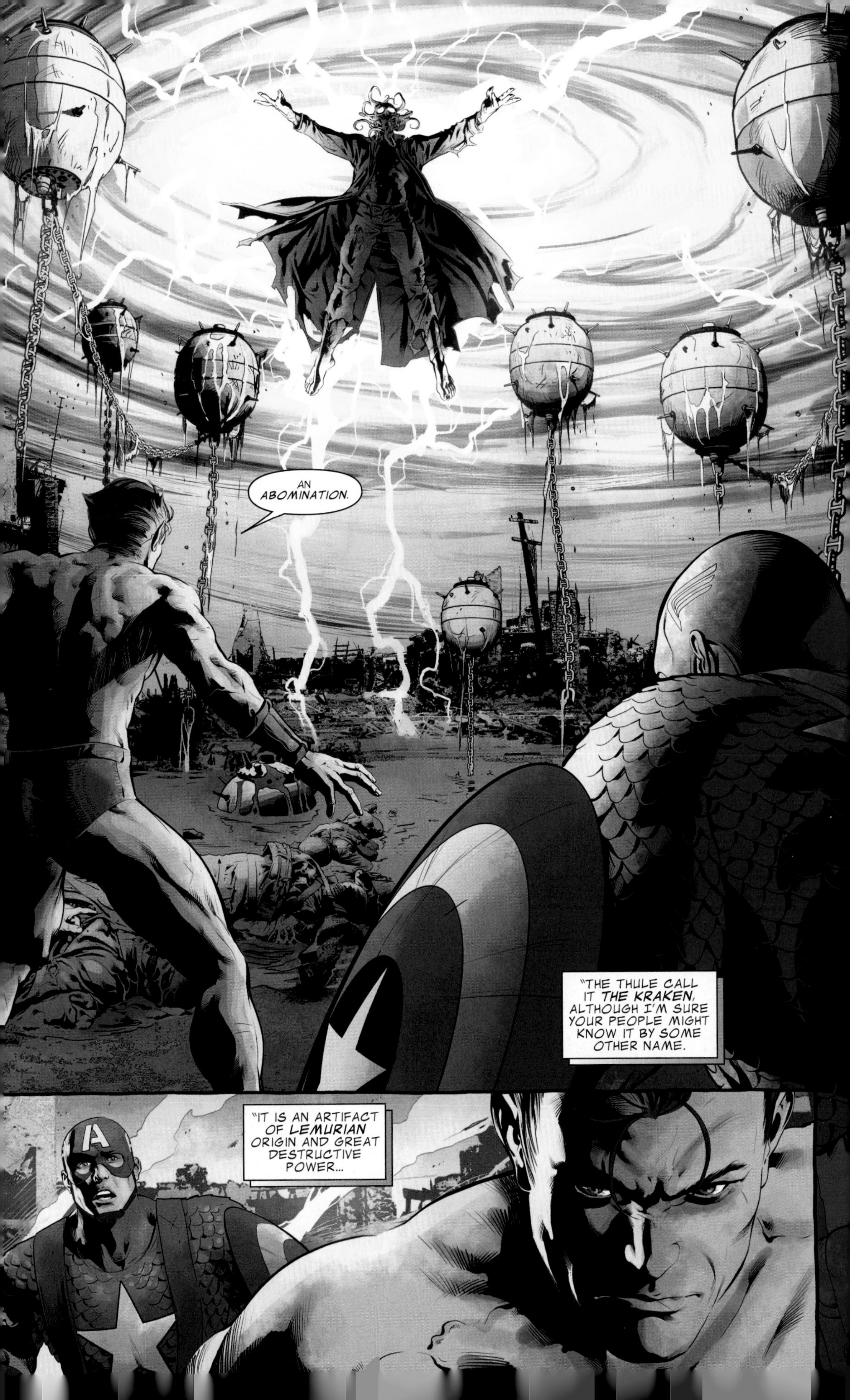
AN ABOMINATION.
"THE THULE CALL IT THE KRAKEN, ALTHOUGH I'M SURE YOUR PEOPLE MIGHT KNOW IT BY SOME OTHER NAME.
"IT IS AN ARTIFACT OF LEMURIAN ORIGIN AND GREAT DESTRUCTIVE POWER...

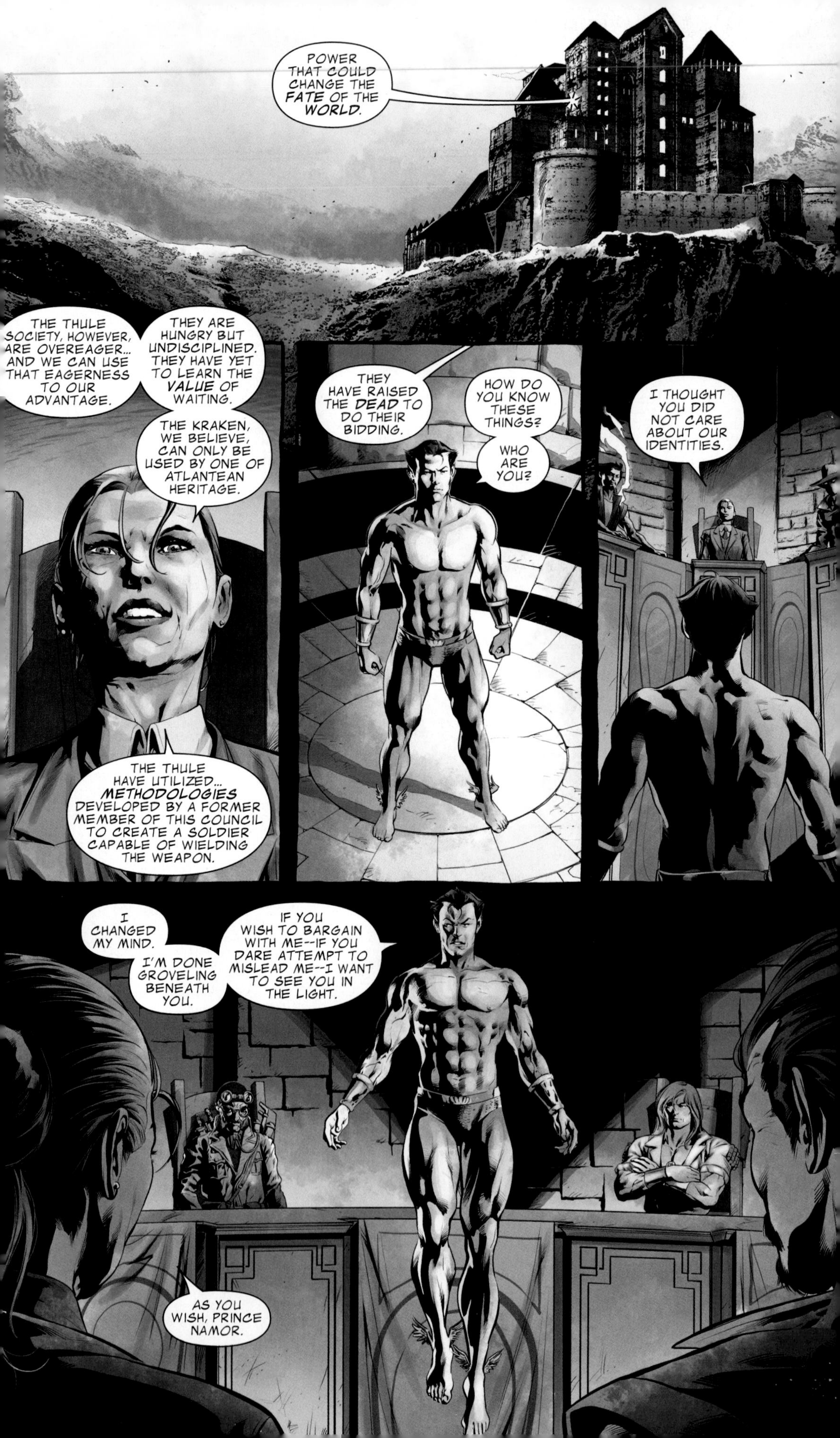
POWER THAT COULD CHANGE THE FATE OF THE WORLD.
THE THULE SOCIETY, HOWEVER, ARE OVEREAGER... AND WE CAN USE THAT EAGERNESS TO OUR ADVANTAGE.
THEY ARE HUNGRY BUT UNDISCIPLINED. THEY HAVE YET TO LEARN THE VALUE OF WAITING.
THE KRAKEN, WE BELIEVE, CAN ONLY BE USED BY ONE OF ATLANTEAN HERITAGE.
THE THULE HAVE UTILIZED... METHODOLOGIES DEVELOPED BY A FORMER MEMBER OF THIS COUNCIL TO CREATE A SOLDIER CAPABLE OF WIELDING THE WEAPON.
THEY HAVE RAISED THE DEAD TO DO THEIR BIDDING.
HOW DO YOU KNOW THESE THINGS?
WHO ARE YOU?
I THOUGHT YOU DID NOT CARE ABOUT OUR IDENTITIES.
I CHANGED MY MIND.
I'M DONE GROVELING BENEATH YOU.
IF YOU WISH TO BARGAIN WITH ME--IF YOU DARE ATTEMPT TO MISLEAD ME--I WANT TO SEE YOU IN THE LIGHT.
AS YOU WISH, PRINCE NAMOR.

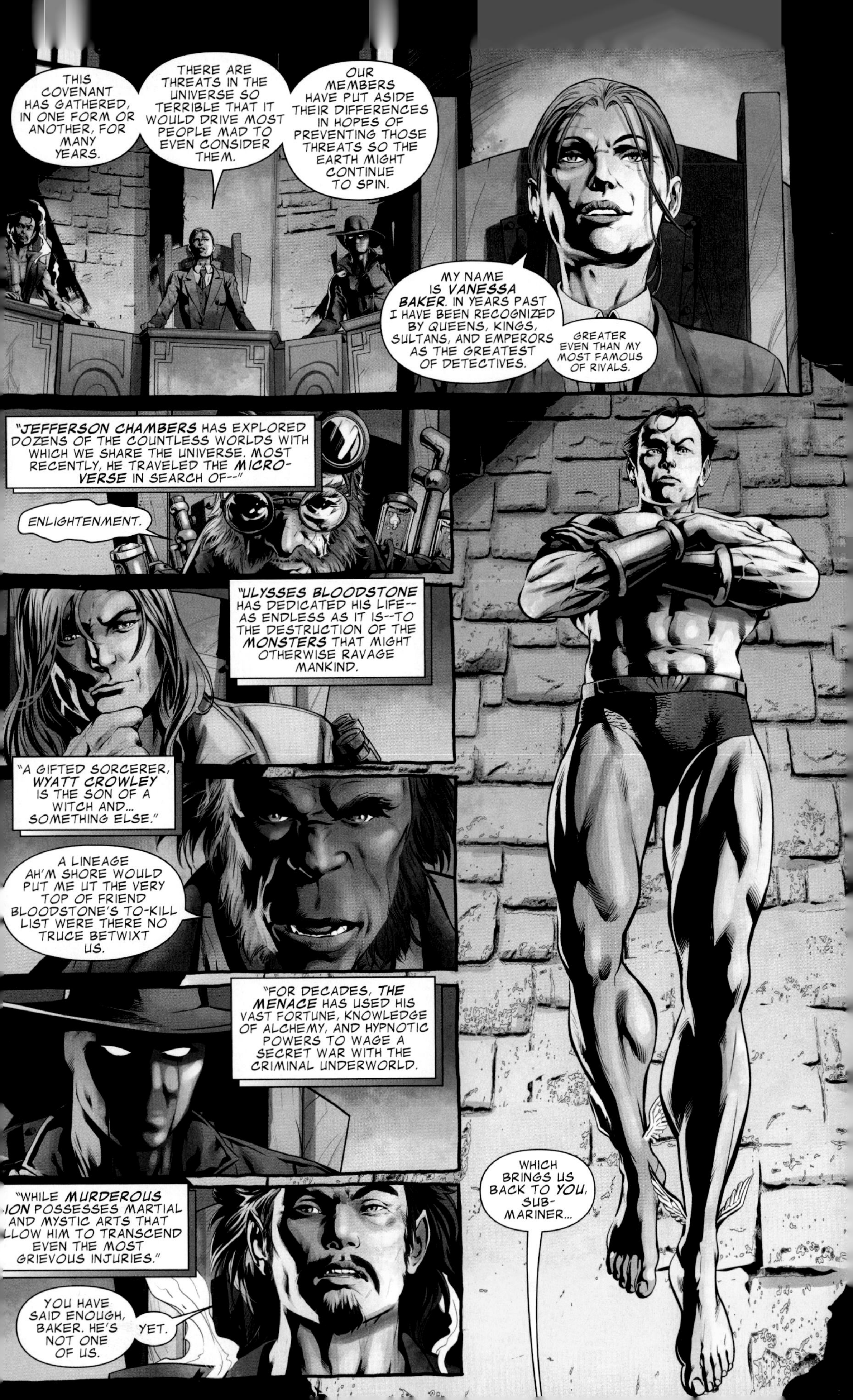
THIS COVENANT HAS GATHERED, IN ONE FORM OR ANOTHER, FOR MANY YEARS.
THERE ARE THREATS IN THE UNIVERSE SO TERRIBLE THAT IT WOULD DRIVE MOST PEOPLE MAD TO EVEN CONSIDER THEM.
OUR MEMBERS HAVE PUT ASIDE THEIR DIFFERENCES IN HOPES OF PREVENTING THOSE THREATS SO THE EARTH MIGHT CONTINUE TO SPIN.
MY NAME IS VANESSA BAKER. IN YEARS PAST I HAVE BEEN RECOGNIZED BY QUEENS, KINGS, SULTANS, AND EMPERORS AS THE GREATEST OF DETECTIVES.
GREATER EVEN THAN MY MOST FAMOUS OF RIVALS.
"JEFFERSON CHAMBERS HAS EXPLORED DOZENS OF THE COUNTLESS WORLDS WITH WHICH WE SHARE THE UNIVERSE. MOST RECENTLY, HE TRAVELED THE MICRO-VERSE IN SEARCH OF--"
ENLIGHTENMENT.
"ULYSSES BLOODSTONE HAS DEDICATED HIS LIFE--AS ENDLESS AS IT IS--TO THE DESTRUCTION OF THE MONSTERS THAT MIGHT OTHERWISE RAVAGE MANKIND.
"A GIFTED SORCERER, WYATT CROWLEY IS THE SON OF A WITCH AND... SOMETHING ELSE."
A LINEAGE AH'M SHORE WOULD PUT ME UT THE VERY TOP OF FRIEND BLOODSTONE'S TO-KILL LIST WERE THERE NO TRUCE BETWIXT US.
"FOR DECADES, THE MENACE HAS USED HIS VAST FORTUNE, KNOWLEDGE OF ALCHEMY, AND HYPNOTIC POWERS TO WAGE A SECRET WAR WITH THE CRIMINAL UNDERWORLD.
"WHILE MURDEROUS ION POSSESSES MARTIAL AND MYSTIC ARTS THAT LLOW HIM TO TRANSCEND EVEN THE MOST GRIEVOUS INJURIES."
YOU HAVE SAID ENOUGH, BAKER. HE'S NOT ONE OF US.
YET.
WHICH BRINGS US BACK TO YOU, SUB-MARINER...

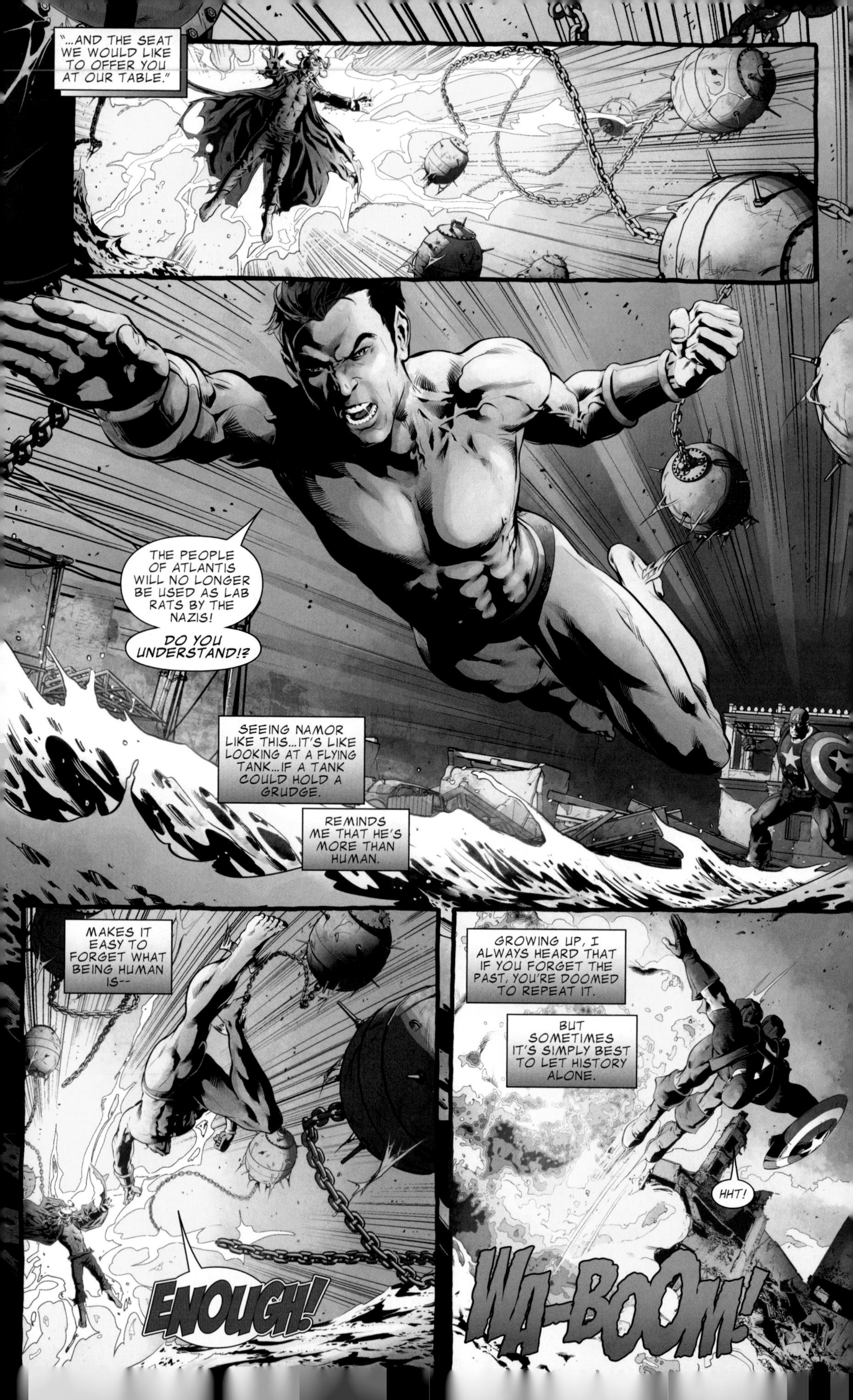
"...AND THE SEAT WE WOULD LIKE TO OFFER YOU AT OUR TABLE."
THE PEOPLE OF ATLANTIS WILL NO LONGER BE USED AS LAB RATS BY THE NAZIS!
DO YOU UNDERSTAND!?
SEEING NAMOR LIKE THIS...IT'S LIKE LOOKING AT A FLYING TANK...IF A TANK COULD HOLD A GRUDGE.
REMINDS ME THAT HE'S MORE THAN HUMAN.
MAKES IT EASY TO FORGET WHAT BEING HUMAN IS--
ENOUGH!
GROWING UP, I ALWAYS HEARD THAT IF YOU FORGET THE PAST, YOU'RE DOOMED TO REPEAT IT.
BUT SOMETIMES IT'S SIMPLY BEST TO LET HISTORY ALONE.
HHT!
WA-BOOM!

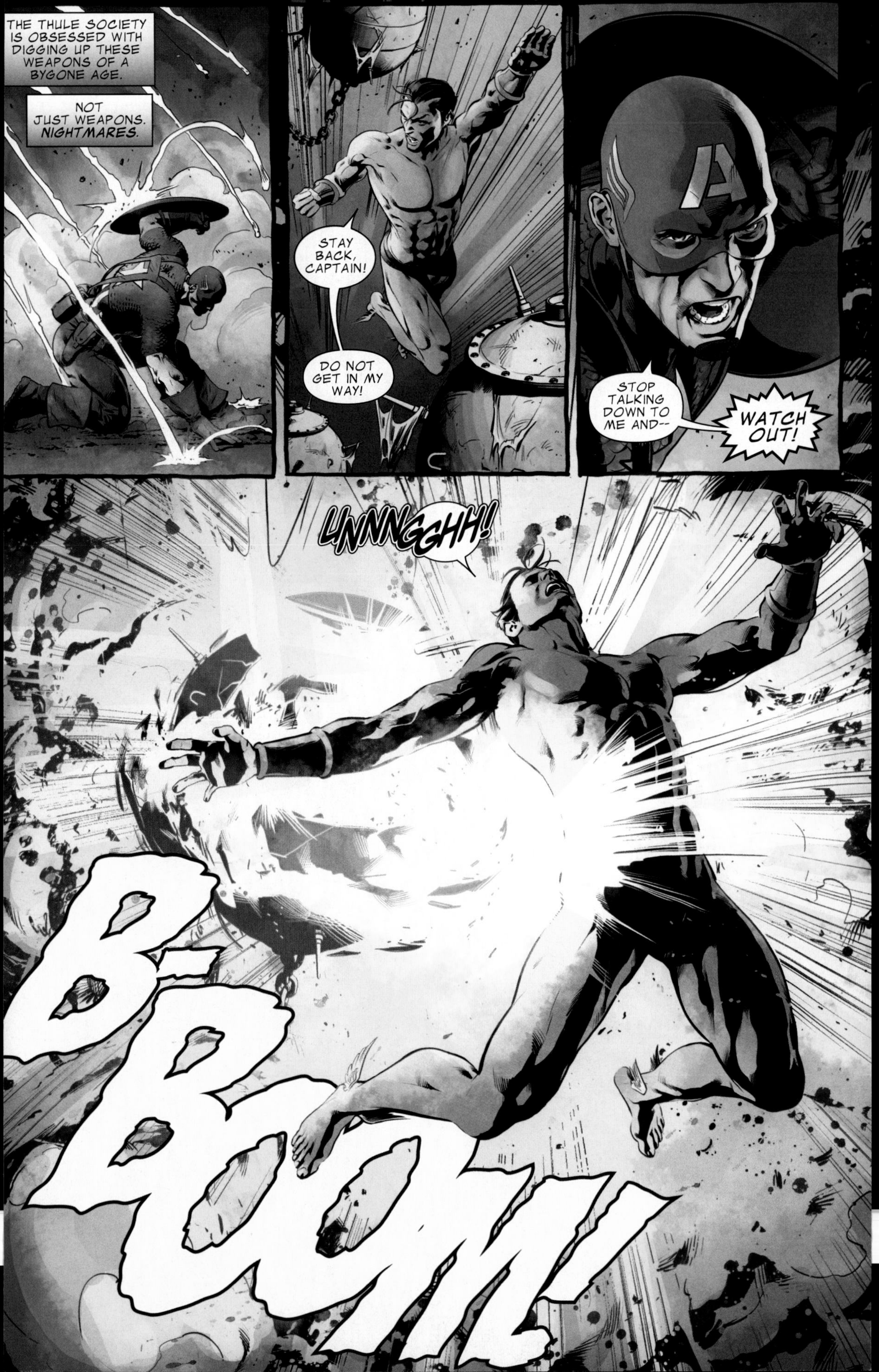
THE THULE SOCIETY IS OBSESSED WITH DIGGING UP THESE WEAPONS OF A BYGONE AGE.
NOT JUST WEAPONS. NIGHTMARES.
STAY BACK, CAPTAIN!
DO NOT GET IN MY WAY!
STOP TALKING DOWN TO ME AND--
WATCH OUT!
UNNNGGHH!
B-BOOM!

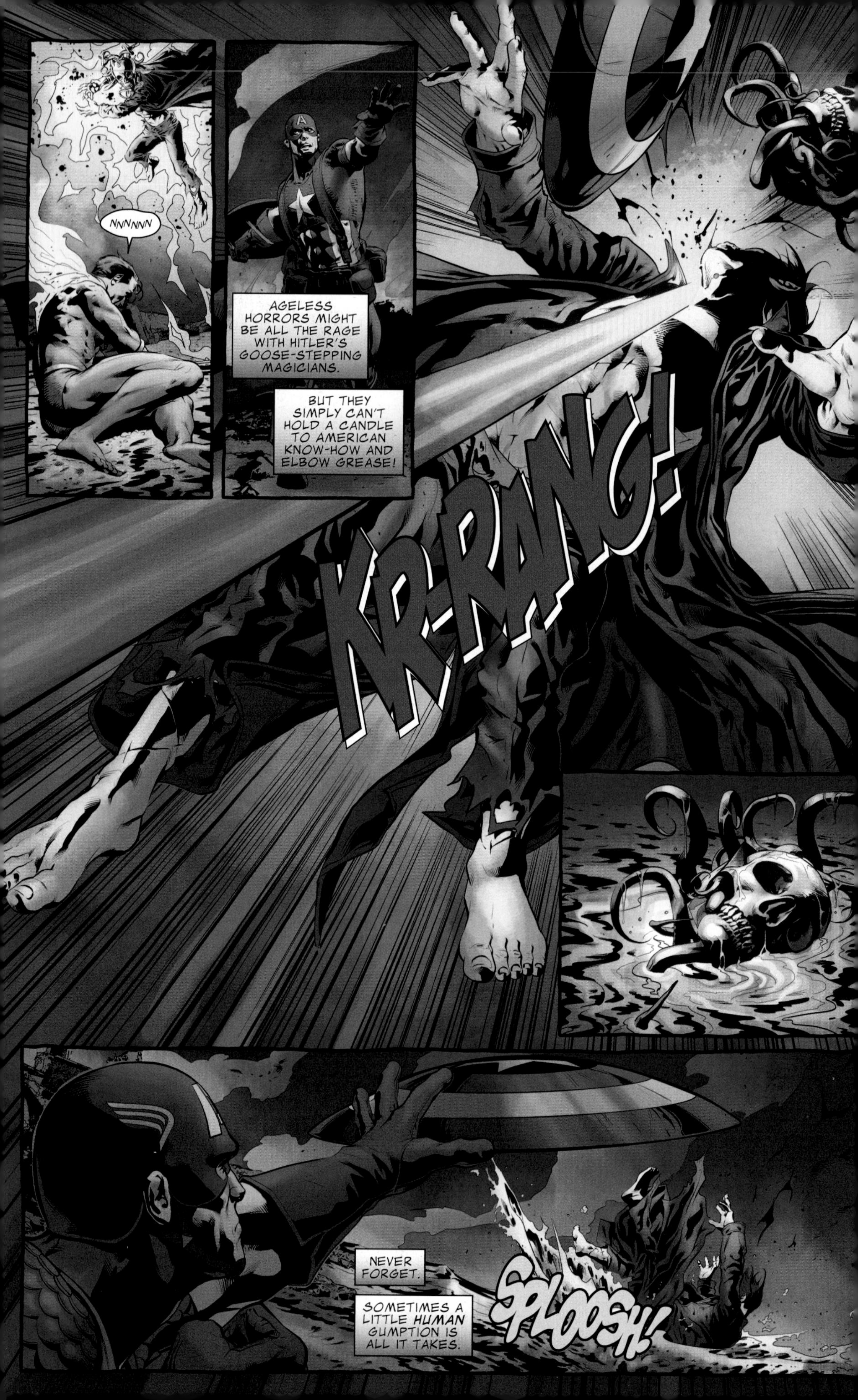
NNNNNN
AGELESS HORRORS MIGHT BE ALL THE RAGE WITH HITLER'S GOOSE-STEPPING MAGICIANS.
BUT THEY SIMPLY CAN'T HOLD A CANDLE TO AMERICAN KNOW-HOW AND ELBOW GREASE!
KR-RANG!
NEVER FORGET.
SOMETIMES A LITTLE *HUMAN* GUMPTION IS ALL IT TAKES.
SPLOOSH!

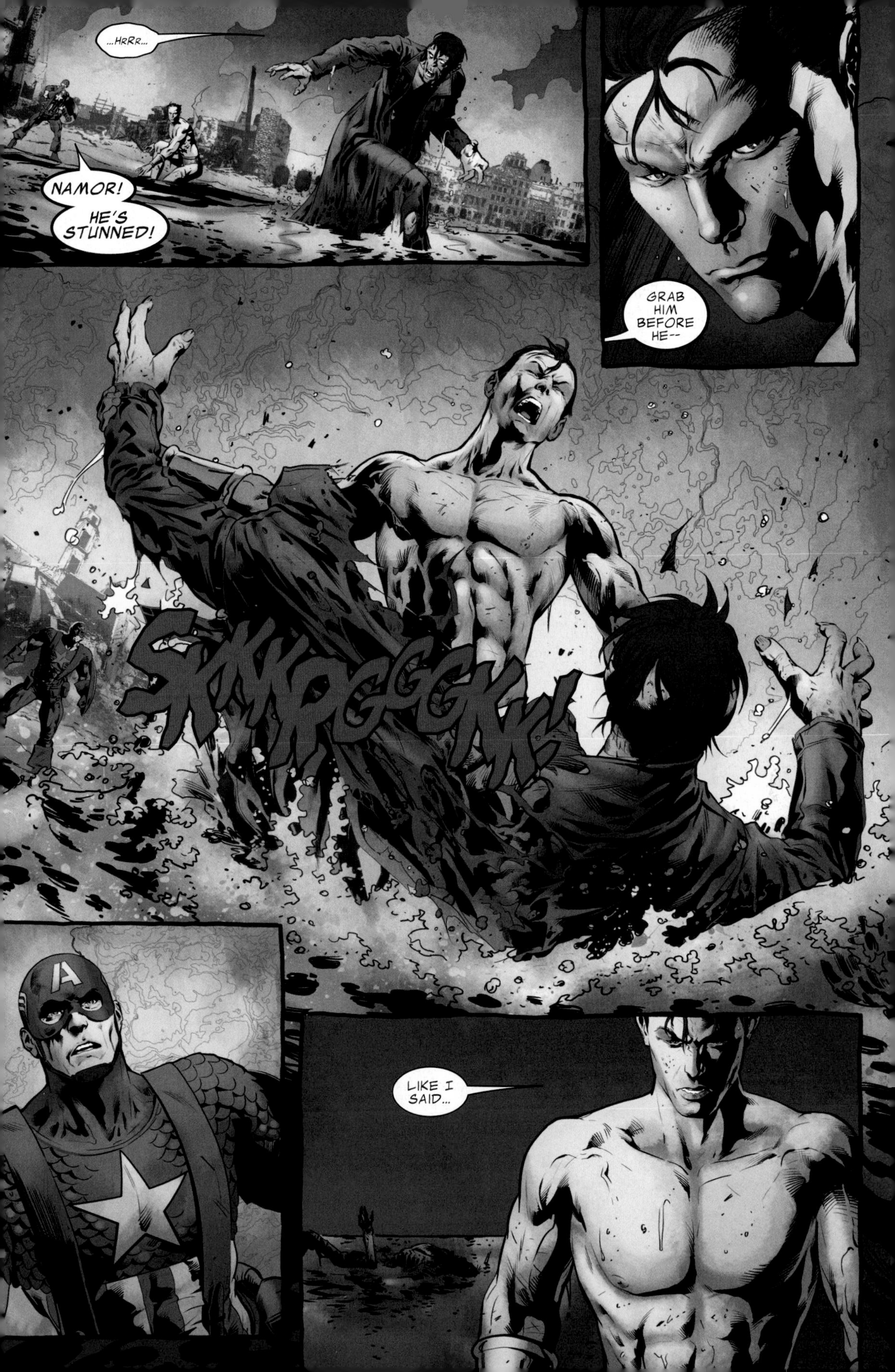
...HRRR...
NAMOR!
HE'S STUNNED!
GRAB HIM BEFORE HE--
SKKKRGGGKK!
LIKE I SAID...

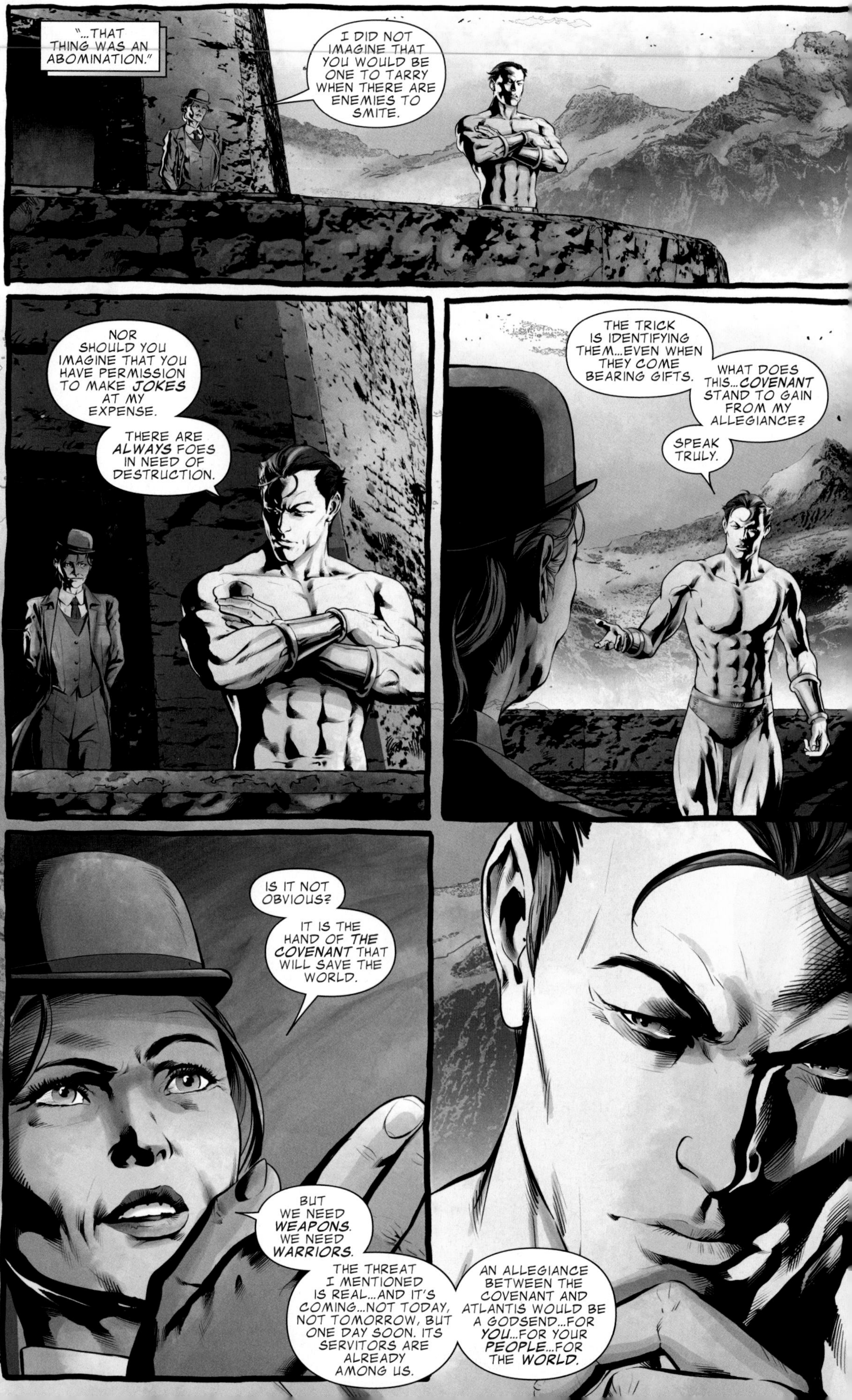
"...THAT THING WAS AN ABOMINATION."
I DID NOT IMAGINE THAT YOU WOULD BE ONE TO TARRY WHEN THERE ARE ENEMIES TO SMITE.
NOR SHOULD YOU IMAGINE THAT YOU HAVE PERMISSION TO MAKE JOKES AT MY EXPENSE.
THERE ARE ALWAYS FOES IN NEED OF DESTRUCTION.
THE TRICK IS IDENTIFYING THEM...EVEN WHEN THEY COME BEARING GIFTS.
WHAT DOES THIS...COVENANT STAND TO GAIN FROM MY ALLEGIANCE?
SPEAK TRULY.
IS IT NOT OBVIOUS?
IT IS THE HAND OF THE COVENANT THAT WILL SAVE THE WORLD.
BUT WE NEED WEAPONS. WE NEED WARRIORS.
THE THREAT I MENTIONED IS REAL...AND IT'S COMING...NOT TODAY, NOT TOMORROW, BUT ONE DAY SOON. ITS SERVITORS ARE ALREADY AMONG US.
AN ALLEGIANCE BETWEEN THE COVENANT AND ATLANTIS WOULD BE A GODSEND...FOR YOU...FOR YOUR PEOPLE...FOR THE WORLD.

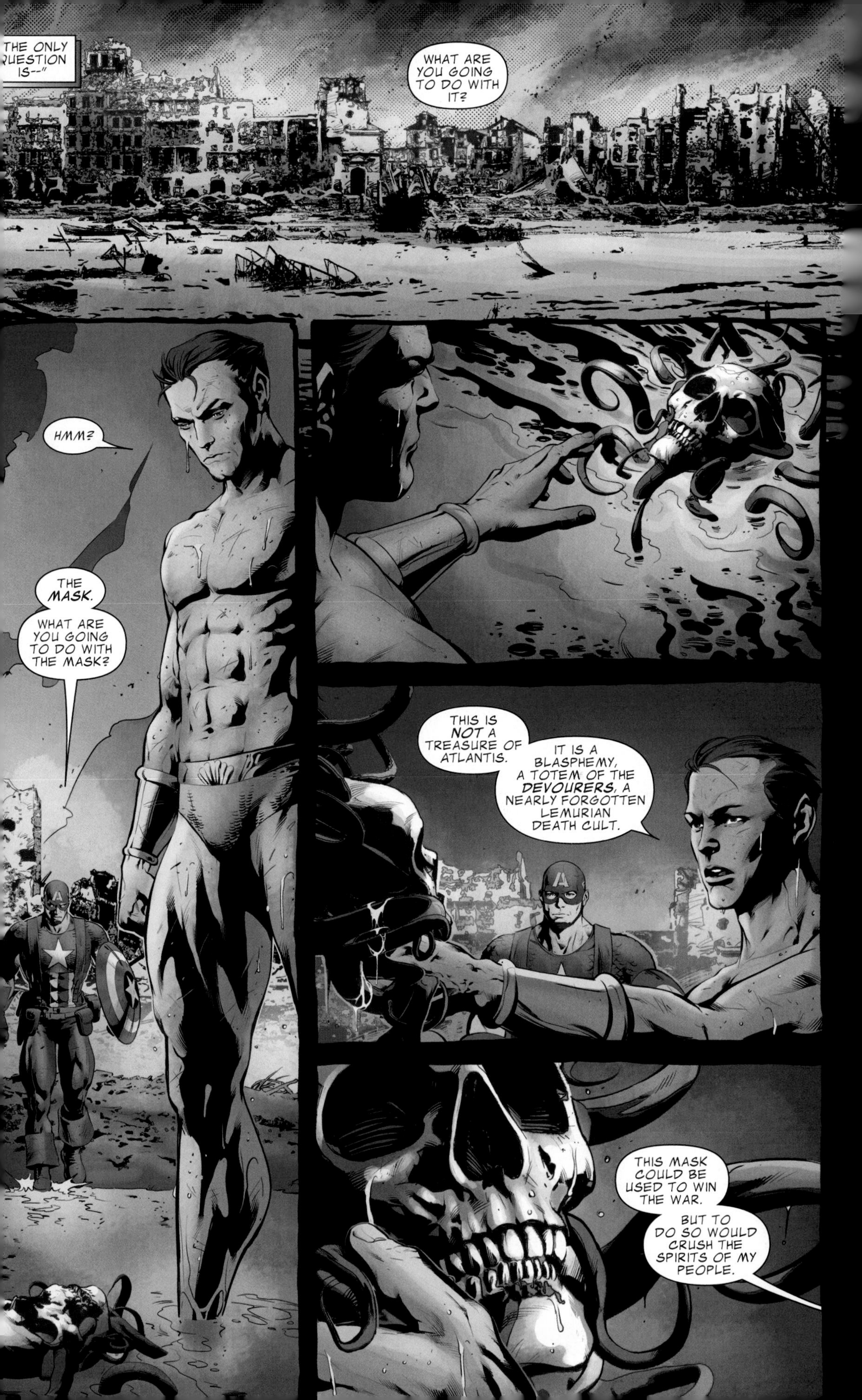

THE ONLY QUESTION IS--"
WHAT ARE YOU GOING TO DO WITH IT?
HMM?
THE MASK.
WHAT ARE YOU GOING TO DO WITH THE MASK?
THIS IS NOT A TREASURE OF ATLANTIS.
IT IS A BLASPHEMY, A TOTEM OF THE DEVOURERS, A NEARLY FORGOTTEN LEMURIAN DEATH CULT.
THIS MASK COULD BE USED TO WIN THE WAR.
BUT TO DO SO WOULD CRUSH THE SPIRITS OF MY PEOPLE.

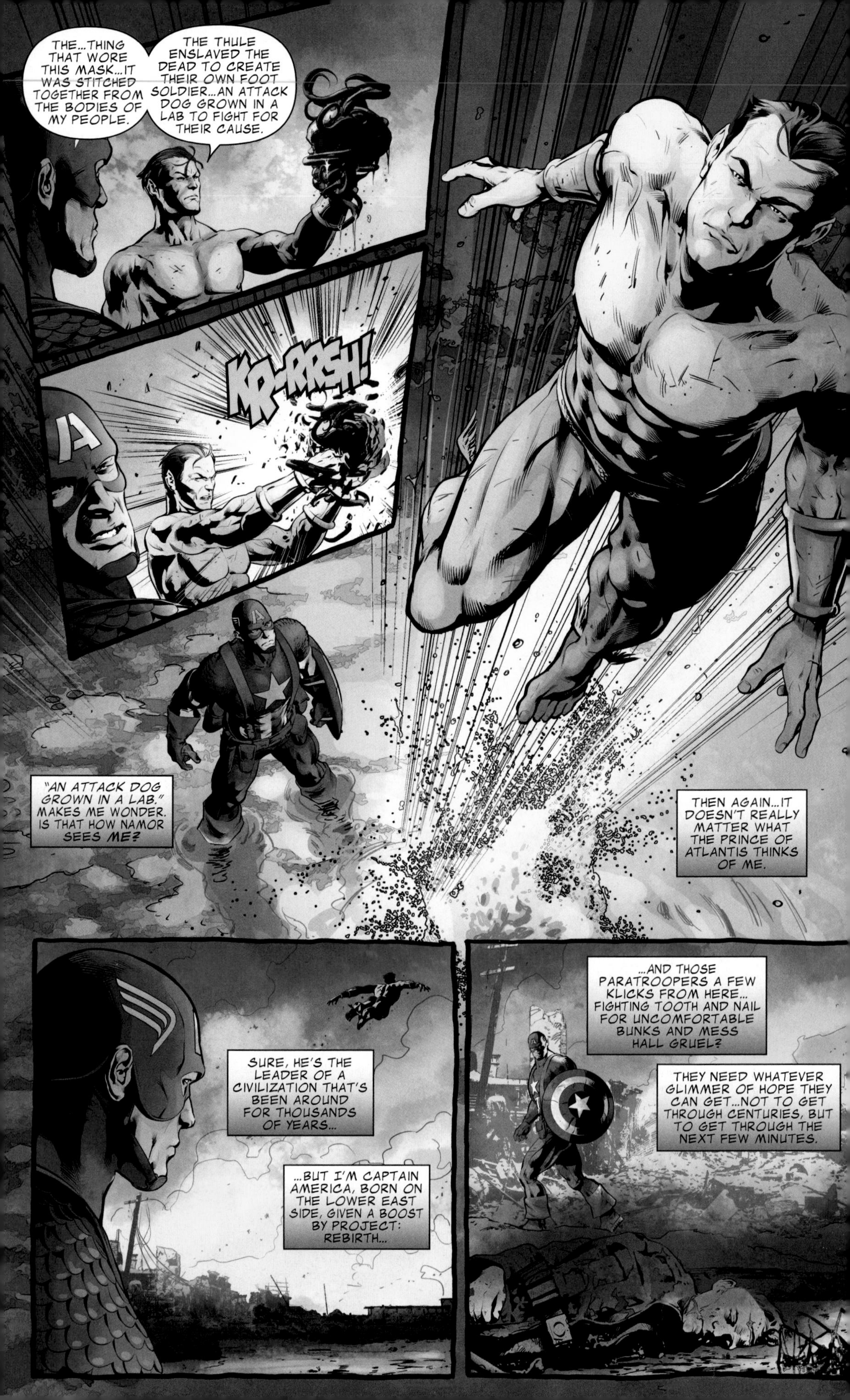

THE...THING THAT WORE THIS MASK...IT WAS STITCHED TOGETHER FROM THE BODIES OF MY PEOPLE.
THE THULE ENSLAVED THE DEAD TO CREATE THEIR OWN FOOT SOLDIER...AN ATTACK DOG GROWN IN A LAB TO FIGHT FOR THEIR CAUSE.
KR-RRSH!
"AN ATTACK DOG GROWN IN A LAB." MAKES ME WONDER. IS THAT HOW NAMOR SEES ME?
THEN AGAIN...IT DOESN'T REALLY MATTER WHAT THE PRINCE OF ATLANTIS THINKS OF ME.
SURE, HE'S THE LEADER OF A CIVILIZATION THAT'S BEEN AROUND FOR THOUSANDS OF YEARS...
...BUT I'M CAPTAIN AMERICA, BORN ON THE LOWER EAST SIDE, GIVEN A BOOST BY PROJECT: REBIRTH...
...AND THOSE PARATROOPERS A FEW KLICKS FROM HERE... FIGHTING TOOTH AND NAIL FOR UNCOMFORTABLE BUNKS AND MESS HALL GRUEL?
THEY NEED WHATEVER GLIMMER OF HOPE THEY CAN GET...NOT TO GET THROUGH CENTURIES, BUT TO GET THROUGH THE NEXT FEW MINUTES.

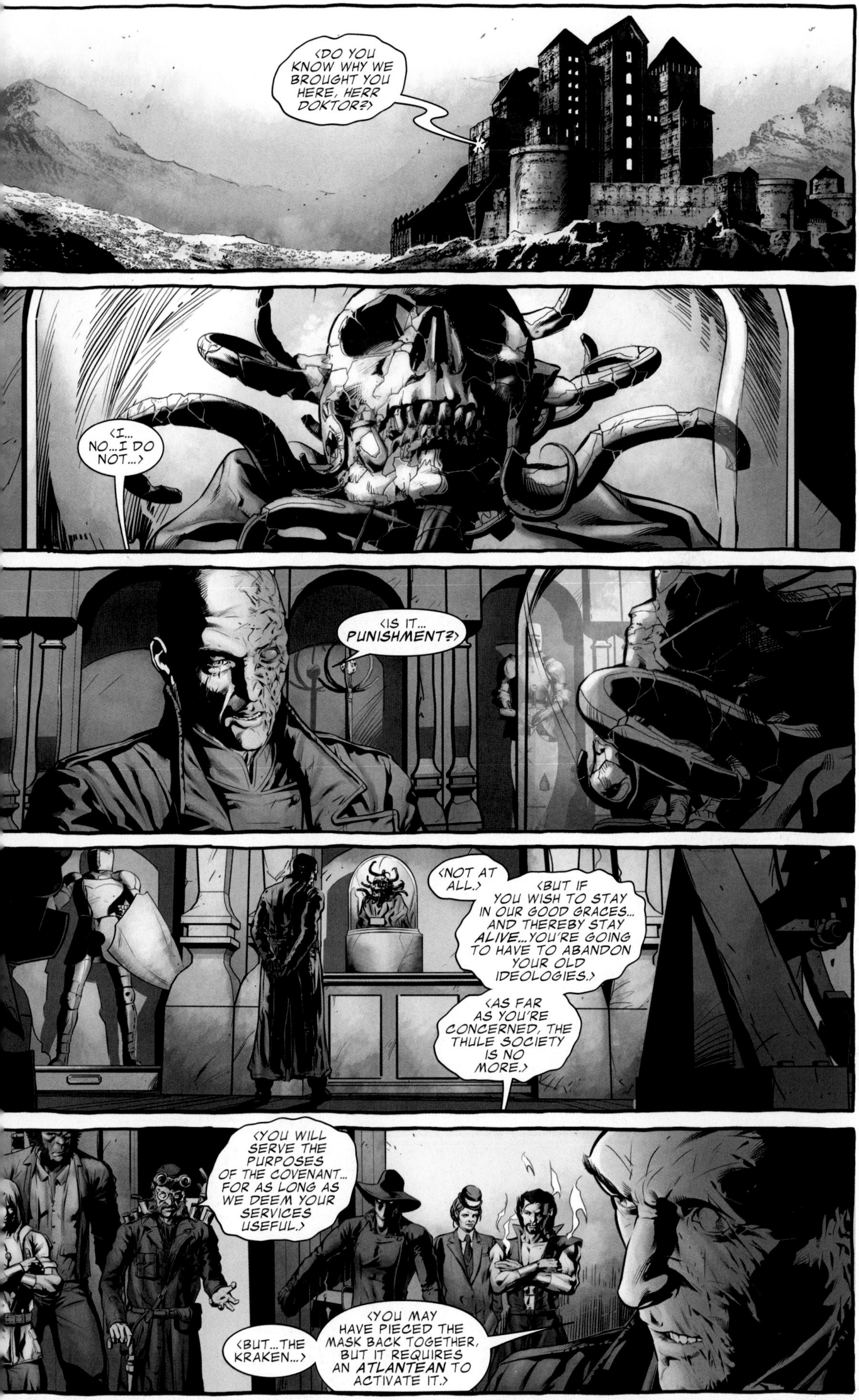
<DO YOU KNOW WHY WE BROUGHT YOU HERE, HERR DOKTOR?>
<I... NO...I DO NOT...>
<IS IT... PUNISHMENT?>
<NOT AT ALL.>
<BUT IF YOU WISH TO STAY IN OUR GOOD GRACES... AND THEREBY STAY ALIVE...YOU'RE GOING TO HAVE TO ABANDON YOUR OLD IDEOLOGIES.>
<AS FAR AS YOU'RE CONCERNED, THE THULE SOCIETY IS NO MORE.>
<YOU WILL SERVE THE PURPOSES OF THE COVENANT... FOR AS LONG AS WE DEEM YOUR SERVICES USEFUL.>
<BUT...THE KRAKEN...>
<YOU MAY HAVE PIECED THE MASK BACK TOGETHER, BUT IT REQUIRES AN ATLANTEAN TO ACTIVATE IT.>

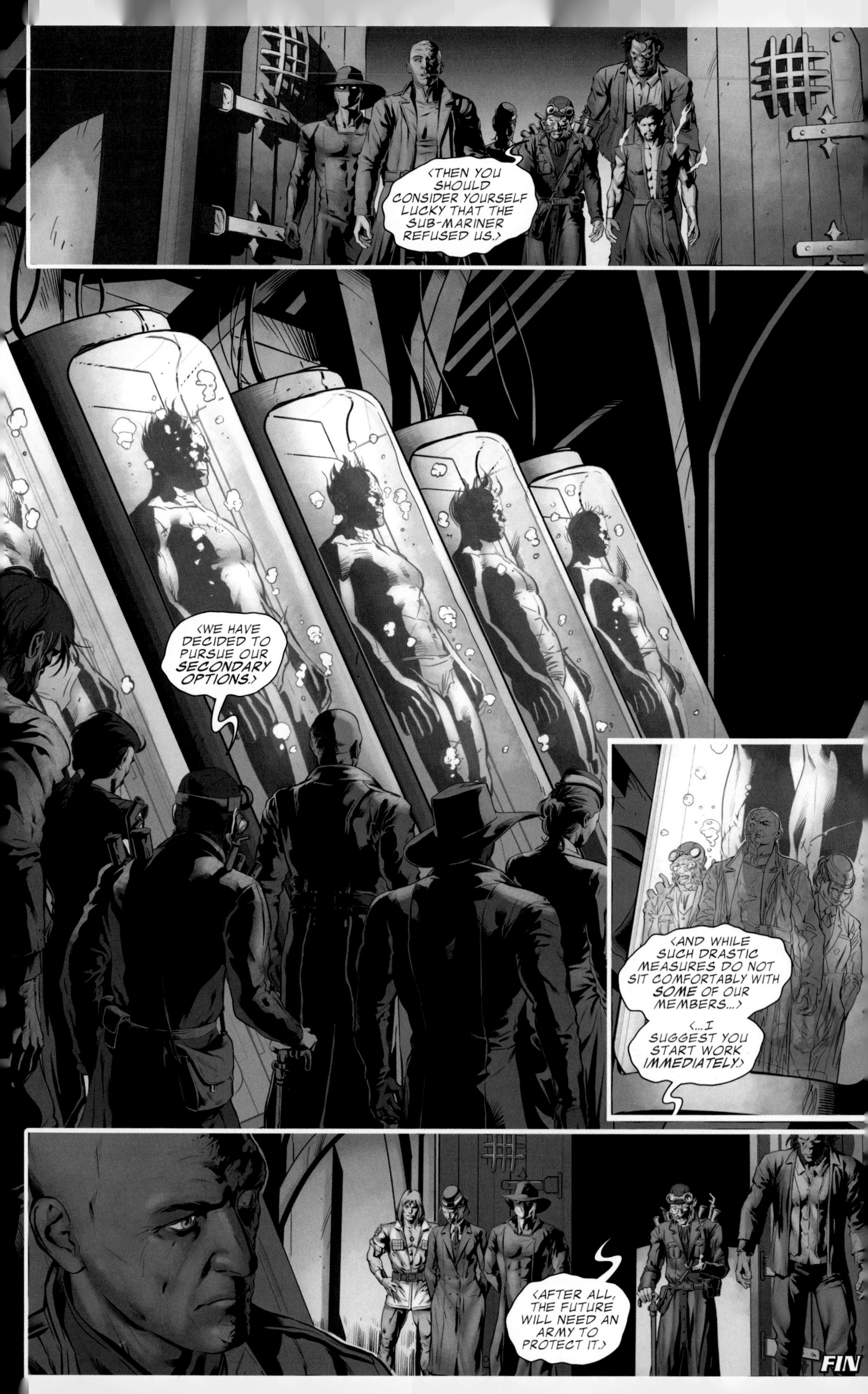
‹THEN YOU SHOULD CONSIDER YOURSELF LUCKY THAT THE SUB-MARINER REFUSED US.›
‹WE HAVE DECIDED TO PURSUE OUR SECONDARY OPTIONS.›
‹AND WHILE SUCH DRASTIC MEASURES DO NOT SIT COMFORTABLY WITH SOME OF OUR MEMBERS...›
‹...I SUGGEST YOU START WORK IMMEDIATELY.›
‹AFTER ALL, THE FUTURE WILL NEED AN ARMY TO PROTECT IT.›
FIN

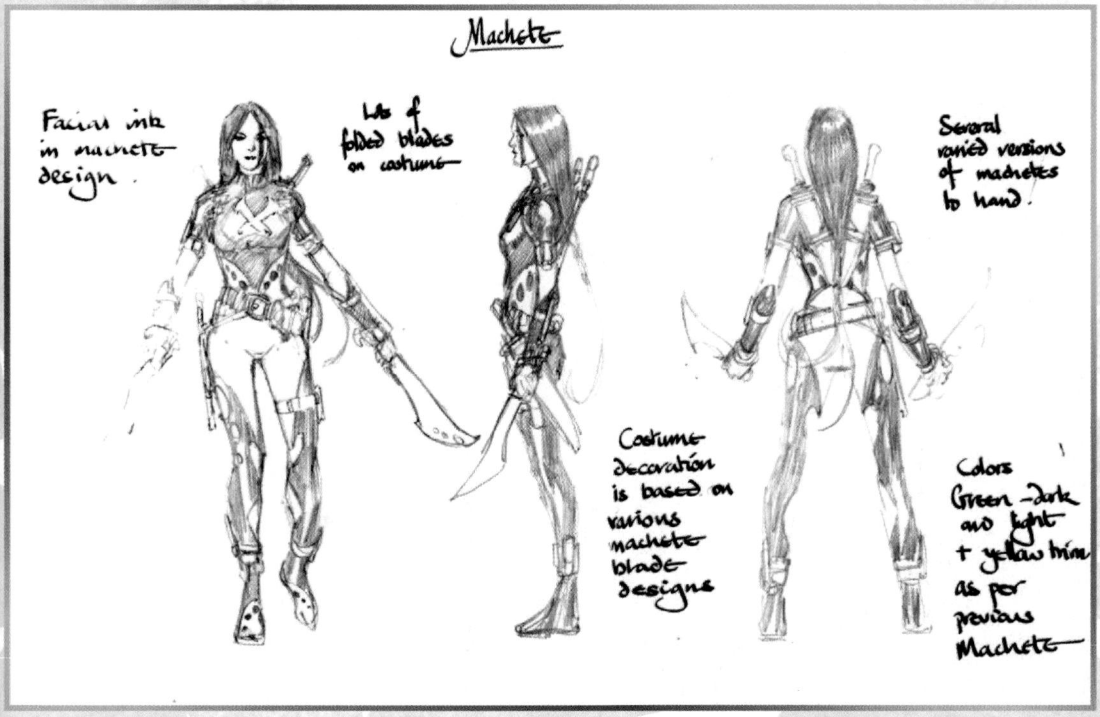
Machete
Facial ink in machete design.
Lots of folded blades on costume
Several varied versions of machetes to hand.
Costume decoration is based on various machete blade designs
Colors Green - dark and light + yellow trim as per previous Machete

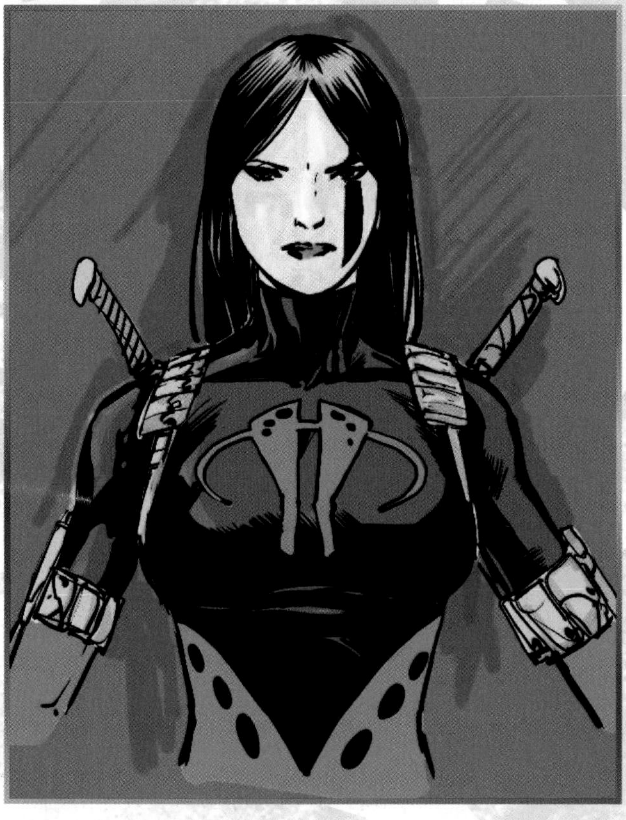

MACHETE CHARACTER DESIGNS BY BARRY KITSON

#633 & #634 COVER INKS BY KALMAN ANDRASOFSZKY

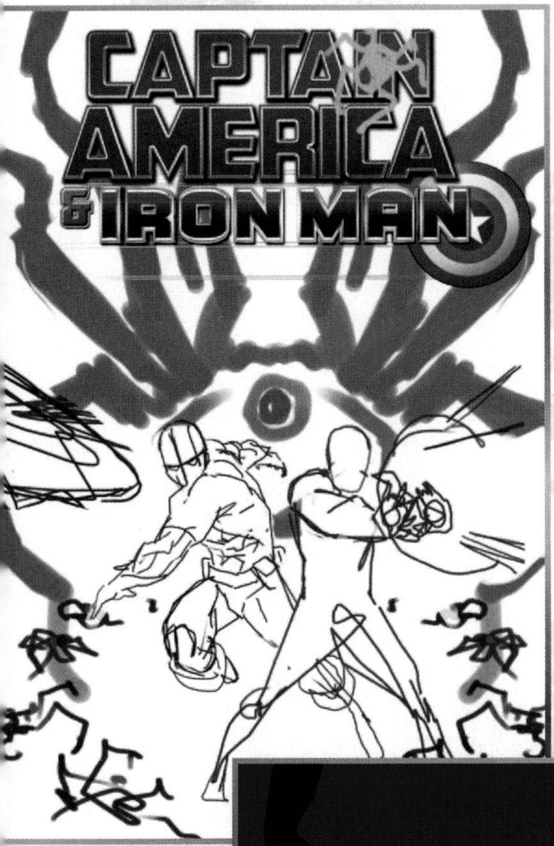
CAPTAIN AMERICA & IRON MAN

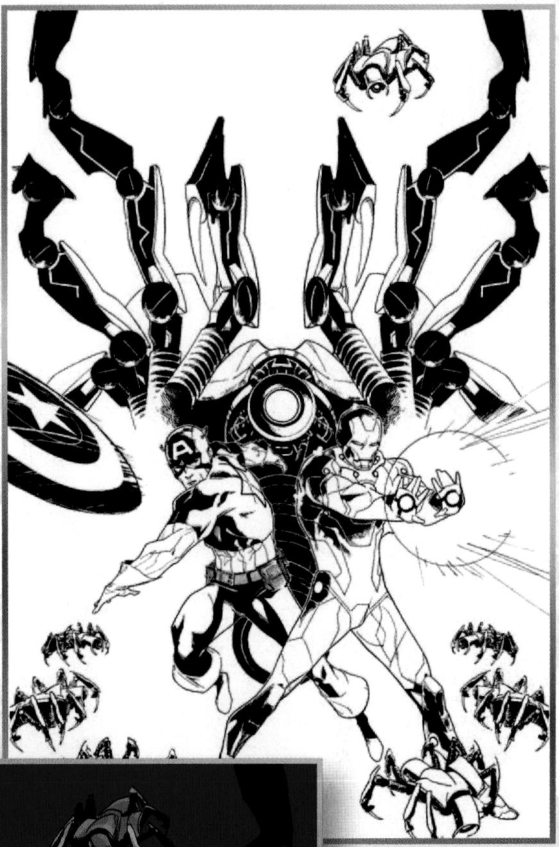

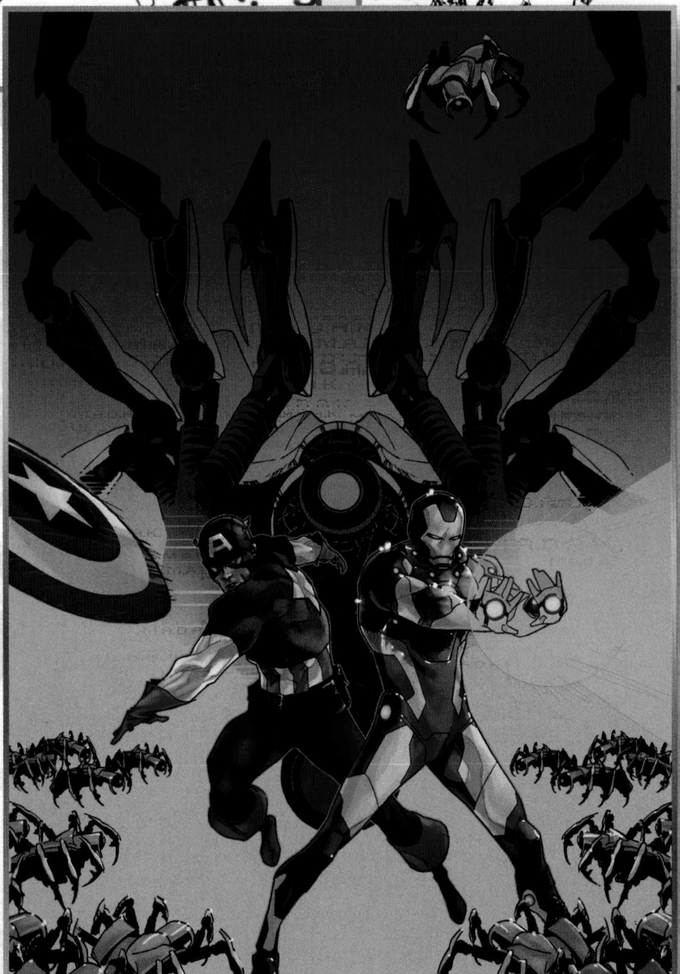

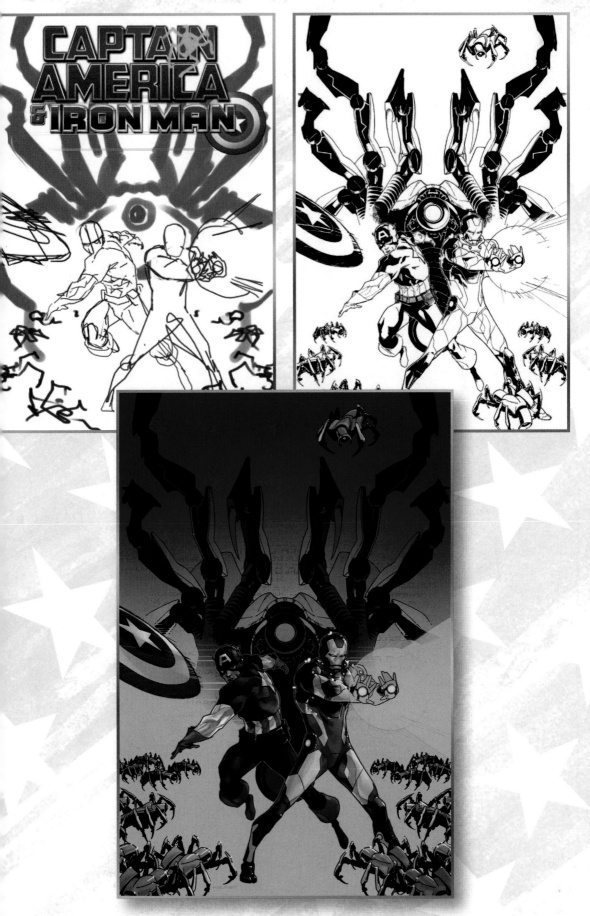

#635 COVER PROCESS BY KALMAN ANDRASOFSZKY

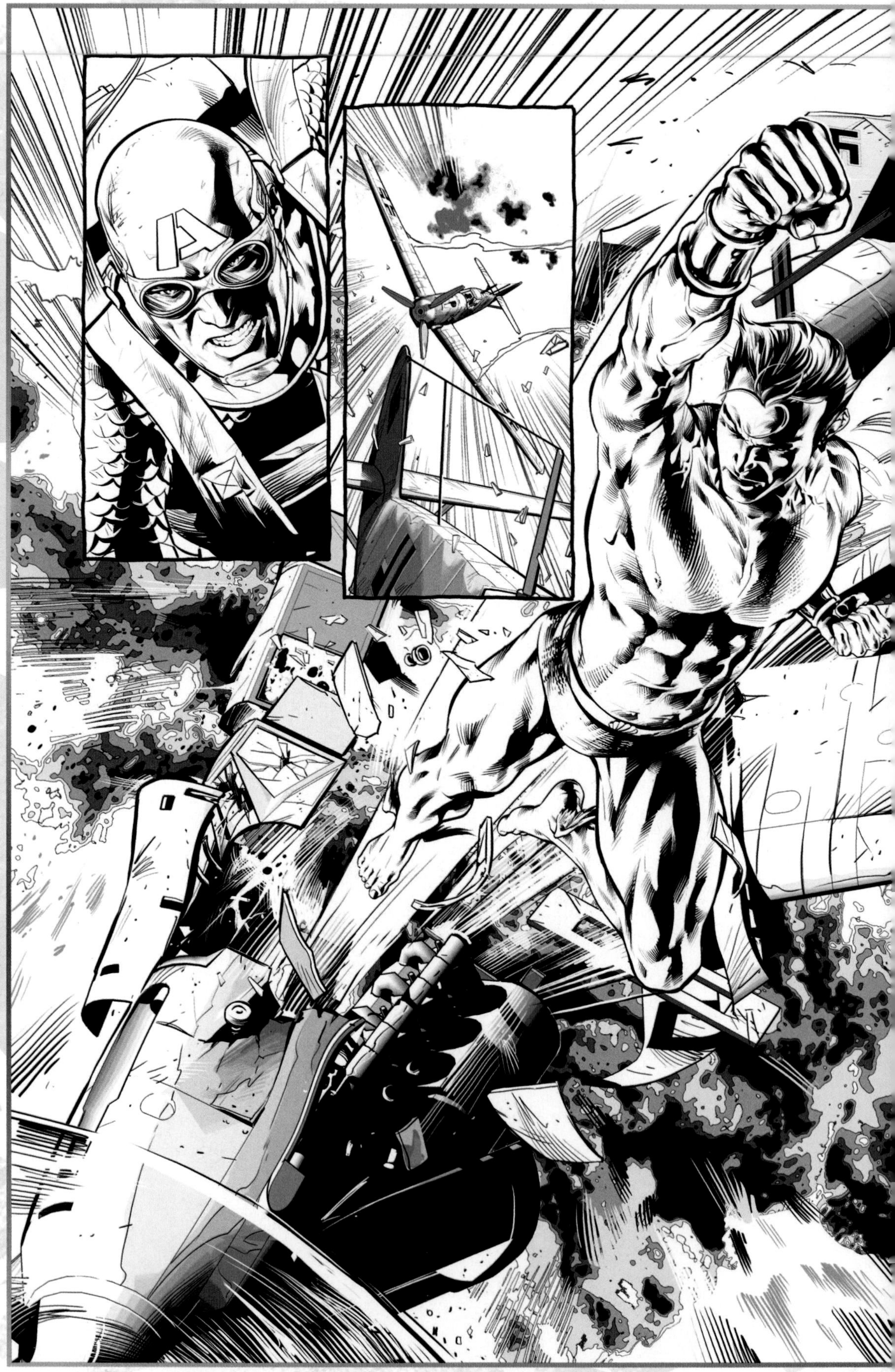

#635.1, PAGE 5 INKS BY WILL CONRAD

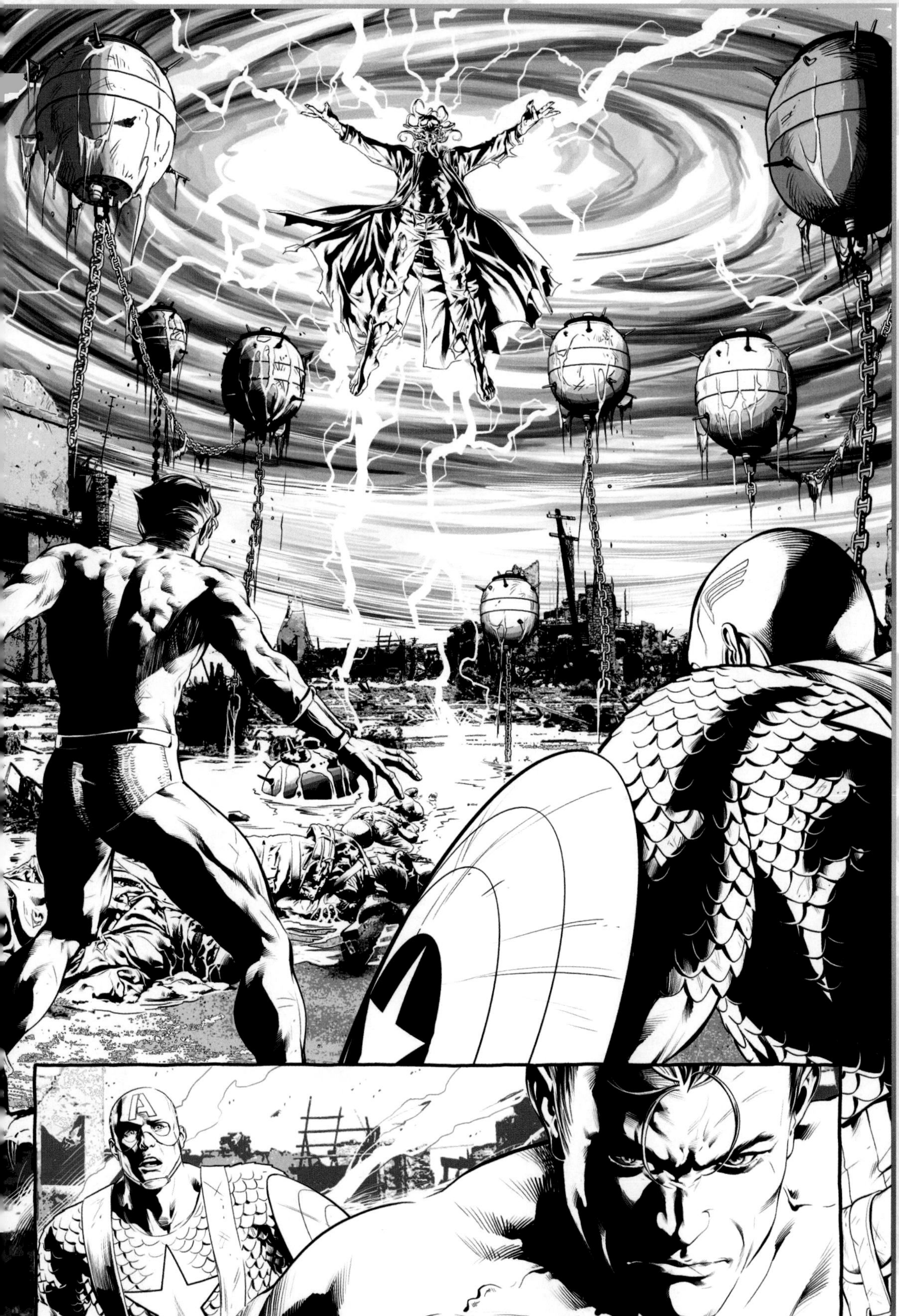

#635.1, PAGE 9 INKS BY WILL CONRAD

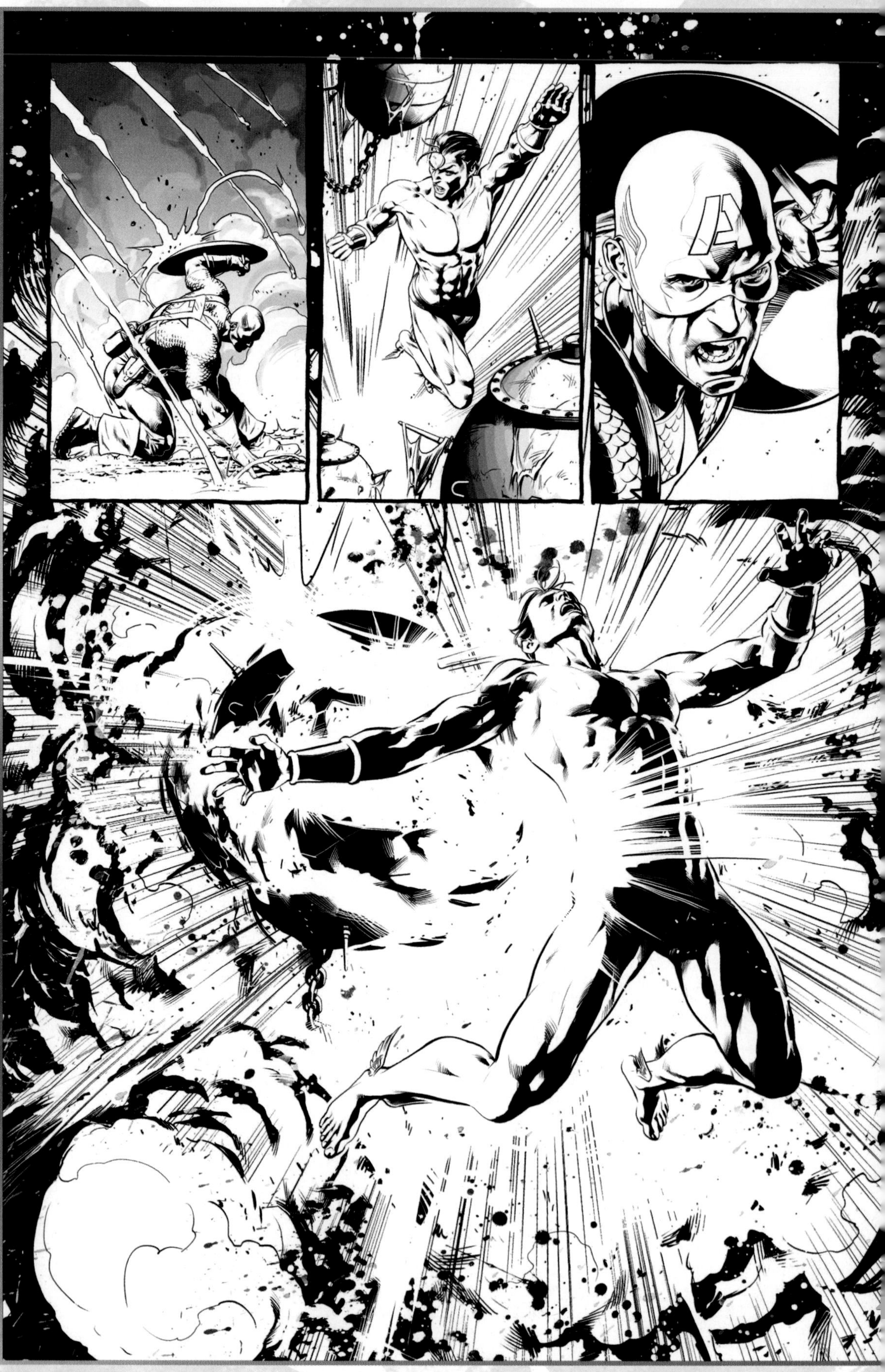

#635.1, PAGE 13 INKS BY WILL CONRAD